Making an Inter-American Mind

HARRY BERNSTEIN

Making an Inter-American Mind

University of Florida Press
Gainesville-1961

To Dr. Carl O. Sauer

INTER-AMERICAN SCHOLAR,
SCIENTIST, TEACHER, AND
FRIEND

A University of Florida Press Book

*T*HE THREE-WAY cultural kinship of the Latin American, Iberian, and North American segments of the Atlantic world is a permanent part of the intellectual history of the Western Hemisphere. It existed, and exists, alongside the geographic factor by which the southwestern and southeastern United States were discovered, entered, and settled by Spain. These two parallel contacts, studious and physical, place the whole inter-American tradition within the United States upon these twin pillars of history.

The Eastern seaboard, lacking any Hispanic influence of place-names, language, and settled places, created original intellectual efforts which carried across ocean and sea to Old Spain or the New World. These ties were man-made. In the "Old Southwest," on the other hand, the heritage and speech of Spain lay in the sun, waiting to be found, tasted, and acculturated, while Spain fell into shadow. In old New York, Boston, and Philadelphia, crossing over to another culture was a bold journey to the frontier of ideas, quite different from the frontier of physical contact.

I have carried my interest in cultural history and contact down to 1900—the point where organized teaching, monied foundations, and early government and inter-American government interest also arrived at the rediscovery of the Americas. But first the pioneer road carried American scholars and scientists, acting as individuals and not associated with any council of learned societies. Organization, like mass media, came after 1900 and conveyed additional messages. It might at some time be possible to carry the story of greater growth and enlargement of this inter-American school for study down to 1960, adding newer factors of theatre, moving picture, radio, television, information, propaganda, education. But first of all this is a history of precedents and patterns.

218365

What I wanted to do was to show how the study of the magnificent subject matter of the New World possessed a respectable and admirable antiquity of its own, giving those who teach and investigate in it quite a lineage and intellectual tradition. Next, a more public intention, was to show that cultural interest in Latin America and Spain is as valid a part of North American life as is capitalism, expansion, the material standard of living. The inter-American mind in fact was born even before there was a nation and a national interest. I have purposely called this civilized spirit Jeffersonian, but it might better be named Franklinian. Certainly, the rational, secular state of mind is the best mirror of inter-American culture.

Like the cultural anthropologist, the cultural historian finds the stuff of growth in contacts, exchanges, and innovations in knowledge. This is history. But this change and exchange had the force to last only as it fitted in with the already established, the historical. I believe that in the earlier cultures of man, as well as in recent Western, the new experience joins with tradition and becomes a way of mental life. This is the history of how an inter-American mind was made. Often enough there is clash between the new and old, between the American and European, the English and Hispanic, the Indo-American, Afro-American, and all-American parts. This is especially so in the psychology and behavior of individuals, groups, and even scholars. Still, it is from this polarity and interaction of view that we have reached the pause on the plateau, the look around. We have the freshness of historical "second wind." From this intellectual ancestry and cultural mestizoism has come the inter-American mind.

I want to acknowledge a grant of the Carnegie Corporation to Brooklyn College for area studies which provided opportunity for help in publication arrangements. I must also give notice of the good will and lasting support of former Dean William R. Gaede, a friend of Latin American and inter-American studies. I thank the editors of the University of Florida Press for their cooperation and careful work. It was the patience and toleration of my wife Florence, my daughter Stefanie, and my son Walter that made the writing possible. The research and the ideas are all my own. So are the errors.

H. B.

Contents

Chapter 1

FIRST STEPS

*A*FTER THE Discovery and Conquest of America, Englishmen and their North American colonials projected their mental image of Spain and her Indies upon New World culture. Not always a clear picture, it lasted as late as the nineteenth century in Western European countries and the United States before getting a title and a name. Spanish historians, outraged by hostile criticism of Spain's work in America, called it the *leyenda negra* (the black legend). In the United States, where opinion about Hispanic culture was inherited from England and Europe but was also conditioned by Spanish imperial possessions along the desired frontier, popular psychology gave rise to a mystic, nationalist term, Manifest Destiny. Both the European and North American conception of Spanish civilization drew from many stores: first reports of Spanish cruelty to the Indians of America, public scorn for the Iberian lust for gold, private and public envy of Spain's visible territories, the dreaded Inquisition's reputation for fanatic religious intolerance, and other instances of man's inhumanity to man—in the Old and in the New World. The record, from 1500 to 1800, showed both fact and exaggeration in the examples. By 1800 the history of Spanish colonization was well-enough known in the United States to feed strong arguments to an anti-Hispanic opinion. Written reports were sensational and widely believed.

Making a myth is easier than denying or disproving it, especially since written history, literature, and even some early science reprinted and circulated the idea in all the modern European languages. Thus the black legend was circulated and fixed for centuries on both shores of the Atlantic seaboard. So much had been put into print and rumor about the *leyenda negra,* and particularly about the hurtful trauma of the

1

Spanish destruction of a weak Indian people, that feelings against Spain lasted down to the present. These attitudes were then displaced on to the Latin American sons of Spain. The prolonged repetition and republication of the "Big Myth" from 1700 to 1900 had convincing effect in Europe. In the United States such popular notions were handed down from one generation to the next, perpetuating the Great Myth in religious opinion, political propaganda, written history, formal education, and folklore, as well as the lasting influence of the grandfather's tale.

The angry defense of the good and worth-while in American Indian culture against the aggressions of Spaniards was first brought together in the sixteenth century by the Dominican friar Bartolomé de Las Casas. He gathered from his experience and books the legal arguments against the Spanish Conquest. Las Casas' picture of the shy and passive Indians established him as their Protector in the eyes of the Spanish Crown. This did not content nor quiet him. His bitter verbal war against the secular soldiers and settlers of Spain had the catching quality of headlines; he provided eager critics with convincing propaganda, pseudohistory and powerful eyewitness attacks upon some conquering Spaniards. Las Casas was a churchman and theologian, Roman Catholic to the core. But his polemics were readily seized and handled by those Atlantic nations which fought the many religious, territorial, and commercial wars with Spain. British, Dutch, French, and later North American rivalry with Spain employed and gave new broadcast to the move to isolate Spain. The black legend was put down into wartime tracts, peacetime books, pamphlets, histories, sermons, essays, dramatic poetry, state papers, and eighteenth-century "scientific" works. It was early psychological warfare.

The early wars against Spain were filled with profit motives and aims for territorial gain, which ultimately drove a wedge between a steadily weakened Spain and her American colonies. Spain failed to keep out intruders, contrabandists, privateers, and foreign invaders; in the same way she failed to exclude books and their ideas from Latin America. Spain and her Church could not exclude reason, republican thought, modern letters, and the influences of science. Iberian taboos were ignored in both cases: on one hand, European and North American strangers carried their cargoes right into forbidden Indies waters. In addition, invigorating ideas found the right way to the Latin American mind. The new achievements of Western Civilization overspread both shores of Columbus' Ocean Sea. Scientific and profit motives brought the proud house of Castile to earth.

That was the seventeenth- and eighteenth-century world into which

North American colonials were born. That was the world from which Latin America acquired her ideas, partly from Spain, and partly smuggled and brought in from England, France, and the early United States. Britain's North American subjects also grew up with many of the books and conceptions which Europe bequeathed: Las Casas, Thomas Gage, Richard Hakluyt. These were the writers whose tracts thundered an anti-Spanish din decade after decade as they were read. It is true that for early North Americans the armed empire of Spain in America was near enough to awaken anxiety, but it was an imported Old World bogey which conditioned their psychology long before Americans ran into any real Spaniards over here.

North Americans already accepted the prevailing propaganda thesis about Spain, just as they regularly and dutifully took part in England's wars in America. Consequently, as some sort of colonial stir in the existing psychological warfare directed against Spain, North American feelings bordered upon panic during the land and sea battles of Anglo-Spanish wars. Some of these even threatened invasion of the New York and New England seaboard, although that never happened. Finally, there was a considerable body of religious warfare which underlay North American opinion. Puritan New England, much more than the Anglican Middle Colonies, kept alive all those historic fears of Catholic Spain, the Inquisition, the Jesuits, and the Counter Reformation, which had long before disturbed Elizabethan Old England. The strict Puritan lived by the theological argument. All in all, however, a blend of European theology, Old World royalist rivalries, European trade interest in the Indies, historical myth, mass psychology, and the real nearness of Spain-in-America ought to be used to explain the whole attitude of British Americans towards Spanish Americans.

The myths about Spain lived for a long time; there was little change in the belief. For those who believed it, the points were the same in the nineteenth century as they were in the sixteenth, when they were born. Such ideas, or rather, images, never seem to grow or evolve. They depended upon a static nightmare of Spain, an abnormally enduring fear, timeless and stubborn. Even the weakened and dying Spain kept the spell alive. Like the well-known iceberg, two-thirds of the real force of the fear was below the surface, invisible and hidden from history, science, and the illuminations of reason. Of course there was method and logic to the madness of anti-Hispanic feelings: it was properly based upon a real and tangible dread of Spanish naval and military power. To the North American and Englishman, Spain was both a psychological force and an enemy religion, reinforced with enormous sea power. Behind that Most Catholic Majesty lay the might of galleon dreadnoughts, the proved battle prowess of Spanish infantry, anchored firmly by the chain of world-renowned fortresses in the strategic Caribbean. The shadow of the giant hid the feet of clay, however. It was a credulous world, easily influenced by the propaganda of a dogma and widespread popular superstition.

Nevertheless, even while the black legend climbed to its height, a friendly attitude toward Spanish culture had also appeared. This was the white legend, so to speak, impelled by science and knowledge towards a rational and intelligent curiosity about the civilization of the distant Indies, the tropics, the great Indian societies, and the vast and impressive geography of the Latin American continent. Its European origins were soon renewed and advanced in the United States. Founded upon European study and researches from 1500 to the present, it found its own place in thinking and learned circles here. We may call this parallel process inter-American cultural relations.

The older psychology of the black legend, which first arose in Europe, also became Americanized under the name of Manifest Destiny. Other factors explain why the attitudes of Manifest Destiny merely visited the sins of sixteenth-century Spain upon her nineteenth-century descendants in Latin America. The verbal and unarmed attacks of the black legend from across the ocean were nothing compared to the land hungers, expansionist drives, and ambitions of the North American frontiersmen who confronted the Spaniard from one end of the frontier to the other. Puritan and Protestant zeal was largely dependent upon ideas, words, and feelings. Spiritual and theological teaching held the stage, and did not, or could not, act. European ideology, when transplanted to America, was bookish. It lacked the active fire and expanding dynamics of real life down at the frontier crossroad of Spanish and North American contact. Still later, in the nineteenth century, a restless popular psychology further agitated those political questions which had to do with Spanish America. A loud and effective *vox populi*, strong in both volume and numbers, rattled sabers and slogans on editorial pages and in the halls of Congress.

It was not the only Americanism, however. The gentler persuasion of inter-American cooperation and good will always was alongside anti-Hispanism and just as much a part of American thought. The cultural relations approach, resting upon knowledge, not emotion, and upon reason, not feeling, was the opposite of both Manifest Destiny and the *leyenda negra.* Many North Americans rejected the latter. They were more skeptical about this propaganda than Europeans were. Indeed, cultural inter-Americanism arose in the very earliest North American historical moment, when England still held the colonies. The regard for Latin America developed in the days of the thirteen colonies, so that its history is as old and as American as Manifest Destiny. These Hispanophile ties, resting upon poise and not noise, stood their case upon reason and upon humanistic and scientific values in the North American mind.

These two attitudes—Manifest Destiny and inter-American cultural interest—are forever paired in American history. Manifest Destiny made better use of spoken and written propaganda and self-interested nationalism, using war, patriotism, agitation, and the temptations of territorial expansion as the lure. In contrast, the inter-American mind, idealized chiefly by literary and scientific people, occupied a quiet and dignified place among the intelligent few. It is true, of course, that the drives behind North American nationalism and expansionism dominated the center of the main historical stage, taking over the drama of New World history. But that is no reason to forget its more rational rival. Manifest Destiny did give high color to a freely moving frontier, seeding the ancient Elizabethan and anti-Hispanic legacy broadcast along the Spanish American borderland.

In contrast, in New York, New England, and Pennsylvania—English in derivation—friendlier concepts of Spain developed from study.[1]* In the academies, societies, and libraries of the North Atlantic seaboard, far removed from deposits of Spanish cultural influence in the neighborhood or from Spanish place-names in the vicinity, a significant community of scholarly and appreciative contact arose. Here was North America's Rediscovery of the Americas. Since 1700 this has been a peaceful process, lively and lasting. In the two hundred years between 1700 and 1900 the diffusion of culture moved freely to and from both Americas. Scientific and cultural relations took their historic place without exciting catchwords, separated and detached from economic, political, and territorial pressures—and, unfortunately, unnoticed. Possessing the proudest aspects of Jeffersonian democracy, cultural inter-Americanism sought harmony between two different cultures. Not even the religious conflict of Puritan Protestantism with Roman Catholicism could prevent scientific rationalism, secular culture, and liberal thought from crossing the Caribbean into the South American world. The secular spirit, in

*Notes to this chapter begin on page 169.

fact, replaced the original and earliest bridge over the Americas, which was religious.

Religion is a part of culture. As religions precede science in making faith the roadway to belief, so did Protestantism get the first start in inter-American culture history. Our story begins with those Puritan Protestants who tried to achieve religious unity in America by converting Latin Americans to their way. Puritan action in this instance was not only a forerunner of nineteenth-century missionary work; it was also the earliest North American intellectual effort to win the Latin American mind. Protestantism in New England tried optimistically but vainly to invoke a religious solidarity for all Americans.

Familiar names, such as Cotton Mather and Samuel Sewall of Boston, head the list of pioneers in inter-American relations. As part of the Puritan paradox which paired anti-Hispanic fears with the desire for a Christian conversion, New England theologians conceived a strange plan for hemisphere oneness. The year 1700 marked the renewed European struggle for the Spanish Indies, whose climax was the War of the Spanish Succession. At about that time, two Boston Puritans, Cotton Mather and Samuel Sewall, also felt the call of Spanish America. They did something peaceably, creating and initiating the first North American program directed toward South America. Puritan religion in New England was militant, looking southward for an inter-American spiritual force.

Mather, Sewall, and a "Number of Gentlemen who make the best figures in this Place [Boston]" began their work in 1699. On the eve of that world-wide war against Spain, called the War of the Spanish Succession, these New Englanders determined to direct and finance the group which carried their view of the Gospel into Latin America. Although it coincided with wartime, the psychology was benevolent and eager. Looking backward from the present, we may see that the enduring by-product was even more important than the proselytizing aim: the earliest North American study of Spanish language and Spanish American literature. Naturally their purpose in reading the language and literature was to help their theological work. This is no objection. Their religious design may have been premature, but more than anything it introduced Boston and New England to a historic reputation for interest in things Hispanic.

Out of the Puritan effort came the first book printed in Spanish in these United States. Cotton Mather was its author; he wrote it to win converts in Latin America to the Puritan form of Protestantism.

Mather was a leading member of the Boston group. Gifted and literate, his hopes to convert Latin America were high, zealous and optimistic, as he frankly confided to his *Diary*, January, 1699:

About this time understanding that the way for our communication with the *Spanish Indies* opens more and more I sett myself to learn the *Spanish Language*. The Lord wonderfully prospered mee in this Undertaking; a few liesure Minutes in the Evening of every Day in about a Fortnight, or three weeks time, so accomplish'd mee, I could write very good Spanish. Accordingly I compos'd a little Body of the *Protestant Religion*, in certain Articles, back'd with irresistible sentences of Scripture. This I turn'd into the Spanish Tongue; and am now printing it with a Design to send it by all the ways that I can into the several parts of South America . . . as not knowing whether the time of our Lord Jesus Christ to have glorious Churches in America bee not at hand.[2]

Mather was bright enough to master Spanish very quickly. He also gave his book an appealing title. He combined Spanish and English to call his broadcast *La Religión Pura to which is added la Fe del Christiano*.[3] This is the simplest version of the lengthy title. Other subtitles regale the reader with a sense of the book's importance, renewing Mather's fervent call to Spaniards in Latin America "to open their eyes and be converted from the shadow into the light, away from Satan to God." The message was bold and self-confident, but there is now no way of knowing whether Mather's appeal for Christian unity in America was read by a dozen, a hundred, a thousand—or by no one at all.

Samuel Sewall was another one of the Boston circle of the missionary-minded. Sewall was one of its firmest, most influential, and long-lived members. His spiritual search went even further: to the founding of a New Jerusalem in America. Sewall, indeed, always dreamed that he had found New Jerusalem in Mexico City, and he spent his years hoping that he could get there. The combination of Cotton Mather, churchman, and Samuel Sewall, merchant and member of the Council of the Massachusetts Bay Colony, gave the project blessing and strong backing. Like Mather's, Sewall's physical being never travelled far from Boston; but their two mind's eyes took spiritual flight and soared. His seventeenth-century ancestors in New England had earlier fought with Old England against Spain in the Caribbean and Central America; now he fixed his sights upon the religious territory of the Indies. He went beyond Mather, hoping that their successful propaganda might induce Latin America to separate from Spain.[4]

Sewall's hopes for the independence of Latin America were as premature and doomed to failure as Mather's design for conversion. Nevertheless, Sewall also studied the Spanish language and acquired a curiosity about the history of Latin America, gleaning information of all sorts about life in the Indies. By 1700 there were several books in translation which he read. The best known (in Old England) were the tract of Bartolomé de Las Casas, circulated since the sixteenth century, and the polemic of the apostate Dominican friar Thomas Gage, printed in the seventeenth century. Sewall sent to London for these books. By reading them he not only acquired the information he sought; he also found arguments against Spanish Empire in America. To this secular arsenal which supplied Europeans with the *leyenda negra* Sewall added the fire of Protestant ideas: he prepared for the "coming advent" into the New Jerusalem at Mexico City by ordering from London the books of the sixteenth-century Spanish Protestant Cipriano Valera.

In 1704, some five years after Mather's little book had broken trail, Sewall kept the large design alive by writing to the Society for the Propagation of the Gospel in London, urging that

it would be well if you could set on foot the printing of the Spanish Bible in a fair Octavo, Ten Thousand Copies; and then you might attempt the bombing of Santa Domingo, the Havanna, Porto Rico, and Mexico itself. I would willingly give five pounds toward the charge of it. . . . Mr. Leigh commends the translation of Cipriano Valera, which I am the Owner of in Folio.[5]

The request for ten thousand copies—an enormous edition—supplemented earlier orders for Las Casas and other works on the Spanish Indies. Then the "Bostonese" (as an anti-Protestant Chilean would call Yankees a century later) "bombed" Spanish America, using the New Testament as their secret weapon in psychological conflict. Their aims were earnest, but the times were changing: the climate of eighteenth-century thought began to favor science rather than religion, free trade instead of war, and rationalism instead of Puritanism. The Boston project did not get far. Not until the Protestant missionary of the present day entered Latin America did the Protestant Bible gain any importance in the circulation of ideas in America. But by that time the Boston precedent was long dead, and colonial New England's experience was forgotten. Puritanism did not succeed in uniting the Americas; it only originated New England's traditional interest in the Hispanic mind.

The hindsight of history can easily point out the flaw in their approach, but these Puritans were optimistic in their time. The carriers of propaganda for their faith were not mystic visionaries. Among them the worldly force of the future—commercial and expansionist interest—was also present, as Samuel Sewall honestly revealed in his *Diary* and *Letter Book*, but the religious motive was greatest. Mather, Sewall, and their Boston associates of 1700 mingled their conscious aims with the reality of the contemporary situation. They took advantage of England's imperial policy during the War with Spain, hoping to penetrate the Spanish Empire under the British flag. Almost all modern wars involving Spain have bettered the growth of inter-American relations, and all during that war from 1700-1714 the Puritan move toward Latin America spurred the hopes behind the ideas contained in some "Notices of the True Christian Protestant Religion . . . by a Sheet which one of their Number did in the Spanish Language fit for that Intent."[6]

One episode will show how long and lovingly Samuel Sewall sheltered his idea. With the coming of peace in 1714 British wartime protection fell away and disappeared. This did not daunt Sewall, who, more than anyone else, strove mightily to keep the project alive and going. In 1709, Carlos Sucre y Borda, the Spanish governor of Cartagena in the Indies, arrived in Boston. Sucre, interestingly enough, was ancestor of Marshal Antonio José de Sucre, chief aide to Simón Bolívar when independence came to Latin America a century later. Sucre had not come to Boston as a visitor—he was a prisoner of war. Captured during the War of the Spanish Succession, he was taken by the British to Boston, rather than to Jamaica or London. This may suggest the role that the British and New Englanders hoped Sucre would play for them. But if British officials and proselytizing members of the Boston group had plans in mind for Sucre, they were in for disappointment.

Samuel Sewall was alert enough to seek an advantage from this unexpected stroke of luck: he tried to get Sucre to become his first Latin American partner and associate. As long as Governor Sucre remained in Boston there was always a chance. But, after the British released him and returned him to Cartagena, the Spanish government lost its trust in him and did not allow him to stay there. Sucre had been living too long under Anglo-American influence and custody. Hence he was recalled to Spain "upon some suspitions of his keeping a correspondence with the enemies of his Master."

So it all came to nought. Had it been successful it might have changed the religious destiny of the Americas, influencing hemisphere culture and history. Since it did not, we may call it a precedent, a reveal-

ing incident. To Mather and Sewall, of course, the plan had flesh and
blood; they never thought of it as cold precedent. To them it was of
great and living importance. How hard Sewall worked at it is told in
his *Letter Book* and *Diary*.[7] Over and over again Sam Sewall went to
visit Carlos Sucre, talking, questioning, explaining, arguing, speculating
aloud, and always trying to learn more about Latin America, and
especially Mexico. He not only sought information; he tried to convert
Sucre. He cultivated Sucre far more intensively than North Americans
75 years later were to go after Francisco de Miranda, another New
Granadan. The Las Casas book, the Spanish Grammar and Dictionary,
which he had received from London, were not enough for Sewall. He
wanted to know about New Spain, the Aztec civilization, Mexico City.
So ardently did he cling to his belief in Mexico as his New Jerusalem,
so necessary was this faith to him, that at the end of his long life, when
twilight settled around him and his program, and long after Carlos
Sucre had left Boston and Sewall's life, the old Puritan wrote from
Boston to Governor Burnet of New York, "I rather hope that America
Mexicana will be the New Jerusalem."[8] This was in 1723.

With the passing of Mather and Sewall, a deeper and more secular
interest arose. Commerce, political ideas, and science replaced religious
zeal and the vision of conversion. The Age of Reason, natural history,
and natural philosophy showed how an Enlightenment and the revival
of rationalism could forget the road to a "New Jerusalem." The language of constitutions and social and political thinking vied with the
language of the Gospel. Religious inter-Americanism sank from view.
Puritanism in practice was a little too grim to win over Latin Americans,
just as it was no longer able to attract any more North Americans. But
this is not the only reason for the failure of Mather and Sewall. The
further, and probably truer, fact was that religion in general was not very
successful at stirring the inter-American mind into a consciousness of
self and interest. The discipline of churches was, if anything, divisive
rather than unifying. This was the continuing legacy of the Reformation and the Counter Reformation.

A more earthly pull towards Latin American history, ethnology, and
the natural sciences was felt. There was a genuine curiosity about the
secular world of Spain, Portugal, and their New World colonies. An
intellectual and cultural expansion followed the eighteenth-century trails
of explorers, navigators, merchants, and scientists right into Latin
America, enlarging the map and widening the boundaries of North
American knowledge about the Indies. Discovery and rediscovery of

Latin America shrank that formerly unknown world and extended its known traits. The misty eighteenth-century curtain which had once veiled Spanish and Portuguese America began to dissolve. North Americans could see and appreciate the outlines of Iberian civilization.[9]

Direct contact with the Indies was possible only for the adventurous few. Colonial North America was able to read about Latin America in books, newspapers, magazines, and the representative collections (such as Harris or Hakluyt) found in the libraries of the time. The catalogues of these libraries clearly reveal the steady—and secular—growth of an inter-American interest. In Massachusetts, New Jersey, New York, Rhode Island, and Pennsylvania, Hispanic titles stood on the bookshelves. Philadelphia libraries had some good books. In fact, for most of the years before Latin American independence and the Monroe Doctrine (1823), Philadelphia more than Boston was interested in Hispanic materials. When Puritanism yielded to worldly science, history, and literature, Philadelphia overtook and passed Boston. Literally a capital of Hispanic studies and inter-American connections within the United States, Philadelphia, with its well-stocked libraries and scientific societies, possessed a cultural level which raised her intelligent readers far above the ordinary range of travel books. Philadelphia's book collections went in for serious and scholarly literature, although the book for the general reader was also present.

The city's library resources included the standard, early histories of the Indies as well as the later studies about Latin America.[10] Before the American Revolution in 1775, the Philadelphia Library Company already owned copies of Garcilaso de la Vega, the Spanish-Peruvian author of Inca history, and of Juan de Solís, the historian of the Conquest of Mexico, who was the official historiographer of Spain's Council of the Indies. There was also the popular *America* of John Ogilby, as well as Lionel Wafer's description of Panama in 1699, which was a propaganda tract to attract attention to the British settlement at New Edinburgh (Darien). The Frézier (French) account of Chile and Peru in 1712-1714 was listed. Other titles provided special descriptions of Peru (Lima and Quito), Chile, Brazil, and Paraguay. Literary views of Buenos Aires, Bahia, Rio de Janeiro, Havana, and Mexico City were on the shelves. Individual authors included, for example, the Spanish economist Uztáriz, Miguel Venegas (*History of California*), and the *Account of the Spanish Settlements in America,* published at Edinburgh in 1762, and generally attributed to William Burke, brother of the more famous Whig orator, Edmund Burke.

These books, and many others like them, gave North Americans their chief stock of information and knowledge, but at the same time they repeated the elements of the black legend. Even reputable authors manipulated the ever-present Hispanophobe tendency. The North American reader, already excited by Las Casas, Thomas Gage, and some of the works in the Hakluyt Collection, was now subtly and skillfully aroused by Dr. William Robertson in his *History of America*. Robertson's history had a very great sale in the early United States and was just as widely read in book form as in serial reprint in the magazines. It enjoyed several North American editions in the eighteenth and the nineteenth centuries and was many times reproduced in periodicals.

Elsewhere in the United States there were other towns with their own Latin American collections. These also revealed both the sensible and serious history of Latin America on one hand, and on the other, the further spread of hostile ideas about Spain in America. For example, the sympathetic José de Acosta, Antonio de Herrera, Juan de Solís, Garcilaso de la Vega, as well as the critical Las Casas and Robertson were almost everywhere. Often enough, as in the case of Las Casas, apparently sound books by Spanish authors contributed to the literature of criticism. This happened when intelligent Spaniards themselves boldly and honestly wrote the literature of self-criticism, for example, the contemporary, eighteenth-century reports about Latin America by the famous Spaniards, Jorge Juan and Antonio de Ulloa (*Voyage to South America*). Unlike Las Casas, Juan and Ulloa were careful investigators, with good scientific reputations and practical experiences. They were hard critics. The attractive Latin American image now reflected in many books became just as quickly dulled under the attention to old evils and newly pessimistic interpretations of the New World.

Although too much unfavorable criticism, of the kind written by eighteenth-century Europeans, might have discouraged the taste for Hispanic culture, fortunately the opposite took place. Literary and historical collections, so necessary to any idea of the New World, expanded. In the Redwood Library at Newport, Rhode Island, or in the private collection of Thomas Prince at Boston, and again in the Harvard College Library (in 1723), the best-known historical treatises were found.[11] Harvard could already boast of a 1596 edition of the Spanish literary classic, *La Celestina, Tragicomedia de Calixto y Melibea*. Thomas Prince had copies of Bartolomé Carranza, the sixteenth-century Spanish religious reformer, and of José de Acosta, the noted Jesuit historian of Peru and America. At Harvard there also were Spanish theological writings, psalteries, a Bible in Portuguese, and an ecclesiastical history of England which was written in Spanish.

After, as well as before, the American Revolution, the major libraries and the new learned societies returned to the acquisition of South American materials. In Philadelphia the American Philosophical Society, the Medical School, and the College of Philadelphia renewed the inter-American process. Leading citizens gave a personal stamp to the work: John Logan, Dr. Benjamin Smith Barton, and Benjamin Franklin were among them. The College of Philadelphia in 1776 offered the first college course on Spanish Grammar and Literature given in the United States. The libraries kept pace. The Philadelphia Library Company had the Portuguese history of Jerónimo Osorio; also the scientific paper of the French savant La Condamine, given before the Academy of Sciences at Paris in 1745. This paper described the Amazon Valley, Peru, and the interior parts of South America. Even better was the reference work, *Voyage of the Ship Conde de St. Malo to Peru, 1745-1749*, with an invaluable appendix on mines, industry, commerce, and agriculture, describing those regions.

While this gave every proof of a healthy intellectual interest in books of the better sort, popular taste still preferred the exciting themes of Spanish Discovery, Exploration, and Conquest. British accounts of war and naval battles of the eighteenth century were also eagerly read. Libraries had a kind of standard shelf for such works, as for example, the Library Company of Burlington, capital of New Jersey, which assembled tales of such sea dogs as Captains Anson, Bulkeley and Cummins, Dampier, and other heroes of Anglo-Spanish struggle and adventure. North American stay-at-homes had vivid word pictures of Indies ports, romantic old Caribbean towns, naval galleons, commercial treasure. Without going outside they drank their fill of storm, siege, piracy, buccaneers in the Spanish Main, Buenos Aires, Panama, Cartagena, Havana, Lima, and the South Sea. In fact, the call of the Spanish Main and the South Sea found willing readers in the United States at all times. Exploration, privateering, and war also gave some lessons in geography, place-names, and riverways of Latin America. The several eighteenth-century wars between England and Spain aroused and delighted the North American onlookers as well as North American privateers who participated. Since the sixteenth century the famous Hakluyt, Purchas, and Harris collections had given literary immortality to tales of adventure in South America; now there was more to read.[12]

Most but not all of these books were published in England. However, this dependency of North American readers upon English books and publishers was to change. In time there came into being an undeclared independence of North American publishing from English dominance, and books on Latin America were published here. The time would soon come when even books in Spanish were printed in the United States although this was hardly visible at first; the number of books published here from 1700 to 1800 was indeed small. Three titles were issued. The total is insignificant compared to those Latin American items imported from England for the libraries. Nevertheless, from these acorns came an inter-American book trade of amazing proportions. Most beginnings are small yet significant.

Cotton Mather's book was the first one printed in Spanish in the United States. We have already seen how he intended it for the Latin American "market" rather than for the domestic reader. The second book was a Spanish grammar, published in 1741 by Garrat Noel, of New York. This, the first Spanish grammar to appear in this country, was intended to educate the North American reader. Noel's grammar sired an enormous progeny; it was the father of the hundreds of grammars which have been published since then. Garrat Noel was a New York bookseller, Spanish translator for the Provincial Council of the Colony of New York, and teacher of perhaps the first Spanish class in New York. Writing this grammar for New Yorkers was no accident, since Noel expressly intended it for inter-American use "particularly in these parts." The Noel grammar was never reprinted. The next North American grammar came out in Philadelphia in 1798, reproduced from a British grammar. Noel's grammar was really American, one of the first factors in building up knowledge of Spanish here. Noel called his book *A Short Introduction to the Spanish language; to which is added a vocabulary of familiar words for the more speedy improvement of the Learner; with a preface shewing the usefulness of this language particularly in these parts.*[13]

For the third example of early North American book publishing of Latin American works, we turn neither to English nor to Spanish but surprisingly enough to German. Not too far from Philadelphia, with its library collections of Latin Americana, was the German-speaking community of Ephrata. At Ephrata, an important center of publishing, a classic of Spanish American mining technology was translated and adapted for Pennsylvania miners and readers. Álvaro Alonso Barba's seventeenth-century *Arte de los Metales* was buried for so long under a complex German-language title that for all its widespread reputation in Spanish and in English its publication in eighteenth-century Pennsylvania was overlooked.

The *Arte,* whose German-language edition was published at Ephrata in 1763, was almost unknown to contemporaries as well as later students. One can well imagine how the Barba work might have pleased Andrés del Río, dean of Mexican mining geologists and an active member of both Philadelphia's American Philosophical Society and the Academy of Natural Sciences. Del Río, as well as other Latin American scientists, came up to the United States to lecture early in the nineteenth century, but they did not know that a copy of Barba's *Arte de los Metales* existed here.

The involved German subtitle explains how it happened that the Latin American *Arte* remained hidden from the many North Americans who knew something of Latin American science. The Pennsylvania edition was based upon the English translation made by the Earl of Sandwich in 1669:

Gruendlicher Unterricht von den Metallen, Darinnen beschrieben wird, wie sie werden in der erden generirt; und was man insgemein dabey findet. In zwey Büchern. Vormals im Spanischen beschrieben durch Albano [*sic*] Alonso Barba, Pfarrherr zu St. Bernhardi Kirchspiel in der Kaiserlichen Stadt Potosi, in dem Königreich Peru, in West-Indien; in Jahr 1664. Hernach in das Englandische übersetzt durch Edward, Graff von Samperich, Anno 1669. Und nun um seiner Vortrefflichkeit willen zum erstenmal ins Hoch-teutsche übersetzt, und zum Druck befördert, durch G. R. Dieser Kunst beflissenen. Nebst einem neuen Anhang betreffend obige Materie. Ephrata: Gedruckt durch J. George Zeisiger, Anno 1763.[14]

Had the book been reprinted in the Spanish edition it would have been far better known and read than it was. But the *Arte de los Metales* lost its essential identity, in spite of the fame of Barba as its author, and of George Zeisiger as the printer. It may have been intended for good use in Pennsylvania mining practice, but it now serves us only as another bibliographical record of the historic process of inter-American book publishing and collection.

These few books were the "firsts" of a large North American book trade on—and with—Latin America which spread into the hemisphere before 1900. As the next chapter will show, less than a handful of books, concerned separately with religion, grammar, and mining, and published in New England, New York, and Pennsylvania, fell into the rich soil of American and inter-American thought, germinating hundreds, even thousands, of volumes about Latin America which were published in the United States from 1800. Long before the twentieth century, books were the constant commodity of inter-American cultural exchange. They did as much as anything else to foster a permanent North American interest in Latin American history, language, mining, music, fine arts, government, geography, and ethnology. This great growth, of course, was slow. It took time. At the turn of 1800 the largest number of books that North Americans read about Latin America were still imported from Great Britain, where they had been translated or acquired. There is, however, one striking point: there were many more books in the Spanish language, printed in Spain, available here than the few which we have seen printed here.

Returning now to Philadelphia and her libraries, we need only a glimpse of the famous Logan Collection to see this.[15] Spanish-language books, imported from Spain, far outnumbered the tiny North American output. Just one cultured bibliophile, John Logan of Philadelphia, enriched the Hispanic resources of the Philadelphia Library Company in 1792, when he donated the original Spanish volumes of the "Loganian" Library. The Logan Collection was the first library of Hispanic and Latin American materials in the United States. This was a noteworthy class. Although the Logan Library had fewer first editions and manuscripts than the John Carter Brown, John Jacob Astor, and Hubert H. Bancroft libraries proudly possessed in the nineteenth century, the Philadelphia Library was extraordinary for its day. Long before the book-collecting activities of Obadiah Rich, Washington Irving, Henry Stevens, Buckingham Smith, George Ticknor, and others enriched the materials for the study of Latin America in the United States, Philadelphia bookmen prized their Spanish originals above London translations.

To add to its galaxy of Spanish writers such as Baltasar Gracián and Cervantes and the writers of the anonymous *Celestina* and other great Hispanic novels and histories, the Logan Library catalogued the *Historia de Mexico con el Descubrimiento de Nueva Espanna,* published in Antwerp in 1554 and written by the chaplain and one-time historian for Cortés, Francisco Lopez de Gómara. Gómara was the chronicler whom William H. Prescott later called one of the pillars of the historiography of the Conquest of Mexico. The other "pillar" was Bernal Díaz del Castillo, foot-soldier, eye-witness, and companion of Cortés, whose

True History of the Conquest of New Spain—a denial of the claims of
Gómara—was printed in the United States soon after 1800. At the same
time that the Philadelphia Library was proud of its Gómara, the Massachusetts Historical Society in Boston (1790) displayed another classic
of sixteenth-century Spanish America, the *Chrónica del Perú*—the best-
known part of the celebrated Cieza de León narrative.[16]

The unusual Spanish and Latin American titles in the Philadelphia
Library make up somewhat for the glaring lack of Portuguese and
Brazilian books. The Logan Collection included Spanish editions of the
historians of the Indies, Antonio de Herrera and José de Acosta, and
of the Jesuit historian of peninsular Spain, Juan de Mariana. Something
must be added here about the literature of Spain's great intellectual
era in the sixteenth century—the *siglo de oro*—as reflected in the Logan
Collection. Because Spanish America and Old Spain were as closely
associated in the North American mind as they should have been before
the Latin American revolt for separation, the classic histories of the New
World and the great literary works of Old Spain formed parts of the
same cultural whole. The genius of the two together made up Spain, at
least before 1810-1825. The Logan Collection made Spanish-language
classics available to North Americans, although its fame is less than the
important Hispanophile literary journals, the *North American Review*
(printed in Boston) and *Port Folio* (printed in Philadelphia). In literature there were Jorge Montemayor's *Diana* and the adroit, picaresque
adventures of Mateo de Guzmán, *Vida de Guzmán de Alfarache.*

The world of science was also here, and the doorway to Spanish
science in America had been opened through books some years before
Alexander von Humboldt described it to readers. Francisco Hernandez'
remarkable sixteenth-century report on the natural history of New
Spain was in the Logan Collection. Not published until 1648, although
written in the previous century, the Hernandez survey of Mexico and
her mineral and vegetable resources was the first of several European
scientific reports on New Spain. Philadelphia's attention to literature
was no greater than the study of science, and the Hernandez volume
is an early example of it. Dr. Hernandez had been sent to New Spain
by Philip II. He left the medical and scientific world this celebrated
treatise upon Aztec and Mexican pharmacopoeia, minerals, plant life,
and zoology. This copy was highly prized, even if it was abridged.

Is it a striking measure of the rise of inter-American scientific study
in the eighteenth century that the Hernandez report could not then
be found in Spain? In 1777 Casimiro Gómez Ortega, the noted Spanish

botanist and chief of the Madrid Botanical Gardens, searched for a copy to be used as reading and reference material for the famous Ruiz-Pavón scientific expedition, which was investigating the natural history and botany of Peru and Chile.[17] Not until 1790 did another edition of Hernandez appear in Spain. The partial title of the earlier Philadelphia copy was *Rerum Medicarum Novae Hispaniae Thesaurus seu Plantarum Animalium Mineralium Mexicanorum Historia relationibus in ipsa mexicana urbe collecta ac in ordinem digesta. . . .* It was printed in Rome, 1648. As a cyclopedia, the *Rerum Medicarum* systematized and classified botanical, mineral, and zoological data; as a scientific account of American natural resources, it was much superior to the more controversial eighteenth-century treatise by Piso, *De Indiae utriusque re naturalique et medica libri,* which also was in Philadelphia.

Books and book collections were always important indices of current inter-American progress; but intellectual friendships between North American, Spanish, and Spanish American scientists and scholars became just as important and quite as permanent. No doubt books and libraries connected the world of scholarly and scientific ideas, but the personal correspondence of men of reason secured the more human and living touch. Before 1800 the human contact with Latin America was missing; after that, men of science and learning came together in the "republic of letters," to use a contemporary phrase. The American Philosophical Society set the model which all other North American societies imitated and have followed down to the present. A sense of living inter-Americanism led Latin Americans to become members and colleagues of North American learned societies. With Philadelphia's existing position at the head of Hispanic studies, it is no surprise to learn that the American Philosophical Society was the first North American scientific society to count Latin American and Spanish scientists as members.[18]

This big step from library to personal ties was most far-reaching because it set a pattern. Here was the historic norm for cultural action, instantly followed and repeated by other societies. A vast range of nominations before 1900 made more genuine those estimates of worth, appreciation, and intellectual equality which North Americans extended to their Latin American contemporaries, and which the Latin Americans both honored and esteemed. Simultaneously, the selection of European Spaniards showed once again how North American science and learning rejected the *leyenda negra,* while the distinction earned by Latin Americans provided clear denial to those popular prejudices which later flourished under the North American formula of Manifest Destiny.

Count Pedro Rodríguez de Campomanes of Spain, a historian, economic reformer, and liberal statesman of the enlightened era of Carlos III, was the most famous Iberian member-correspondent of the Philosophical Society. He was the author of several works on Spanish history and education, which he had donated to the North American society. Campomanes, a powerful political and educational figure of those days, was president of the Real Academia de la Historia, 1764-1791. When Thomas Jefferson circulated his *Notes on Virginia* among the leading thinkers of Europe, he was quick to give a complimentary copy to the Conde de Campomanes. The Spaniard was one of the brightest lights in Spain's shining eighteenth-century Enlightenment. In 1791 William Carmichael, then attaché of the United States in Madrid, wrote to Thomas Jefferson about the "Ct. de Campomanes, Governor of the Council of Castile, who is, with those he can influence decidedly of the opinion that it is to the interest of this country to form liberal and lasting connections with the United States."[19] Beside Campomanes, other Iberian members of the Philosophical Society before 1800 included Francisco de Gardoquí, auditor at Rome for the Crown of Castile, and Diego de Gardoquí, Spanish minister to the United States. Both Gardoquí brothers belonged to the prosperous mercantile firm at Bilbao in Old Spain which had profitable commercial relations with New England business houses.

Before 1800, membership was extended to the Conde de Caylus, now considered a minor literary figure; to Cipriano Rivera Freire, the Portuguese minister to the United States; to Francisco de Peyrolón and Luis de Urbina, both of the Sociedad de Amigos del País of Valencia; and to José Joaquín Ferrer of Cádiz. A major contemporary patron of Spanish scholarship was José Miguel Flores, the secretary of the Real Academia de la Historia, and a colleague of Campomanes. Another corresponding member was José de Jaúdenes, a former Spanish representative in the United States, who married a New England girl and then returned home to settle in Valencia. This sampling of names illustrates some of the personal as well as institutional connections which had arisen by 1800. From this pattern came that permanent and established North American feeling for Spain and Spanish America which led to the work of Washington Irving, William H. Prescott, George Ticknor, Henry W. Longfellow, Buckingham Smith, H. H. Bancroft, and William Dean Howells. A more complete list of Iberian members will be found in the Appendix.

The Hispanic members reciprocated: they enriched the book and library resources of the Philosophical Society with gifts and donations and helped regularize the trans-Caribbean and trans-Atlantic exchange of scientific transactions. For example, in 1788, the Count of Campomanes gave the American Philosophical Society the *Proceedings* of the Real Academia de la Historia, the works of the sixteenth-century jurist Ginés de Sepúlveda, who had fought against Las Casas and his concepts of Indian liberties. He also donated his own *Diccionario Latino-Arábigo*, a treatise on Spanish historical philology, and some Spanish coins.[20] Similarly, a few years later Dr. Freire, the first Portuguese member, donated the prize-winning publications of the Lisbon Academy of Sciences in addition to the memoirs of that learned society. He also gave a valuable volume illustrating economic thinking in late colonial Brazil: the Bishop of Pernambuco [Azeredo Couto de Coutinho]'s *Ensaio Econômico sobre o Comercio de Portugal e suas Colonias*, in the Lisbon edition of 1794.[21]

Gifts, donations, and exchanges allowed the Philosophical Society (and other North American academies) to increase their holdings in such fields as Portuguese colonization, Latin American science, and even the Philippines. Corresponding members, as a rule, were quite generous and eager to help, because of a pride in their country's cultural achievements. Valentín Foronda, a Spanish liberal of that country's Age of Reason and one-time consul in Philadelphia, sent back from Spain many volumes on political economy, medicine, history, and philosophy. Foronda, whose interesting observations on government, life, and society in the young United States were written down in 1804 (in a manuscript recently published), remained a dependable associate in cultural relations.[22] Together with other Spaniards then residing in the United States, Foronda evaluated North American democracy through Spanish eyes. The age of Jefferson and Franklin won friends for the United States even in monarchical Spain.

The American Philosophical Society and its contemporaries were consequently stimulated to buy those works which were not given or exchanged. For example, the Society had been given two outstanding Peruvian scientific treatises: that of the Spaniard Hipólito Ruíz on the botany and medicine of quinine, and the medical study of the widely-known Peruvian Hipólito Unánue on the coca plant. This was the beginning. In 1803 the Society acquired volumes that are still invaluable for the history of the Age of Reason in Peru, when it ordered the purchase of the rare *Mercurio Peruviano* [*sic*] *from its Commencement*

[*1790*]. And with these printed cultural treasures of the Peruvian and Latin American Enlightenment came such other gems of Latin American liberal-scientific thought as the *Gazeta de Guatemala* and the *Semanario del Nuevo Reyno de Granada*. The *Semanario,* published by the noted Colombian astronomer and patriot-scientist Francisco de Caldas, showed North Americans how far Latin American science and secular thinking had by then emerged from the influence of religion and the Church. Caldas, whose school of science had been singled out for praise by the great Alexander von Humboldt, held a very high opinion of North American science and thought. He had already expressed his specific wish to commence direct inter-American cultural relations, but his life ended early. He was executed by the Spaniards, a martyr to early Colombian republican principles. One of his letters was sent to Philadelphia in 1812 by "Pedro de la Lastra from Santa Fé de Bogotá. Also a Description of the Astronomical Observatory there, in charge of F. I. de Caldas, who seeks correspondence with Astronomers in the United States."[23]

Successful cultural relations have to be two-way, and most of the North American efforts were reciprocated. As early as 1784 the august and monarchical Real Academia de la Historia of Madrid added North American members to its roster. The Academy's first choice was Benjamin Franklin.[24] This selection was significant, a symbolic reward for Philadelphia's growing Hispanism and inter-Americanism. It also proved valuable for the new North American democracy, since Franklin's membership had impressed Spanish and even Latin American intellectuals with the worth of North American science and learning. Benjamin Franklin was thus the first of the line of North Americans elected by the Real Academia, preceding Washington Irving, William H. Prescott, George Ticknor, and others.

Campomanes and Flores, the two leading officers of the Real Academia, were Franklin's intellectual colleagues, keeping in touch with him and sending him Spanish books from time to time. In addition, Carmichael, the North American attaché in Madrid, took on an early cultural relations function by forwarding to Franklin many books published in Spain, including the complete works of Francisco Pérez Bayer, a well-known philosopher of the eighteenth century. So much has been written on Franklin and French culture that his pioneer role in the North American feeling for Spanish culture has been overlooked.

Latin Americans felt the same way towards Franklin as the Spanish did, singling him out for his contributions to modern science. In fact, to many an enlightened Latin American of the eighteenth century Franklin was the living proof of the virtues of science and secular thought, of invention as well as of republican equality. Mexicans knew and praised his work on electricity and optics, while in far-off Chile Franklin was the model and living example of American man's capacity to progress. To contemporaries this meant an effective rebuttal of the European "scientific" thesis of the Fall of Man in the New World. Franklin gave a sense of pride to the Latin American creole, chiefly because he blazoned the grand possibilities of growth for the "new and virile people" in the Americas, North and South. The sophisticated and specious argument of New World degeneration and inferiority before Europe, then being propagated by such Europeans as Buffon, de Pauw, Robertson, and even Abbé Raynal, was earlier and specifically rejected by Jefferson in his *Notes on Virginia*. Franklin was even better known, and he made quite evident the existence of reason and science in the New World. That is why, for one example, the great Chilean creole, Manuel de Salas, put the name of Franklin at the head of his list of great New World figures, in order to show that Western Hemisphere culture was as good as European, or even better.[25]

With this state of mind in the making, along inter-American lines, North American scientific and learned societies soon extended to Latin America the same type of cultural relation that had recently begun with Spain. Technically, of course, the Spanish government could hold any such direct cultural exchanges to be illegal; there were some attempts to censor and restrain them under Spanish laws. But law did not—and probably could not—encompass the flowing nature of ideas, and it was not long before an intellectual bridge connected North and South America. Before Latin America won her independence from Spain and her resultant freedom to act, the currents of inter-American forces were running across the Caribbean. In spite of all the differences of speech, religion, and form of government, and notwithstanding the attempted censorship by Spain, the ties were made. Cultural expansionism had a quiet drive and persistent energy of its own, launching the ever-widening circles of diffusion.

Soon after 1800 the American Philosophical Society found a Cuban friend, Francisco Arango y Parreño of the learned and still-existing Havana Sociedad de Amigos del Pais. Arango was an outstanding leader of the Cuban Enlightenment in his own right, whom the American Philosophical Society persuaded to distribute its *Transactions* among Iberian scientific bodies on his trip to Spain, in 1801 and 1802. The

Philosophical Society's *Transactions* came into Mexico just as success-fully.[26] We know that the Mexican scientist José Antonio Alzate, himself a member of several European scientific societies, knew and read the *Transactions* of the American Philosophical Society when they came to Mexico City.[27]

About 1800, when the exchanges of transactions between societies became as usual and as frequent as library acquisition of Spanish works, inter-American relations took a great step forward: in 1801 the Ameri-can Philosophical Society turned to Latin America to choose a member —the first from Spanish America. He was Alejandro Ramírez, so-called "first secretary of the Guatemala junta." Ramírez was a Fellow of the Real Academia de la Historia in Spain, a well-known botanist and scientist in Guatemala, Cuba, and Puerto Rico, where he had passed most of his life. In each of these places he had also held a government position, once in the key intellectual post of Censor of Press and Publica-tions and in his later years as Intendant of Puerto Rico.

The nomination of Ramírez in 1801 means much as a landmark; it means far more as the first action in the new inter-American pattern. From that time on, an unusual and impressive number of Latin Ameri-can ethnologists, scientists, humanists, and historians were extended membership in United States societies. It is both admirable and striking to notice the great coincidence by which every important society in the United States, by its own and separate interest, without central organi-zation or advice, succeeded in doing exactly the same thing in the same way. These bodies acted on an independent, *laisser-faire,* but parallel basis. There was an unconscious pattern at work among each of them to reach in the direction of Latin American men of science and letters. No government proposed the rules or suggested the policy; it was free and spontaneous. The societies laid down their own aims. In this way, too, they were also free from the praise or blame of North American diplo-matic action, economic and territorial expansionism, or the psychological aggression brought out by Manifest Destiny and war. Most important, to repeat, was the course and process of separated actions, renewed over and over until a tradition was built.

The Appendix, in the list of Latin American members of the North American societies, gives a fairly representative chart of many of the appointments. Here too, the nominations were reciprocally helpful to the development of North American libraries and collections. Latin Americans were as cooperative as the Spaniards; they sent gifts, dona-tions and books. As one example: August 21, 1807, Juan Manuel de

Ferrer of Veracruz, Mexico, shipped to Philadelphia "a box of minerals and sixty three volumes, and four volumes of the *Journal de Physique* accompanied by a letter saying that he had continued the subscription to the same as a donation to the [American Philosophical] Society."[28]

From the start of the nineteenth century, then, we find reports of corresponding memberships, exchanges, library collections, and even early book publishing, which successfully formed and bound inter-American ties. In the republican atmosphere of the New World, which believed in the equality of all the talents, North American and Latin American talents drew closer together. Bodies of like-minded men had rediscovered the Americas, North and South.

Because New England awoke slowly from the early vision of Mather and Sewall, Boston took some time to catch up with Philadelphia in the level and quality of inter-American and Hispanic work. New England's place lay well ahead, in the nineteenth century. But the stages in between were the same for Boston societies as they were for Philadelphia: by 1800 the Massachusetts Historical Society's library catalogued the now-usual and standard titles dealing with Spain and Spanish America. In addition, the library owned two books not found elsewhere in the United States at the time: Peter Martyr's letters describing the news of Columbus' Discovery and Pedro Velarde's *Historia de Philippinas*.

Another important item in Boston was a French translation of the Zárate history of the Conquest of Peru, written in the sixteenth century, as well as the *Chronica del Peru* (cited earlier), which is undoubtedly Cieza de León's. In Cambridge nearby, the Harvard College Library had been improving its position since 1723, by filling in gaps with a fine collection of the literature of travel and discovery. By this time Harvard had also received some scholarly works on Castilian literature and historiography, including the writings of the court historian Pero Mexia, chronicler of Charles V, and the work of Juan Palafox y Mendoza, bishop of Puebla in Mexico, *History of the Conquest of China*. The College Library, which had previously listed *La Celestina,* now had the work of the sixteenth-century Aragonese historian Jerónimo Zurita, *Indices Rerum Gestarum ab Aragoniae Regibus* (Zaragoza, 1578).[29]

New England was also ready for the next step: the American Academy of Arts and Sciences at Boston chose as Spanish corresponding members the Marqúes de Santa Cruz and the Duque de Almodóvar, both of them well-known in their day—especially the latter, who had translated into Spanish the Abbé Raynal's *Histoire des Indes.* The Frenchman Raynal had entered the company of Las Casas, Robertson,

Gage, Jorge Juan and Antonio de Ulloa, and so many others who found much to criticise in the Spanish settlement of South America. However, nothing that these writers had said along the lines of the *leyenda negra* had diminished the North American desire to read about Latin America.

A far more definite proof of New England's parallel (not unified) interest in cultivating Latin American scholarship comes from the very clear plea of the president of the American Antiquarian Society at Worcester, Massachusetts. In 1814 Isaiah Thomas, publisher, historian, and president of the American Antiquarian Society, urged his New England colleagues that it should be "one of our first endeavors to extend membership to gentlemen of distinguished characters in Spanish and Portuguese America, particularly in the dominions of the former, where it is believed many of the valuable antiquities of the continent may be procured."[30]

To be sure that these aims would be carried out, the American Antiquarian Society instructed its Governing Council, in Article II of its first by-laws, to "enquire concerning the character of persons living out of the Commonwealth proper, to be elected honorary members, particularly in Spanish America." The Society did well, and gave additional energy to the historical process which was now hard at work.

New York City did not lag behind Boston and Philadelphia in inter-American interests. As we have already seen, the study of Spanish before the American Revolution was helped by the Noel grammar. Latin American books and book collections in the libraries matched those found elsewhere. The New York Society Library, founded in 1754, also had some of the more recent Latin American works, such as Juan Bautista Muñoz' *History of the New World* (published recently), the *Spanish and Portuguese Letters* of Robert Southey, the now widely read *Celestina,* and the highly regarded *History of Mexico,* written by the exiled Jesuit Francisco Clavigero, lately translated in London, and well-illustrated with reproductions of Aztec pictographs. This library's materials compared favorably with other collections in the United States. However, the New York Society Library was a place for general readers and not a scholarly or learned society. In New York, therefore, the serious task of creating and consolidating the basis of hemisphere ties fell, instead, to the New-York Historical Society.

The New-York Historical Society, founded in 1804, not only quickly came to possess one of the most extensive book collections in the young nation but it also turned attention southward in order to nominate and elect Latin Americans to its membership as well as to promote the exchange of scientific works. Its library owned many books which were written and printed in Spanish (that is, they were printed in Spain, not England), in addition to the usual translations of Latin American and Iberian chronicles, histories, and some literary works. The fact is that so much of the general and secondary source material was available in the United States by that time that something of a specialization by regions could be noticed. If, for example, Philadelphia was interested in Hispanic science and Boston had begun to cultivate a literary bent, then the New-York Historical Society echoed the feelings for history.

The panel of Latin American historians in the library was certainly extensive, even for those days. Among the names we find Muñoz, Solís, Herrera, Robertson, Molina, Clavigero, Bernal Díaz, and several others. Moreover, as though to show that New York preferred the rational, the enlightened, and the liberal, the Historical Society was the only group to have the *Transactions* of the justly famed Sociedad Vascongada de Amigos del País, for 1776, 1779, 1783, and 1787, which acted as a model for those societies of "Friends of the Country" in Cuba and Guatemala which did so much to open their countries to new ideas.[31]

And yet, the patient work of libraries and societies supported and sustained quite different ideas of Spain and Spanish America from those of the *leyenda negra* which inhibited the more popular mind. No bridge crossed this gap between the two. No matter how genuinely the catalogues of books, lists of Latin American colleagues, or the turnover of scientific interchange proved the presence of real inter-American attitudes, we find that prejudice painted still another picture. Mere inheritance of ideas from Elizabethan and Cromwellian anxieties supplied the start which North American newspapers and early magazines kept alive. It would be impossible to measure and compare the educational influence of libraries and societies with the propaganda of the press. The average North American reader held attitudes which were not affected by science and scholarship. Outside the more learned bodies, many newspapers and magazines reproduced and fed hostile views about Latin America. Consequently, the image of Latin America looked one way to one set of readers and meant something else to the other.

Magazines and newspapers sometimes reprinted articles and often serialized books which pleased the existing public taste for stories about Latin America. The newspapers of the colonial period as well as those of the early national were chiefly interested in political incidents and commercial news, but they could always find space to give some sort of impression about the continent and people across the Caribbean. In fact, the stimulating combination of passive (that is, inherited) attitudes, together with current events, gave rise to the popular type of book about South America which was widely sold in the nineteenth century. As we shall see in the next chapter, North American book publishing, like that of the North American magazine and newspaper, had to reckon with the two levels of inter-American interest: the superficial and the studious.

Before 1810 North American newspapers served up a diet far thinner than that offered by the libraries. Before the revolutions for Latin American independence in that year, the newspapers generally confined their free use of serialized articles to the retelling of those tales which hardened already stiffened viewpoints. Not until after Latin American emancipation from European Spain did the papers suggest any sympathy from those events into the mind of the reader. Current inter-American and international pressures brought this about in the years before the Monroe Doctrine. In Philadelphia, New York, and especially Baltimore, newspapers which favored the recognition of independent Latin America presented an attractive picture of Latin American prospects and leaders.

Newspapers of the eighteenth century had little news that was exciting to report; but they found much to repeat and reprinted the now standard materials of the *leyenda negra,* drawn from readable accounts, and mixed with envy of Spain, fear of her power, and the epic of adventure. Before 1800 there was little change from the spirit manifested in 1758-1759 when Samuel Nevill in his *New American Magazine* revived the provocative, anti-Hispanic travelogue of Thomas Gage, seventeenth-century Central American traveler, Spanish friar, and apostate to Protestantism, then propaganda adviser to Oliver Cromwell. Another recurrent theme was the so-called "gold rush" article (really dealing with silver), especially the exciting discoveries in renowned Potosí. Robertson's *History of America* was a favorite serial in many magazines.

In contrast with the many North Americans, probably the majority, who thus regularly replenished their psychological dependency upon a *leyenda negra* and passed it down to the Manifest Destiny hostility of the nineteenth century, there was a small but more stable group of Americans who inherited friendlier feelings and bequeathed a cultural reciprocity to the hemisphere. These few, fortunately, were much better known than "the people" and more influential than the majority. They also gave a personal touch, which compensated both for the impersonal work of newspapers and magazines, on one hand, and for the societies and libraries on the other. Living people breathed life into inter-Americanism. No process is bigger or better than the people who share it, and the historical force in inter-American relations was no exception. Men like Dr. Benjamin Smith Barton of Philadelphia, or Dr. Samuel Latham Mitchill of New York, were so clear and vocal in their scientific friendship for Latin America that it is easy to see why they, in turn, won so much respect from Latin Americans. They were the products of the age and attitude of Franklin and Jefferson.

Their prestige and their active personal efforts gave very real impetus to the building of scientific connections in the New World. After 1800 it was the North American scientist and scholar, the secular heir of Cotton Mather and Samuel Sewall, who sent the message of reason, natural philosophy, and freedom of ideas into Latin America. This later generation secured a good name for the United States throughout Latin America. Mitchill and Barton not only followed the eighteenth century in time; they transmitted a fine tradition to the nineteenth century. Before their day, other Americans, such as the local New England and Pennsylvania historians Jeremy Belknap and Ebenezer Hazard, pushed the horizon of American history to include Ancient Peru and Mexico, just as the libraries and societies near them were doing. American history was already understood to include Spanish American beginnings. Spanish American history and antiquity were part of the history of the hemisphere.

Dr. Benjamin Smith Barton, like his fellow-Philadelphian, Daniel G. Brinton, a century later, was essentially a book ethnologist. He could only be as much of a specialist in Latin American Indian studies as North American library collections then permitted. No one—except specially authorized Spanish scientists, or the unique Alexander von Humboldt—could then get permission from Spain to do field work or carry out local research. Yet Barton's interest and his book studies led him to take a stand in the contemporary Buffon-dePauw-Jefferson polemic over the ability and prospects of New World man. This intellectual encounter between Americans and Europeans was, in many ways, a continuation along scientific and rational lines of the debate begun by Bartolomé de Las Casas two hundred years before: Was the European superior to New World man? For an answer, Barton turned to the evidence of the Indian societies in Peru and Mexico. Two factors limited the scope of his Latin American work: his interest in Indian origins rather than later history and his lack of field opportunity. Still, Barton helped to launch a rudimentary North American knowledge of Latin American ethnology;[32] and he may be regarded as a sort of pioneer here, although his reputation in Latin America was based upon his medical studies, and his work on goitre was extensively reviewed and cited in the *Gazeta de Guatemala,* 1801-1802.

If Philadelphians like Benjamin Franklin won special mention in Mexico—and Dr. Barton extended this esteem southward into Central America—it remained for a New Yorker, Samuel Latham Mitchill, to expand the reputation of North American science and scholarship into continental South America. A scientist of great local reputation in New York, Dr. Mitchill acquired further fame as a friend in Congress of the national independence of Latin America and a confirmed partisan of inter-American cultural relations. From 1802 to well past 1823—independently of national policy and the Monroe Doctrine—Mitchill was officer and member of several scientific and scholarly societies which gladly recognized the cultural equality of Latin America and reached as far south as Havana, Bogotá, Lima, and Buenos Aires for an intellectual solidarity with the other America.

Once he had rediscovered Hispanic and Latin American capacity for science Mitchill used the written and spoken word to urge cultural ties. He took his place on the inter-American stage shortly after 1800, and he never left it while he was alive. His sense of American and inter-American pride was stirred in 1808 when Joseph Alsop of Connecticut translated Molina's *History of Chile* from the Spanish. The book was published in New York City and was dedicated to Dr. Benjamin Smith Barton of Philadelphia. In the foreword Dr. Mitchill became enthusiastic over the achievement represented by the event, feeling that it was "an honor to our age and country that the first translation into our own tongue should have been done at Middletown in Connecticut by one of our own literati and published in this city [New York]." Mitchill may or may not have known at that time that other books about Latin America were then being published and subscribed in Salem, Boston, Philadelphia, Richmond, New York, and elsewhere in North America. Whether he knew or not that this was part of a large cultural process of publishing about Latin America, he had a right to make much of the local "honor" which he emphasized.

In 1813 he lectured before the New-York Historical Society, revealing to the audience his acquaintance with the literature and authors of Latin American botany and natural history. Some of this came from his reading of Humboldt. Mitchill must have impressed his listeners with information about the scientific expedition carried out by Hipólito Ruiz and José Pavón in Chile and Peru and with Humboldt's writings on Mexico and northern South America. He drew some famous Latin American scientists into his lecture: Martin Sessé and José Mariano Mociño of Mexico and José Mutis of New Granada (Colombia).

He could and did separate his scientific from his political ideas. An ardent democrat, and a Jeffersonian Republican elected to Congress, Mitchill nevertheless credited the Spanish monarchy with considerable support for Latin American science. A staunch supporter in Congress of the recognition of Latin American independence (he introduced the first Congressional resolution to that effect in 1810), Mitchill scorned popular Anglo-American notions of *leyenda negra* flavor. He gave full praise to Spanish royalty when it came to the patronage and growth of science in the New World. At the same time that Isaiah Thomas, in 1814, was speaking up firmly for New England's cultural recognition of Latin America, Dr. Mitchill, addressing the New-York Historical Society, said he wished it in his power "to state the particulars . . . for the improvement of American botany made by the Kings of Spain. There is perhaps not a government upon earth that has expended so much money for the advancement of this branch of natural history as that of the Castilian monarch."[33]

Mitchill, and all others concerned with the advance of science and learning in the Americas, never asked the question, "What is the good of all this?" The answer, of course, singles out for special scrutiny the value of science, learning, and the liberating effect of ideas in free circulation. Part of the answer may be tied in with the next question, "How can ideas be transmitted from the educated to the uneducated?" The heart of the answer then points up the alternate strength and weakness of cultural relations with Latin America. For it is a sad fact that the greatest opinion of the greatest number of North Americans continued to assume that Latin Americans were inferior in science and government, and fit only for conquest and violence, but that they were not suited for freedom, republican self-government, and practical science. The myth held fast. In spite of the beneficial interchanges on the learned society level and in the face of an enlargement of real knowledge about Latin America, fact gave way to feelings. Popular notions prevailed in government and in the public state of mind, clinging to familiar taboos and getting them ready for assimilation with the mystic-nationalist ethnocentrism of Manifest Destiny. The negative reaction to

Spain and the positive assertion of a grand Americanism were actually the same psychology: opposite sides of one and the same coin.

It would have been hopeless in the first quarter of the nineteenth century for the friends of Latin America to compete with the psychology of popular and aggressive feeling. That would have meant spending energy, time, reputations, and even money, fighting these viewpoints against the press, the public, traditional church attitudes, and the House of Representatives. After 1815 a group of pro-Latin American newspapers tried to do this. They were in favor of the liberation of South America.[34] The effect of their activity is hard to prove, and their steady propaganda was all right for newspapers; but the scientists, societies, libraries, and learned institutions took no stand. Probably too few politicians, popular figures, and editors would have been found reading Dr. Mitchill's review of Alexander von Humboldt's *New Spain* in the *New York Medical Repository* for 1811. Mitchill's plea had even less effect upon the "common man."

Since Mitchill was already a disappointed advocate in Congress of the political recognition of Latin America in 1810, he took out his feelings the next year (1811) in a plea for cultural recognition of Latin America, combined with a bold, frontal attack on the *leyenda negra*. It is probably the first time that the two basic views about the Hispanic mind were set up for examination in the United States. Dr. Mitchill chose his side and struck hard. He made it very clear in the cited review that

Nothing has been a more trite and erroneous subject of remark than the ignorance of the lazy Dons. This silly cant has been imitated in our country from the English. It has been so frequently proclaimed and so widely repeated that many of our honest patriots sincerely believe that the Spaniards are by a great difference their inferiors.

This is a miserable and unworthy prejudice. A moderate inquiry will evince that New Spain has produced a full proportion of respectable observers and valuable writings. And as to public spirit and patronage it has been manifested in the endowments of learned institutions and in the encouragement of scientific men to an extent of which no parallel exists in our state of society.

The outlook for cultural relations was better than it seemed, although inter-American aims were dimly seen. Little that Mitchill and his scientific contemporaries could do in their own day overcame the endurance and easy circulation of the *leyenda negra*. It was one of the most forceful antigroup formulas in modern history, centuries older than inter-American good will. Books, scientists, and societies could correct the attitude slowly, if at all. The argument that the beneficial role of scientific ideas had little influence upon United States government policy is true. But, in point of historical consequence, this is the very reason for the permanent and enduring vitality of the free association of inter-American minds. The more that North American expansionist and economic pressures ignored the work of culture, the more reason was there for accepting the rule of reason and science in Latin America. As government in the United States responded rather to parties and people at home, the more did policy abroad need to show another side of the North American spirit. There were no strings attached to inter-American cultural relations; they led to no wars; they sought little profit. No better ambassador ever represented the United States in Latin America than the spirit and successors of Franklin, Jefferson, Dr. Mitchill, and the free minds of their time. We shall see more of this in later chapters.

That is why it proved possible for the United States in the nineteenth century, in spite of Texas, Central America, Cuba, and the "diplomacy of the dollar," to keep alive a community of scientific and scholarly partisans in the other America who managed the intellectual relations of the New World so as to get along in one hemisphere. In spite of the difference of religion, language, history, and economic development, the time came when science and serious study took up the job of educating and improving the public as well. Lyceums, lectures, museums, and the schools were good agencies for bringing information to the public. This was a local, domestic development and was handled at home. History, archaeology, ethnology, geography, and the natural sciences came down from the library tower of the eighteenth century, opening the green continent of Latin America to the public eye.

There was another way of doing this—the unique and striking growth of a trade in books about Latin America, and even with Latin America. Recognizing that books provide the most profitable channel for the contact of ideas, North American book publishers went to work to foster a domestic reading public interested in Latin America. Having now outlined and surveyed most of those men and groups which provided permanent lessons in the art of creating and holding inter-American cultural associations, let us examine the success of one of these forces: the Latin American book trade.

Chapter 2

OF MEN AND BOOKS

*W*E HAVE seen that before 1800 less than a handful of the many books dealing with Hispanic civilization were printed in the United States. In the century from 1800 to 1900 there was an enormous upward rise in this ratio; and North American book publishers turned their attention to Latin American readers and multiplied their sales there. By 1825 freedom and independence for both Americas made their interdependence easier. North American publishers, authors, and translators not only produced for the large and growing domestic market in books about Latin America; there was also a large volume of book exports from the United States to Latin America. Domestic and foreign sales combined to make up the whole of the Latin American and inter-American book trade. The three early works of Cotton Mather, Garrat Noel, and Álvaro Alonso Barba were lost among the hundreds of titles of books which later covered the United States and Latin America. The nineteenth century was quite good to the book business in general and to inter-American publishing in particular.

In 1803 a Massachusetts publisher made ready to tap New England for subscriptions to his printing of Bernal Díaz del Castillo's *True History of the Conquest of New Spain*. This was the first North American edition of that famous work, but it was based upon the recent London edition. Five hundred people were willing to subscribe.[1]* Shortly after this, in 1806, the volume of de Pons' *Travels* into Venezuela was published in New York City in an edition said to have been translated by Washington Irving. This New York City printing carried a foreword by Dr. Samuel Latham Mitchill, who stressed to the reader the wisdom of knowing something about Latin America. Published under the title of a *History*

*Notes to this chapter begin on page 171.

of Caraccas, an advertisement of de Pons' book in the *New York Daily Advertiser* of May 1, 1807, urged the New York citizenry "that we should possess a perfect knowledge of Caraccas." The year and the book coincided with Francisco de Miranda's invading expedition from New York to Venezuela. Two years later, in 1808, Dr. Mitchill launched the local publication of Molina's *History of Chile,* as we have seen.

Old wine tasted just as well in new bottles, and the old established titles did reappear in new editions. Publishers found readers over and over again for several editions of Robertson's *History of America.* The many serial reprints in the magazines did not wear out the perennial welcome given to Robertson's history by the domestic market. Robertson could be bought in a better-grade edition of four volumes in 1804 for four dollars; a cheaper edition, in paper covers, sold for one dollar.[2] Readers found other histories of Latin America besides those of Robertson, Molina, de Pons, and Bernal Díaz. Historians, previously known only to library members, now stepped out into the open light of the public book market. Those interested in Mexican Indian antiquities— and they were many—could now purchase Francisco Clavijero's *Historia Antigua de Méjico* from several North American publishers. Interest in the Mexican past antedated William Prescott's later work and in fact supplied him with readers. Publishers at Philadelphia printed Clavijero there in 1806; another edition came out at Richmond, Virginia, in 1817,[3] and other printings appeared at different times and places. Meantime, copies of English editions were regularly imported.

North American readers interested in Latin America swelled the sales of Prescott and Washington Irving in the next generation. They bought the many histories and historical novels on Mexico and Latin America published all through the nineteenth century. Mexico was always an interesting and fascinating theme. It is true that more extreme popular taste, cut along the bias of *leyenda negra* and Manifest Destiny, changed very slowly, but that did not prevent the appearance of sensible values. Publishers from an early date could find intelligent North Americans to read their books. Below the select standards of the scientific and learned society on one hand, and far above the anti-Hispanic mass which knew little and cared less about Latin America on the other, we find a growing middle group which read the better books on Latin American history, ethnology, and archaeology. Some of this group doted on historical novels. Its economic, social, and political nature is not known, but its interest in Latin America brought all its parts together. As we shall see, even textbooks on Latin America occupied a leading place in North American reading habits. Other persons chose to read about the gentler theme of Latin love in the well-sold novel of romance.

Books on serious history were as highly regarded as the novel which had entertainment value. Sober history and romantic fiction about Latin America became the most widely read types of book in the field. North American publishers undertook to please both kinds of reader. Book publishing in these two lines—intellectual and entertaining—settled down upon lines which seemed unrelated and did not meet. One other kind of book had its day in the decade before 1823: the treatment of contemporary hemisphere and world affairs. Current events awakened reader interest in tensions over Latin American Independence, fear of the Holy Alliance, domestic pressures for and against support of Latin America's revolutions, and other vital issues which reached their climax in the Monroe Doctrine. Inter-American and international "crises" determined the nature of books and publishers' titles.

From 1806 to 1823 it was made abundantly clear by journalists and travellers that popular and public interest in Latin American temperament, political revolution, natural phenomena, and geography found some satisfaction in books on those topics. Most books available before 1810 dealt with the sixteenth century and the nature of Spanish and Portuguese Conquest, three hundred years before. In the light of international wars, revolts, and invasions which were challenges to the hemisphere, there was something incompletely nostalgic about a literature that offered a better biographical account of Cortes, Pizarro, Balboa, and the distant *conquistadores* than the nearer epic figures of Bolívar, José de San Martín, Marshal Sucre, and others who were liberating America. The demand for the current had to be met. The renewed opportunity for travel in Latin America provided still another type of literature which the next generation could read.

Books on current history were timely, but the older fondness for Spanish literature and letters was very much alive. This affinity for the culture of Old Spain also helped North American publishers. Moreover, some magazines turned away from the trite reproductions of the eighteenth century and, by reviews and articles, called attention regularly to the best of books on Iberian poetry, drama, literature, and history. In New England, the editors of the *North American Review*, and in Philadelphia the directors of *Port Folio*, replaced the anti-Hispanism of the eighteenth century with an avowed Hispanophilism. They repeatedly pointed out the dignity of Spanish thought and prose, the beauty of the sonnets, the sweep of poetic epic, and the attraction of the drama. The teaching of Spanish in Harvard College, the College of Philadelphia, and St. Mary's College in Baltimore also increased by some number, as yet unmeasurable, those North Americans who could read Spanish books.

Philadelphia sent out the most vigorous plea for appreciation of Hispanic letters and the Spanish spirit behind them. The city of brotherly love was by now so well committed to Hispanic and inter-American things that editorials urging North American esteem for Spanish culture should stir little surprise. We will see soon how a "great awakening" in literature brought about a counterstruggle against the *leyenda negra*, making it possible for publishers to supply the books for the finer tolerance in readers' minds and tastes. Let us go back to the appeal of Joseph Dennie, editor of Philadelphia's literary journal *Port Folio*, who detested the *leyenda negra*, preferred Spanish letters, and tried to teach the North Americans to do the same.

Fifteen years before Boston's *North American Review* won a justly historic fame for educating a literary interest in Hispanic thought and letters, Philadelphia's *Port Folio* had already published the Portuguese sonnets of Luiz Camões, Spanish ballads and lyric poetry, essays of Benito Feijóo, the thoughts of Cervantes, and samplings from the dramatic writings of Spain's better-known playwrights. Literature replaced the legend. More important, in 1809, two years before New York's Samuel Latham Mitchill heaped his praises upon Spanish science, and five years before New England's Isaiah Thomas opened the eyes of Puritan descendants to the antiquities and memberships to be found in Latin America, *Port Folio* had already smashed hard at the false image of *leyenda negra*. Thus historians, scientists, and the literary leaders all felt the same admiration for the greatness of Spain, and disagreed with the legend.

Port Folio argued angrily and impatiently:

Nothing can be more deplorably stupid than the *vulgar* idea which has been cherished respecting the character and habits of the modern Spaniard. From simple and unprejudiced travellers we have heard so much of Castilian jealousy and Castilian laziness, of the insolence of the clergy, and of the insolence of the laity, of Inquisitorial horrors, of the broiling Philip and his gridiron Escurial. . . .

Nothing is more common than to listen to very sturdy declamations against the state of letters in Spain and nothing can be more atrociously false than these *unfounded* invectives. The fact is that Learning has her temples in Spain as well as in Scotland. Literary societies and men of genius are more numerous than ever. Publications of uncommon merit are constantly issuing from the presses in all the cities of Spain. . . .

As at the present juncture men are particularly solicitous about everything respecting Spain, we feel an extreme desire to make this country better acquainted with the other. . . . Their noble language, an idiom incomparably superior to that of two of their nearest neighbors, an idiom which often-times for dignity, energy, and magnificence challenges a comparison with the purest dialects of Greece and England, is a rich exchequer. . . .[4]

Port Folio never won the national influence attained by the *North American Review*—nor was it published for so long a time. As a forgotten man in cultural relations, Dennie was eclipsed by larger figures such as Samuel Mitchill and Isaiah Thomas. Boston's friends of Spain, including George Erving, Edward Everett, George Ticknor, William Prescott, and Henry W. Longfellow, were far better known. Joseph Dennie, however, struggled to break down a legend, not to write great literature; he tried to build up a Hispanic-mindedness among his countrymen. He hit early upon the happy phrase which is also today's formula for cultural relations: "to make this country better acquainted with the other." This process he started as early as 1801. When the American Philosophical Society of Philadelphia was ready to nominate its first Latin American to membership in that year, *Port Folio* introduced its readers to the classic poetic epic of the Conquest of Chile: Alonso de Ercilla's *La Araucana*.

Philadelphia was not a town to forget tradition, and book men there soon consolidated their share of the rising inter-American enterprise. Philadelphia publishers, among whom were Carey & Lea, "Guillermo" Stavely, "Juan" Hurtel, Palmer, and Dorsey, took up the task. The Spanish names are taken from the title pages of the Spanish-language books which some of them published. Publishers' book lists, here and in other cities, give us an idea of the reading public which existed alongside the scholarly and scientific.[5]

Several such firms arose in Philadelphia and elsewhere, specializing almost entirely in Hispanic titles. Unfortunately, their permanency is hard to trace, since publishers in those days changed their partnerships whenever death, illness, estrangement, or other reasons broke up the firm. Publishing houses were individually owned; they were partnerships, rather than corporations. When Simeon Ide issued his *American Bookseller's Complete Reference Trade List* in 1847, most of the Philadelphia firms pioneering in the Latin American book trade had either gone out of business or broken up the partnership. For example, Matthew Carey, one of Philadelphia's leading publishers, had left Henry Lea and formed another partnership, Carey & Hart.

Carey & Lea of Philadelphia were probably the largest of the early North American book publishers dealing in Hispanic sales. As publishers they put out lists in Spanish and English, serving the Latin American book field year after year. Book lists in Spanish were for the Latin American reader; another part of the catalogue had the English titles. Some domestic readers could by now read Spanish and bought Spanish-language books. Carey & Lea turned regularly and seriously to Hispanic and Latin American themes. After 1811 they put out a somewhat lengthy book list. Titles in the catalogues mirror both the variety of taste and the many-sided reader interest. There were many levels of demand. Some wanted grammars, some were fascinated by legendry, ballads, and the warrior-hero (partly the influence of *Port Folio* as well as the romantic era and the literary vogue of Sir Walter Scott). Others wanted tales of the Spanish Conquest of America or current accounts of Mexico and the Latin American revolutions of the day. Historical novels and fiction about Latin America were perennially popular. A small sampling of Carey's output included Antonio Agapida, *A Chronicle of the Conquest* (1829); T. F. Goodwin, *The History of America, containing the History of the Spanish Discoveries prior to 1520* (1831); Edward Temple, *Travels in Peru* (1833); and the romantic novel, *Calavar: Knight of the Conquest, a Romance of Mexico* (1835).

As for current events during the crisis of the hemisphere, Fayette Robinson gave Carey & Lea his timely volume of biographical sketches of the leaders of the Mexican Revolution of 1810. Carey & Lea also introduced contemporary Brazil to readers in 1816, reprinting John Mawe's *Travels in Brazil*. Englishmen living in Latin America also wrote other books that Carey & Lea made available. Years later, when the firm's name changed to Carey, Lea and Blanshard, it issued a Philadelphia edition of J. P. Robertson's *Four Years in Paraguay* (1839) and the account called *Francia's Reign of Terror*, which was taken from the London edition (1839) called *Letters from Paraguay*.

The other side of this important inter-American book business was the printing of books in the Spanish language. These were very clearly intended for export to Latin American schools and readers, although some small but unknown part of it went to North Americans able to read Spanish. Even if we could suppose that Carey & Lea knowingly carried out the advice of *Port Folio* or consciously followed the lead of the scientific societies, the publishers could not have done any better. Bookmen stimulated a further diffusion among North Americans of ideas congenial to Spanish culture. The first of the nineteenth century's countless books in Spanish now started on their way to domestic and Latin American readers.

Carey & Lea republished the now-forgotten novels of Athanasio de Cespedes y Monroy: *El Desafío, La Paisana Víctima,* and *La Presumida Orgullosa*. They were originally printed in Madrid in 1800 in eleven volumes as *Lecturas Útiles y Entretenidas*. We have to assume that this Philadelphia printing was a pirated one, and also that it was well worth Carey & Lea's while to issue them. Published here in 1811, they are the first novels printed in Spanish in the United States—the beginning of a lengthy list. They are mentioned here only to introduce the Hispanic work of Carey & Lea, because it is tedious and impossible to cull their entire list. There were many other titles—several Spanish dictionaries and grammars, as well as the *aguinaldo* (Christmas gift list). Proper classes in the Spanish-speaking world (or rather, hemisphere) selected from books on manners, styles and fashion, morals, etiquette, conduct—all of them in Spanish.

Other Spanish-language books carry different firm names, but historical research is tricky here because some Spanish American agents, propagandists, and writers during the struggle for independence used to falsify a North American publisher's name in order to slip by Spanish censorship and confiscation. There are many such misleading imprints which have to be separated from the distinct and legitimate ones. However, the North American publishers described here are those who did not disguise their names or origin. Certainly Carey & Lea did not. They put their name on the title page of one of the most subversive and trouble-making of Spanish-language books: the *Espíritu del Despotismo* (1822), one of the Spanish versions of Rousseau's *Contrato Social*, specifically intended for North American export to Latin America.

Publishers, like their contemporaries in the libraries and learned societies, had neither centralized organization nor unity. Individualism and a *laisser-faire* sense of private enterprise gave publishers the characteristic of independence, and they worked by themselves. Generally, this was the spirit of business in the nineteenth century. There was no grand government plan nor was a governing body instituted. Consequently many firms came and went, sometimes as colleagues, again as competitors. Just as the libraries and learned societies followed their individual, specialized instincts toward a hemisphere goal, so did each book publisher unconsciously shape and fit into a "national" pattern and the now-widespread cultural approach. Let us now look at some other Philadelphia publishers who won a share of the Latin American book business.

William Stavely, John Hurtel, and the firm headed by someone named Palmer, were among the others who made their way in the book trade. Their piecemeal, private profits, however brief, give a large inter-American meaning to the whole story. Parry & McMillan, for example, printed and sold the history of the Cuban Pedro Guiteras, whose other work, also a history, was later printed by George Lockwood of New York City. Some publishers lasted a long time; others soon disappeared. As early as 1822 unknown Philadelphia publishers put out the famous picaresque account of *Lazarillo de Tormes*. In 1828 there was a Spanish-language edition of the Latin poet Horace. Several concerns printed one or sometimes two books and then left the inter-American scene without applause and without trace. The total and permanent influence of their contribution did not vanish, however, although the opportunity to give them credit for their work now appears to be lost.

William Stavely of Philadelphia, among those who remain known, was a fairly close rival of Carey & Lea in activity and quality. Stavely seems to have come into the inter-American book field in 1824, as a publisher of books and of Spanish-language newspapers. Like his contemporary W. S. Steward, who published Spanish books and the newspaper *Revista de la Crónica* in New York City, the Philadelphian Stavely combined the publishing of the newspaper *Habanero* with a book business in Spanish and English. He published novels, treatises, and other types of book. Sometimes his firm's name would appear as Stavely & Bringhurst; oftentimes it would be as Spanish as "Guillermo" Stavely. As other publishers were doing, Stavely supplied the North American reader with works written in English and the Latin American reader with works written in Spanish.

In 1828 Stavely published the Mexican romantic novel *Jicotencal* in two volumes—a tale of Indian struggle and bravery against the conquering Spanish and of courageous Aztec resistance. Before Prescott came along to write his serious history of Mexico, the historical novels of romance, such as *Jicotencal*, together with the call of the legends and ballads of Old Spain, combined to modify public attitudes. These books softened the psychology of the North American reader. Long before this time, *Port Folio* had begun to stress the heroism of the Indian in the struggle of the "good" Inca against the "bad" Spanish knights. In odes and poetry, *Port Folio* made an epic American symbol of the dead Indian of long ago, just as Latin Americans were doing with their Indian glories (of the past). The novel of ancient Mexico did the same sort of thing. Stavely's *Jicotencal*, one of the better-selling historical novels of that day, has an importance far beyond its trite plot and standard character structure. In fact, the combination of historical novel and current romance about Old Spain and Mexico began to glorify the past, softening its harsh *leyenda negra* with tender romance, lovers' tragedy, and other devices.

The historic Elizabethan-Cromwellian anxiety towards a powerful Spain now lost some of its tense severity, helped and reassured by the visible signs of Spanish weakness in America. North Americans, instead of rushing to trample on the fallen giant, did just the opposite. To get rid of their fears they opened their minds to new ideas. The *leyenda negra*, originally projected along lines of fear psychology, now acquired the softer outlines of the romantic image of Spain, bathed in the fountains of Andalusia, colored with romance and balladry of the *cancionero*, mingling the *caballero*, the *morena*, and the Indian in a new literature. The structure of the fabled "castle in Spain" came into view. We know how sensitive were Washington Irving and other travellers to the attractions of Spain. Somewhat in the same way, continuing the "noble savage" naturalism of the eighteenth century, the historical novel about Latin America now had the effect of turning the other cheek. *Port Folio* and the novels raised on high the symbol of the brave New World through the appealing heroism of the dying Indian and the proud, "republican" virtue of the chieftain. In one case the love of the brown-skinned Moorish maiden for the Christian Spanish knight, in the other the sacrifice of the Indian girl for love of the Spanish conquistador, was repeated often enough to change the legend of three hundred years into another myth: owning a gentler mood, somewhat unreal and exaggerated.

The proud Spaniard in the Old World and the New, as seen by the novelist and noted North American travellers, lost his fierceness. Calavar, Jicotencal, and many other fictional creatures had their psychological effect, so subtle and continuous that it did the same work as schooling, education, and science in the long-range task of making Spain and Spanish ways more attractive to North Americans.[6] Literature brought to the surface less of a nationalist and more of a universal sympathy, especially for tragic lovers. The travellers brought back a greater feeling for Andalusian warmth and Moorish art, less for Castilian austerity. This romantic love of nature, Toledan architecture, Moorish buildings, and Iberian history created a more understandable Spain, in some cases even lighter and warmer than the black, inquisitorial symbolism arising from Philip II and the fear of Roman Catholicism. Similarly in the New World, the romantic novel and the pleasant literature of the travel book came to life at the same time as scientific archaeology and Indianist ethnology, in a joint, or rather parallel, account of the "American" virtues of courage and love of freedom from European (that is, Spanish) intrusion.

Publishers printed other books besides the romantic novel. William Stavely, to return to him, published the plays of the Latin American dramatist Felix Megía and sent them to Latin America for reading and for performance. At another time, Stavely shared with Carey & Lea the writing talent of the North American diplomat who had lived in Chile and Mexico for years: Carey & Lea had published Joel Poinsett's *Notes on Mexico* (1822), while Stavely, in 1826, brought out Poinsett's comments on the instructions given to the United States delegation to the Panama Congress of that year. Stavely rendered Poinsett's views, as well as the instructions, into Spanish, and sent them to Latin America. Stavely also gave a few North Americans, and many more Latin Americans, a chance to read his Spanish edition of the Colombian José María Salazar's *Observaciones sobre las Reformas Políticas en Colombia* (1826).

Publishers in Philadelphia, Boston, New York—and we can even include Charleston, South Carolina, in this national as well as regional development—[7] had a share of the inter-American book trade. Both the times and the situation were opportune. The output as well as the quality of books spurted, because of the freedom of the new Latin American nations and the decline of Spanish political power (that is, the censorship) in the New World. New opportunity made it possible for Latin American intellectuals to reside in the United States in greater numbers than ever. Some of these residents were political exiles who wrote and said little or much, depending upon their fervor. Culturally, as Latin America was separated from Spain, writers in Spanish and their North American publishers could join in a more sympathetic atmosphere of liberty from censorship, freedom of thought, and independence from ecclesiastical restriction. Spain still reminded Latin Americans of European tyranny and oppression, although North Americans could now afford to take Spain less hostilely. Latin Americans found freer expression in the United States than they could get in Old

Spain, where clericalism, Bourbonism, and the powerful vestiges of reaction still led to open or subtle control over the ancient publishing guild of Spain. There was no censorship in North America; and authors, publishers, and readers of Hispanic books communicated freely, in spite of their different cultural and political origins.

All was not milk and honey in these relations. An occasional publisher of books on Latin America might also publish magazines that catered to the harsh tones of *leyenda negra*. True, examples are few, but they should be pointed out just the same. Making a living from an inter-American book market did not disturb the private opinion of some publishers. Carey & Lea provide us with a shining example, a sort of protective coloration that found two answers to the same problem. The case of Mexico, always a subject for controversy in the United States, may be taken. Strain between the United States and Mexico along diplomatic and political lines arose early. While Carey & Lea sponsored the palliating books and novels on one hand, on the other they used their own magazine, the *American Quarterly Review*, to keep alive an anti-Mexican attitude that would have shocked those who read friendlier opinion in *Port Folio*, the *North American Review*, and the affirmations of Dr. Samuel Mitchill.

The hostile side of North American psychology was far from dead, just because a new light was dawning on inter-American attitudes. It was quite alive and animated in 1827 when the *American Quarterly Review* wrote bitingly about Mexicans: "In civilization and intellectual improvement far behind the rest of the world, yet with the most dilated ideas of their own capacity and general intelligence, the Mexicans, whilst in a state of dependency and debility, imagine themselves gifted with superior energy and readily conceive themselves the objects of universal envy and admiration."[8] When this was written Samuel Mitchill and Alexander von Humboldt were still alive. So were those noted Mexican scientists who, in spite of this attitude, had been chosen for membership by Philadelphia's scientific societies. Consequently, this attitude was a far cry from *Port Folio*'s and Mitchill's attack on that "silly cant . . . imitated in our country from the English."

Fortunately, however, these adverse sentiments neither hurt nor hindered scientific good will; nor was the Latin American book trade adversely affected. It is unlikely that a combined source of intellectual profit and benefit, by now a regular part of North American cultural, scientific, and reading habits, could be seriously set back any more. The disappearance of a feeling born in the sixteenth century had to be gradual. Belief dies hard and the myth seeks to be permanent. A rival confidence in the New World and its values had come into the Americas since 1700 and had grown up the hard way—independently. Finally, along purely human lines, what one publisher had to say usually fell upon the deaf ears of other publishers and not at all upon those who had come to different conclusions about Mexico and Latin America. The book business, like that of newspapers and magazines, was individualistic and competitive. Cultural relations remained very much alive, now supported by interconnecting foundations.

Progress could not be stopped but it could be influenced within the whole inter-American process. One of these was in the aspect of regional influence in the total picture. By 1850 a significant change had taken place: most Spanish-language books were now printed in New York City. New York overtook and passed Philadelphia and Boston in the Latin American book trade. How many books were printed and how great was the volume? No one can say. Only a general answer is possible, because publishers' catalogues and book lists for that period have disappeared or are hard to find. But we can assume a fairly high output. The Bossange catalogue and several other lists, by naming the place of imprint as Brussels, Madrid, Paris, and New York City, indicate that New York City had already become a prominent center of Spanish and Latin American book activity. This may not come as news, since Manhattan (New York City) already excelled in economic, financial, and commercial relations with Latin America.

In the practical side of literary culture—the size of the Latin American book trade—New York took the lead. New York publishers did not come anywhere near to matching the high standard of Spanish typesetting and printing artistry, but the number of titles which were printed made up for shortcomings in the graphic arts. New York publishers also made little effort to compete with Boston in getting scholarly authors with reputations for high literary performance. Instead, they confined their efforts mainly to large production, bookselling, and Latin American distribution. Exactly or approximately how many books were printed? It is impossible to be exact, even where contemporaries help us with a guess or make estimates which might be open to question. One guess, made by the Argentine Domingo Sarmiento, asserted that as many as two-thirds of the books published in Spanish came from New York City.[9] By all odds this ratio was too good to be true and must have been exaggerated; but the point behind the claim is quite accurate: New York City became the undisputed North American center for inter-American book circulation in the nineteenth century. It is a great loss to the full record of North American and Western Hemisphere intellectual history that the files and records of most of these book firms have been lost. Some records vanished, others were burned. All we do know is that there were many publishers who made and sold books, and they gave New York a reputation for Spanish book selling that brought credit to the openmindedness of free publishing and liberal friendliness with the culture of Latin America.

For example, during the 1820's, Behr and Kahl of New York continued where still earlier firms had begun, and would follow: they printed novels in the Spanish language, histories, poetry, and essays. Without statistics and with no figures to reconstruct their activity, we can at least show that Behr & Kahl reprinted the widely read and widely studied *Fábulas Literarias* of Tomas de Yriarte. This firm revived a Spanish literary duel by printing the *Fábulas* of Felix Samaniego, Yriarte's eighteenth-century contemporary and rival. There were other ways in which nineteenth-century publishers brought Spanish and Latin America to Manhattan. Not only did they reprint the earlier writers of the *siglo de oro*, Spain's Golden Age of the sixteenth century, but they also published Latin American works. Behr & Kahl, for example, published a volume of Mexican poetry in 1828, under the title *Poesías de un Mexicano*.[10] In 1828 New York was the proper place to publish the work of the great colonial poet of New Spain, Bernardo de Balbuena. Balbuena lived too early to have ever heard of New York, but his poetic epic of the founding and situation of Mexico City, *Grandeza Mexicana*, was issued by Lanuza y Mendía in Manhattan. Publishers' stock included poetry, history, grammar, literature, and science. Lanuza y Mendía, for another example, published the treatise of the famous Cuban botanist and naturalist, Ramón de la Sagra, already well known in scientific circles of the United States where he was corresponding member of several learned societies and where he visited and lectured. Without statistics the record of activity is clear from contemporary advertising, as in 1831, when a certain José Desnoues of New York published a *Diario Histórico* of La Salle's discovery of the Lower Mississippi Valley and Texas, a book which was very expressly announced "for the Mexican market."

Some first-rank names in Latin American history, science, and letters gave prestige to the New York book lists. The work of the Mexican historian Lorenzo de Zavala, *Ensayo Histórico de las Revoluciones de México desde 1808 hasta 1830,* first published in Paris, 1831-1832, was twice printed in New York, once by Elliot & Palmer (20 William

Street) in 1832, and again in 1833. Considering the limited number of books in English upon Mexican affairs and history, it would have been better had a publisher translated this book for North American readers. But events and the profits of book exports to Latin America proved otherwise, and only Spanish language editions were handled. In fact, another of Zavala's works, also in Spanish, and dealing with the Mexican scene was issued by C. S. van Winkle of New York in 1830. Sometimes the contact between Spanish American authors and North American publishers was direct and personal, especially if the writers were in the United States as travellers and visitors. This was true of the Cuban poets José de Heredia and Gabriel de la Concepción Valdés, and also of the historians Lorenzo de Zavala of Mexico and José Antonio Saco of Cuba. In most cases their choice of publishers was voluntary and mutually advantageous; in some cases these local editions of their work were unauthorized. In either event the publishers' desire to print these books proved the existence of an inter-American market for them.

As a final example, we cite the New York printing of the history of New Spain by the Mexican archbishop Lorenzana, which contained the letters of Hernán Cortes, Conquerer of Mexico. First published in Mexico City in 1770, while Lorenzana was still archbishop, the second Spanish edition appeared in Manhattan in 1828, the same year in which Balbuena's *Grandeza Mexicana* was published.

The New York edition of the Lorenzana-Cortes narrative appeared as the *Historia de Mejico escrita por su esclarecido conquistador aumentada con otros documentos y notas por D. Francisco Antonio Lorenzana, antiguo Arzobispo. Revisada y adoptada a la ortografía moderna por D. Manuel del Mar.*//Neuva (*sic*) York la publican los sres White Gallaher y White en la imprenta de Vanderpoel y Cole, 1828.//[11]

This New York edition was neither known nor used by North American historians of the Cortes cycle. William H. Prescott, for example, and others who could read Spanish easily do not seem to have been aware of the work. Instead, they relied upon George Folsom's English translation of the *Letters* of Cortes, likewise printed in New York in 1843. From this it would appear that such Spanish-language histories were exported out of the city to Latin America. From separate sources it is definitely established that the Lorenzana volume was exported. On the flyleaf of one copy of the valuable and scarce work is an inscription to Buckingham Smith, the noted Hispanist of the next generation, dated at Tampico, Mexico, 21 November 1851. Obviously the book was intended for Mexican readers and, indeed, was sent to Mexico.

Just as authors of the books might have been Spanish and also North American, so the publishers were either Anglo-American or Spanish American in ancestry. Men and firms of different origins had contributions to make to the inter-American book community. As in the case of Philadelphia, however, those publishers who were English-speaking became the leaders of the Latin American book trade. New Yorkers who took over this branch of book publishing were chiefly North Americans by birth. Of all the New York publishers during the period before the Civil War, Roe Lockwood of 411 Broadway did the most with Spanish books. Publishers from 1815 to well past 1850, Roe Lockwood did a surprising amount of business in Spanish books.[12]

George Lockwood's name holds a permanent place high up on any honor roll of inter-American relations. Many other North American booksellers and publishers are eligible to fill such a rather crowded community, but Lockwood's leadership reached a level that had no equal—for that time. Only two publishers would catch up with him in time and even pass him, but that did not take place until after 1850. Headed by Stephen Hallet and D. Appleton, those later firms had far-reaching reputations and business connections, due to special advantages. Until they came along, George Lockwood had this field practically to himself, and he did important things with his opportunity. Some outstanding Spanish and Spanish American histories carried the Lockwood imprint. Lockwood, for example, published the *Obras* of Cuba's famous historian José Antonio Saco, and as already stated, the history of another Cuban historian, Pedro Guiteras. José Saco's celebrated history of the rise of Negro slavery in the New World appeared in 1853.

Lockwood's work marks a change for the better in the development of North American attitudes and Latin American relations. It supplied greater and deeper understanding of Hispanic culture. He, and other publishers, printed and sold Spanish grammars, literary essays, and many novels, as well as histories intended for export to Latin America. A good many books were sold to North American students in the colleges, academies, and schools. In schools and outside, language awakened any existing feeling for Hispanic life, leading in some subtle way to closing the religious and psychological gap between the two American cultures. Grammars and novels came into their own. With the aid of Lockwood and other publishers, North American interest in the Spanish language was the bright and shining key to understanding Spanish civilization, in Europe and America. Thus grammars, together with those books published in Spanish and English (to be described below), fed their specific values into the general cultural current. We must never let the lowly study of grammar be obscured by the brilliant literary sentences of William H. Prescott, Washington Irving, Henry W. Longfellow, and George Ticknor. Spanish grammar supported the structure of publishers and scholars, building up to the higher levels.

It is a serious oversight to think that Prescott, Irving, Longfellow, and Ticknor created North American interest in Latin America and Spain. The fact is that dozens of authors, sponsored by numbers of enterprising publishers, wrote about Spanish America and Spain throughout the nineteenth century. Because they did not have the fame and scholarship of those greater names, almost all of them have become obscure, but their influence was once felt and their books were read. Before, as well as after, the gleaming era of New England's Hispanic scholarship in the middle of the nineteenth century, the circulation of many books served and built up the general interest in Latin America. Here was a rediscovery of Latin America. The "revival of learning" in the New World, partly developed by scientific individuals and learned societies, needed the book trade to stimulate wider public interest.

Latin America had everything that the general reader would want: stalwart adventure, bold and startling discovery, clash-of-arms among men-at-arms, brave leaders of other men, cultural and individual drama and tragedy, and—certainly not least for the generation of '49—a vast and unending silver and gold rush which apparently lasted forever. North American stay-at-homes of the nineteenth century found exciting elements of native courage, stories of *criollo* chivalry, wild and imposing landscapes, the gentler stage of love and romance, and the incredible achievements of the semifeudal Conquest. Themes and plots beautifully suited to readers' tastes in that day emerged from both historical and imaginary situations. Love, too, won a stronger hold over the reader, toning down the harshness of Las Casas' and Gage's estimate of Spanish America. At the same time, tales of piracy, war, buccaneering, and the sea which had fascinated the North American reader of the eighteenth century now lost a good deal of that early popularity. As a matter of fact, a kind of Indian "classicism" appealed to writers, readers, and even to scholars who were eager to find an aboriginal American civilization somehow equal to Graeco-Roman virtue, stoicism, and republicanism. The idea was for the hemisphere to reflect and mirror the finer values of Western Civilization; this was the corollary of the "noble savage" ideal. Books also carried appeals for exemplary or moral conduct.

Even North American children's books dealt with Latin America. The adult generation bought many novels, tales of romance, and lighter histories; children usually read about individual heroes. The younger reader was more easily impressed by examples of fanatic courage and types of conduct that the fearless adventurers of Spain displayed. For both young and old there were some thrilling tales. The authority of the adult generally pulled books for younger people into the popular book market. Children's biographies of Balboa, Columbus, Pizarro, Cortes, and other Spaniards in America appeared at the same time as the more serious adult histories by Washington Irving, Brantz Mayer, and William Prescott.

Children's books conditioned coming generations to future views about Latin America. In 1830, when Simón Bolívar brought his energetic and colorful career to a close, a children's edition of his life was prepared at Boston from the *Memoirs* of the Baron of Ducoudray-Holstein, a military aide to the famed Liberator during the Latin American wars for Independence. Since the psychology and aims of children's books intended to bring out the moral and exemplary, this book stressed the patriotism, sacrifice, and tenacity of Bolívar's character. On the other hand, the invariably popular, best-selling Peter Parley (S. T. Goodrich) also supplied the children's book market with his *Primary History of Mexico and South America*. In his *Wonders of South America,* Peter Parley steered the young, impressionable mind towards the green continent with its curious customs and many Indian peoples. Even the learned and staid Dr. Francis Hawks, historian of the Protestant Episcopal Church, executive member of the American Geographical, Ethnological, and New-York Historical societies, tried his hand at a library of Latin American books for the young child. A Hispanist of still unrecognized importance, Dr. Hawks published for children in 1855 his *Adventures of Hernán Cortés*, in line with the current adult interest in Mexico and New Spain.

For those youngsters who had to learn about Latin America the hard way—through the classroom—a rather long-lived outline book, called Grimshaw's *Question and Review Book,* was sold at ten cents and must have been proportionately useful. Then there were others, such as Eliza Robbins, who turned away from historical facts about dates, names, and memorized items in order to point up those traits of desperate courage and cruel purpose that were supposed to characterize all the Spanish conquerors and settlers. In this way those "young persons" for whom these books were written obtained some of their ideas about the men who pioneered in Latin America. Sometimes the facts of history were invented in order to convey a desired impression. That was how it was possible in 1833 for someone in New England to telescope into one name the two Spanish scientists Jorge Juan and Antonio de Ulloa, who had reported on Latin America in the previous century. The unknown author misnamed his book the *Adventures of John Ulloa.*

Many children's books were obviously lifted from those better-known standard histories, memoirs, and narratives meant for their elders. Juvenile inter-Americana formed the junior part of the book trade. This was to be expected, since American children were looked upon as little grown-ups, who were to absorb simplified versions of their parents' likes and beliefs. Of course, there were some books which did not sacrifice historical truth for children's attentiveness and which found it possible to keep these two essentials together. One such example, conforming to the best traditions of New England, was E. Sedgwick's *Stories of the Spanish Conquest of America. Designed for the Use of Children,* printed in 1830 in three volumes. Children of all ages browsed through and read the rich offerings and the exciting themes of Latin American stories.

Such books did not incite children to run away from good North American homes to seek fortune, fame, or adventure in Latin America. Books tended chiefly to change or entrench existing opinions by copying both the good and the bad models. The use of examples for youth made it necessary to retouch the Latin American picture with stress upon grim wars, conquerors, and military men, which aroused in the young reader the same vision of exaggerated militarism, personal heroism, and constant fighting in Latin America that his parents already had. Violence and struggle were made congenital in Latin Americans. This was nothing but another way of perpetuating from father to son traditional prejudices and legends about Latin American psychology and behavior.

Nevertheless, because of the trend of tender ideas in the romantic novel for adults and the folly of being too violent in children's literature, the over-all attitude toward Spanish America improved. The too sharp visage of religious rivalry and the vestiges of Elizabethan legacy gave way to more tolerant feelings which accepted the coexistence in one hemisphere of the bitter residues in the cup of the different Christian churches. The Reformation and the Counter Reformation were known but left alone. While the territorial expansionism of Manifest Destiny had much of the field of North American politics and policy to itself, the sentiments of moral message and literary interest moved away from this attitude, settling down with both scientific and scholarly understanding as neighbors. If Manifest Destiny psychology was then winging with the eagle, the Latin American book trade, combined with the even more effective work done by science, history, and the learned societies, ultimately educated the North American mind further and further away from *leyenda negra* and closer to a New World, American basis for affinity.

It is true that reality spoiled the picture, with Latin American civil war, *caudillismo*, and clericalism casting shadows in the path of progress towards republicanism and liberal self-government. The aggressions of Manifest Destiny in Mexico and in the Caribbean and Central America threw double doubt upon the strength of Latin American governments. Ideals of republican fraternity and "good neighborhood" in the Americas underwent the acid test. Perhaps it was the Monroe Doctrine, perhaps the liberal optimism which accompanied republicanism, which made it possible to look hopefully from one America to the other. The events of the day were important, not drastic. Publishers propagated new themes for North Americans in books about Latin America, taking attention away from the clash of cultures and concentrating upon more peaceable and harmonious terms of love, romance, the gentle and noble Indian, and especially the acceptance by human nature of missionary entreaty and moral teaching. Finally, the Latin American Indian came into his own, sharing the lights of history and archaeology with the scholar, as early ethnologists and travellers praised the high achievements of pre-Columbian and pre-Cortesian civilization in the Americas.

In short, the book trade—in its domestic, North American aspects —did not undo or try to change the fundamental cultural differences between the United States and Latin America. The general reader, true enough, added his own sentiments. What happened was that the North American who read books about Latin America became tolerant in his impressions and jumped to fewer or no conclusions about human beings below the equator. This did not necessarily improve his opinion about their governments. The level of sympathy rose, but not because of any strong desire to proselytize politically, force a common cultural pattern, or identify Latin America with a North American spirit. The two Americas were known to be different and were accepted as such. They needed to be understood. The inter-American book trade used that means of communication, that medium, to bring them together.

Conditions creating the book trade about Latin America within the United States were not quite the same as they were for the export of Spanish-language books abroad, or for the sale of Spanish-language books in this country. North American book interest in Latin America was not only a manifestation of continuous relations with the trans-Caribbean world; it grew without any assistance from government and without an organized book council or centralizing agency. In spite of this, the self-reliance and independence of publishers nurtured their impulse and profit until, after a while, the sale and export of Spanish books became the greatest part of some publishers' business. In fact, the specialist took over the Latin American book market. By the middle and late years of the nineteenth century, publishers had already come and gone, leaving behind little but important precedent. Slowly, other publishers put a definite structure together. After 1850 the early pioneers of inter-American publishing whom we have seen doing business in New York and Philadelphia surrendered their place to the high, energetic success of the specialist.

To return to New York, and George Lockwood: three such firms illustrate the new export specialization in books abroad. George Lockwood, Stephen Hallet, and Daniel Appleton were bookmen who discovered Latin America through books. Their unique success marked an unusual cultural advance. The three of them, acting separately and individually, underwrote the prestige and leadership of New York City as the publishing center for Latin American books. If Boston was the hub of the universe, Manhattan Island was contented to be the intellectual heart of the Americas. These publishers made this possible: the hemisphere scope of their business, their Latin American authors, and the profitable marketing of their books in Spanish and Portuguese America.

Selling Spanish books was the specialty of George Lockwood. Some of these he published directly, as we have seen. But others he purchased from Spain and distributed to Latin America. As publisher and as bookseller-proprietor of the Librería Americana y Extranjera (the revealing name of his firm), Lockwood supplied Spanish-language books. Fortunately he was able to combine a useful life with a long one, and from 1850 to 1869, he pushed his efforts to a great climax: the medium of exchange for books and their ideas. Unfortunately, his business records are scanty; but it seems, from the little source material left, that he sponsored very few books in English. He was chiefly concerned with Spanish-language publications.

Lockwood's entire catalogue was in Spanish, issued as a *Catálogo de los Libros Españoles que se hallan de Venta en su Librería* (Nueva York: 1869), obviously a list of what he was then selling to Latin Americans and those North Americans who could read Spanish. This *Catálogo* is a first-class record of a bygone era in the book business. Lockwood's wealth of Hispanic titles was broad enough to satisfy every contemporary interest in language, literature, and history. The catalogue showed how he made New York City the center of supply for Hispanic books. The study of grammar and language paid cultural as well as publishing and bookselling dividends. Students and teachers in the United States bought their books from him; Latin American libraries and readers depended for their supply upon George Lockwood. He advertised for students, supplying college classes with Spanish books. In the store he displayed volumes and sets on science, arts, biography, history, law, religion, education, in addition to grammars, literary works, and *cancioneros* and *romanceros*. From Spain he imported Spanish versions of *Uncle Tom's Cabin;* and from Mexico came Prescott's *Conquest of Mexico* and the *Conquest of Peru* for re-export to Latin American book dealers, since the original editions already had an ample market here and in other English-speaking countries.

One of the finest historical works by a Cuban scholar came out of Lockwood's press—again a study which was exported, not imported. The New York book man published Jacobo de la Pezuela's, *Diccionario geográfico, historico, estadístico y biográfico de la Isla de Cuba* (Nueva York: 1842). Volumes by individual authors sold well, because Lockwood announced many other single works on such Latin American topics as Cuban sugar and coffee agriculture, Mexican geography, the Chilean scene, and aspects of Peru and Bolivia. The authors were Spanish Americans; the editions were in cheap paper for export to Latin American buyers. The sale of sets, however, was also quite profitable, and Lockwood featured small and large collections of manuals on art, the professions, and the celebrated literary series, *Colección de los mejores autores Españoles antiguos y modernos.*

Through the sale of books to Latin America, Lockwood also took part in the guidance and instruction of Latin American youth in the exemplary conduct and patriotism of their national heroes. We have seen that books in English for the education of North American children reflected one attitude. But unlike the North American children's market, Lockwood's volumes awakened and directed the patriotism of Spanish American children toward their national fathers instead of toward

the distant conquistadors who came from Spain. The younger generation of Spanish America needed a more American basis for their at-
tachment, and books taught them to admire their republican liberators
rather than the founders of the royalist, Spanish regime.

Lockwood therefore promoted a *Biblioteca de la Juventud ó Colección de Historias Morales para la Niñéz.* Individual titles in this filiopie-
tistic series sold in New York City at sixty-five cents each. Latin American
libraries, schools, booksellers, or buyers for ministers of education
could buy the whole set. Others, who could not afford to pay for the
collection, would order single volumes of the lives of such patriotic
examples as Bernardo O'Higgins, José de San Martín, and Simón Bolívar. It was an educational and nationalistic series, and Lockwood found
a large school-age market in Latin America that wanted these books.
Business was good as long as Latin Americans appropriated the money
to pay for these orders.

The educational needs of Latin American schools and libraries were
very steady, but from 1860 to 1900 Latin American ability to spend
money on books fluctuated too much. Consequently their financial
credit declined in North American publishing and bookselling circles.
As Latin American intellectual liberalism, with its interest in schools,
morality, and educational reforms, gave way to economic liberalism,
with its emphasis upon material prosperity and progress through roads,
public buildings, foreign loans, the effect upon book orders and cultural
relations was harmful. An unfavorable balance in book trade reduced
the sales of Lockwood and other New York publishers. Books, that is,
schools and libraries, were apparently less important than railways,
shipping lines, concessions, and the money to pay for them. Investments
had more influence than ideas, and bankers would do better than booksellers.

We do not know how Lockwood obtained his clients and connections in Latin America or how he was paid. His Spanish-language
catalogue alone may have won the orders for him, or Latin Americans
may have sent their orders to him directly. But this, if likely, could account for only a small number of orders. His business was too large
and covered too much of Latin America to be left to occasional individual orders. Book orders in volume, sufficient to have kept this firm
in business for so long a time, should have required salesmen, advertising, and active sales promotion, perhaps (anticipating another New
York publisher) some agency or representative in the big Latin American cities. But there is no evidence that Lockwood had such an organi-

zation. On the contrary, his firm was local, personal, and individual. It may be, however, in the light of what is known about Latin American consuls in New York, that some of them, or special travellers in the United States, passed their orders to Lockwood on behalf of buyers in Latin America. We know only too little about this successful publishing leader. He was one man in the small but excellent company of publishing equals. He perpetuated his work in his advertising, which reads in Spanish:

Libros de Textos . . . publicados en español al uso de los Españoles, franceses e ingleses por George R. Lockwood 812 Broadway, Editor, Librero e Importador de toda clase de libros. . . .

That is all we know of him.[13]

We are just as much in the dark about "Esteban," really Stephen Hallet, of Buenos Aires and New York. Called Don Esteban after a quarter-century's residence in Buenos Aires, Stephen Hallet finally came back home. If our information about Lockwood is scanty, for all his work in the United States, Hallet is more elusive because of his life and work outside the country. Fortunately, Argentines have found and printed what North Americans did not know about him. General material about Hallet's life reveals that he was a far bigger publisher in Argentina than he was in the United States, when he returned after 1852. But whether he worked in the Argentine or in New York, Hallet never lost the inter-American connections with the political and intellectual lights of the day. He made use of them when he set up in publishing in this country, after his years of activity "down under."

Stephen Hallet was born in the southern parts of the United States, according to Argentines. He left this country—for reasons unknown— setting out for Buenos Aires in 1821, the year when Bernardino Rivadavia and a liberal generation were to reform intellectual, university, and economic life in Buenos Aires province. Hallet stayed there for the next thirty years, achieving success and close friendships with famous writers, political leaders, and business people. Sometimes a business visit brought him back to the United States, but these trips were short. Hallet was not a political exile; nor was he a literary self-expatriate. He was a business man, a publisher, who located a vastly profitable field for himself. After more than a generation of publishing books, newspapers, and magazines in Argentina, Latin America, and the United States, Hallet possessed an unusual reputation in Hispanic America. The renowned and excellent Argentine printing and graphic arts industry owes a great deal to the North American Stephen Hallet. He could never leave the smell of printer's ink and continued to publish in New York City from 1852 to nearly 1870. For him the transition from Buenos Aires to New York was an easy one, as it has been for many others.[14]

In Argentina, Hallet's editorial and literary associates included, at different times, the greatest of intellectuals, such as José Rivera Indarte, Manuel and Bernardo de Irigoyen, the noted Domingo Sarmiento, and Pedro de Angelís, historian, journalist, archivist, and propagandist for the dictator Juan Manuel de Rosas. (Pedro de Angelís was also a corresponding member of the American Philosophical and Massachusetts Historical societies.) Hallet either mastered the way of staying clear of internal Argentine politics or successfully adapted himself to either party. He had come into Argentina during the Liberal era of Bernardino Rivadavia, built up his business during the regime of Rosas, and was invited to stay there by the new leaders who overthrew Rosas in 1852. He held the friendship of the second generation of Argentine liberals, especially of Domingo F. Sarmiento, educator, minister to the United States, and later president, who knew Hallet quite well.

From 1829 to 1852 the Argentine *caudillo* Rosas awarded the North American foreigner Stephen Hallet the lucrative printing contracts of the Argentine government. It may have been the well-connected Pedro de Angelís who helped him get these nearly-monopolistic contracts. In any event, Hallet prospered as a result. But that was not his whole story. Hallet made his own enterprises, and as far as can be ascertained now, was the leading publisher in Argentina at that time. His private and newspaper business was very extensive and his "chain" of newspapers and magazines included:

El Argentino, 1824-1825.	*British Packet,* 1826-1835.
El Avisador, 1826-1827.	*Statistical Register,* 1822-1825.
The American, 1827-1829.	*The Observer,* 1831.
The Anglo-American, 1829-1832.	*Star of the South,* 1829.
L'Abeille, 1832-1834.	*Le Spectateur,* 1829.
Correo Nacional, 1826-1828.	*El Lucero,* 1829-1834.
Current Prices, 1824-1825.	*The Mirror,* 1829-1833.
The Cosmopolitan, 1825-1827; 1831-1833.	*The North Star,* 1834.
	La Verdad, 1826-1829.
Cincinnatus, 1825-1827.	*La Gaceta Mercantil,* 1823-1852.

The Pilot, 1825-1826.

Beside being a forerunner of newspaper and publishing magnates, Hallet also printed the first illustrated magazine to appear in that region of South America, *El Museo Argentino,* which came out from 1835 to 1837.

About this time he went back to the United States, possibly to visit but certainly on a business trip. During that period of commercial depression in the United States, Hallet kept his optimism about the growth of publishing and bought up modern printing presses for his Argentine publications. He did not stay here very long, returning to Buenos Aires, where he introduced the Hoe steam-printing press into his own enterprises, especially the *Gaceta Mercantil,* one of the most successful and lasting of his newspapers. His initiative, contacts, editorial experience, and long residence in Buenos Aires assured Stephen Hallet, owner of the most modern publishing plants in Latin America, an immense prestige among Spanish Americans.

But "Don Esteban" soon overtaxed himself physically, and after the overthrow of Rosas in 1852 he came home to stay. Rosas went to permanent exile in Southhampton, England; Hallet gave up an "exile" to resume a North American life. Whether he lost his money is hard to prove; he lost his high political associations. Hallet left behind him forever the Argentina of Juan Manuel Rosas, which looked eagerly towards a new, liberal era. He settled down in New York City, seeking quiet amid Manhattan's friendly atmosphere towards Hispanic and Latin American culture, where he had so high a reputation. New York was almost as proper a place as Buenos Aires for him to keep his stake in Spanish and Latin American publishing. Hallet could not be idle, and he turned again to books. He set up a publishing firm to publish Spanish-language books for readers here, or following the established pattern, to use Manhattan as the center for a contribution to the Latin American book trade.

During the decade from 1860 to 1870 his firm of Hallet and Breen, 107 Fulton Street, took a prominent role in that book trade. Hallet had much better direct contact with Latin Americans than George Lockwood had, and his firm knew prosperity. Latin Americans from all over the continent knew him and sent their manuscripts to him. He also had first call on the works of leading literary and political exiles in New York City. Latin American Freemasonry also relied upon the Hallet press. The firm printed many books, pamphlets, and discourses in Spanish and shipped them to Latin America to be circulated, read, and discussed there. Hallet & Breen published little in English. Their list of

Spanish books strengthened the place of New York City as an inter-American clearing-house for books and ideas about Latin America.

The Venezuelan ex-president José Paez brought Hallet his *Autobiografía*. The Peruvian Minister to the United States gave Hallet his source study of *Relaciones* (reports which the colonial viceroys of New Granada left to their successors)—a valuable historical collection. Hallet & Breen published historical, political, and literary works. Their best-known literary client was Antonio José de Irisarri, the poet-político of Guatemala and Chile, who was then (1861) living in Brooklyn, New York. Hallet printed several of Irisarri's poems, and also brought out his critical study on Latin American Spanish, *Cuestiones Filológicas sobre algunos puntos de la Ortografía de la Gramática y del Origen de la lengua Castellana*, a Latin American's criticism of "Oxford," that is, Castilian, Spanish, to be compared with the Andrés Bello grammatical study written a generation before.

Hallet employed many Cubans in his business and, in fact, when he retired in 1870, his publishing business was taken over by his editor and proofreader, M. M. Zarzamendi, who continued to print Masonic books and articles for export. Zarzamendi was well known among Latin American groups in New York.[15] One of the first books that he printed in Spanish after Hallet's death was a Spanish edition of the *Political Science* by Francis Lieber, then at Columbia College. Lieber's ideas about strong central government, as against states' rights and sectionalism, found many friendly readers in Latin America. Even these books could not hold Hallet & Breen at the level it had once attained. No one could inherit Hallet's personal reputation and friendships. His successors failed to hold his business together. Hallet & Breen, like a predecessor, George Lockwood, became a stationery-printing concern, turning out some Spanish newspapers, books, and pamphlets, but definitely abandoning the Latin American book trade. Stephen Hallet followed George Lockwood into the unwritten archives of inter-American cultural history.

By this time, fortunately, other publishers dealt with Spanish America even more directly, and successfully. They could pick up the trail of the earlier publishing pioneers of the nineteenth century. Stephen Hallet and George Lockwood filled the gaps left in the contribution of Behr & Kahl, Stavely, Carey & Lea, and the other known and unknown firms in New York, Boston, Philadelphia, and Baltimore. They overcame many cultural obstacles, but there were other hurdles ahead. The chief weakness of early publishing lay in individual and unorganized promotion. It is true that adding up each publisher's separate output summed up the whole inter-American picture, but these unilateral efforts, based upon partnership, did not have any definitely expressed aim. By 1850 the most positive and aggressive of North American publishers took over the book trade with Latin America. D. Appleton & Company framed older and historic book relations into an organized, composed plan of expansion.

D. Appleton & Company gave North American sales methods, business organization, and inter-American cultural goals to the book trade. Appleton was a success almost from the start. No other publishing house in the Western Hemisphere and hardly any in Spain or France ever matched the high regard which Appleton won and maintained for fifty years in Latin American book, library, and school circles. For almost the second half of the nineteenth century Appleton's publishing success dominated and directed the inter-American book trade. The books they sold were varied enough to suit even the special type of demand. Appleton differed from Lockwood, Hallet, and all the others; yet these predecessors had initiated and built up so many small successes. A combination of Appleton's own business talents, plus connections, coupled with the market already won in the book trade, set Appleton's business upon so sound and reputable a footing that it lasted down to 1900.

As early as the 1840's, Appleton began to set up the machinery for export of books to Latin American schools, colleges, and libraries. Their specialty, really the new factor in the enterprise, was quite original: publication, translation, and sale to Latin America of school and college textbooks adopted and used in North American institutions at the same educational level. By using North American business techniques and drive, Appleton excelled in that line. Overcoming the differences of religion, language, and culture between Latin America and the United States, Appleton & Company found a welcome place. Educators and students shared in a sort of hemisphere schoolroom because the same books were used throughout the Americas. One can say that Appleton was publisher and purveyor to Latin America's schools.[16] This was a remarkable step toward that standardization of curricula and textbooks which twentieth-century educators and international conferences have sought repeatedly in the Western Hemisphere and in the world. Private publishing enterprise once achieved the goal of a unity of ideas through textbooks.

Employing Latin Americans as editors, translators, and writers,

Appleton had an outstanding advisory staff of literary stylists. Most of these editor-writers—some of whom were Domingo Sarmiento, Eugenio Hostos, and José Martí—were later to reach the zenith of fame throughout Latin America. Their literary skills, even though they protested in letters at being underpaid, built up and held Latin American good will and respect for their employer. Several of them, especially Sarmiento, went back to their native lands as political leaders and promoted book orders of texts and the series for students. Appleton could have had no better kind of sales promotion than that which these literary men gave.

Along more business lines, Appleton went into Latin America proper, setting up branch agencies of the firm. This is one of the earliest examples of the migration of North American business into Latin America. Appleton founded branches in Brazil, in Spanish American cities, and in European Spain. Now the inter-American book trade had a marketing system, a sales method, and an organization. Sales promotion moved in with cultural and intellectual relations—at least in the book trade.[17] The efforts paid well and business was good. The volume of books sold by Appleton was never again reached by a North American publisher—even when cultural relations with Latin America attained new heights under government assistance after 1933.

As in the case of George Lockwood, Appleton & Company issued Spanish-language catalogues to advertise large book imports from Spain as well as their own export lists for Latin America. The scattered catalogues, now well tattered, throw only a tantalizing light upon the business. No attempt will be made here to itemize the number of books or the titles of the individual works that were announced. The total was impressively large, reaching into a variety of topics, exactly as we have seen in the catalogues of George Lockwood and other booksellers and publishers. Favorite subjects were Castilian poetry, essays, drama, and the novel. Occasionally a few of these books were published here. Most of them, however, bore imprints from Madrid, and Appleton sold them to Latin Americans and to the many readers of Spanish in the United States.

Appleton's original accomplishment was the textbook series called *Appleton Educational Series for Hispanic America*. This was the special inter-American line, existing alongside the regular Hispanic list, cited just above. It was this unprecedented project which really made Appleton's high reputation in Latin America. In fact, so successful was the textbook business that, after a while, Appleton cut down on the standard

Hispanic titles in order to concentrate on the supply of Spanish texts for Latin American schools and *colegios*. These texts were published in Spanish, received careful editorial supervision, and were attractive in appearance, style, and content. The inter-American text series included many subjects, such as spelling, grammar, literature, manners, drawing, arithmetic, bookkeeping, biology, morals, geography, as well as dictionaries and even catechisms. Probably the finest practical index to the success and profit of the *Educational Series for Hispanic America* was the number of individual titles in the series which rose from 21 in 1860 to 244 in 1890.

Appleton's discreet advertising was very aware and conscious of what the publisher was doing in these educational cultural relations:

The Editors take pleasure in offering to those persons interested in education their new Catalogue of Textbooks for Teaching . . . with the object of promoting between the United States and Hispanic American countries those relations of friendship and commerce which are becoming each day more necessary and important. . . .
The majority of these books have received the highest recommendation and praise not only in the United States, where they are known and commonly used in the schools, but also in Havana, Mexico, and the provinces of South America.

The fact that these books were the same as those used in classrooms in the United States is of very great significance. North American historians, for example, wrote texts used in Latin American schools. Furthermore, that these texts were widely distributed and employed to bridge the differences between the Latin-Catholic and the Anglo-Protestant halves of the hemisphere is both a historic precedent out of the past and a historic guide for the present. Here, in a nutshell, is the actual uniformity of textbook treatment of American and Latin American history.

The books sold to Latin American school children were quite different from those overly prim and moralizing children's books that were sold within North America. The high standards of North American educators and authors won the confidence of Latin American educators and parents. It is a notable tribute to cultural relations that a *yanqui*, Protestant country—supposed to be crassly materialist and technological!—supplied authors and books for the education of tender, young minds in Latin America. Latin American schoolmen turned to North America in matters of the mind, not only to Europe.

A simple example of this is in the correspondence of Domingo Sarmiento, who supplied one of the strongest testimonials on behalf of Appleton. Sarmiento, a former editorial employe of Appleton, one-time Argentine minister to Washington, president of the Argentine Republic, and its foremost educator at the time, had only good words to say. Sarmiento, who was also a good friend of Stephen Hallet, called upon both North Americans—Appleton and Hallet—several times to supply Argentine schools and libraries with their books—which they did. He had great influence and prestige; so that in 1867, when the citizens and parents of Paraná, Argentina, wanted to found a *colegio* for their youth they turned to Sarmiento to recommend the textbooks which they wished to order. In the voluminous correspondence of Sarmiento, his reply to this request has long been unnoticed; but it can be quoted now. Sarmiento replied from New York, September 22, 1867, in a letter to the governing board of the *colegio*:

The Appletons here have published texts on chemistry, physics (in Spanish), and geography, astronomy (for secondary schools). There are excellent books for Latin, with English notes. And since this language ought to be diffused among us as a medium of education, students will profit by North American texts which are considered excellent.[18]

The reputation of the firm climbed as high as the standards of the texts themselves. Appleton, for its part, never lowered these standards. What was being used in North American schools went out to Latin America. The writers of the textbooks were occasionally Latin Americans writing especially for the Hispanic series, educators, teachers, or outstanding North American authors. One of their best-selling geography books was written by Ramón Páez, son of the former president of Venezuela, and a well-known contributor to North American magazines of the day. Appleton advertised his geography as being "prepared expressly for the Spanish American schools . . . widely introduced in South America, and should become the universal textbook in those countries in which Spanish is spoken."

Other texts were written by North Americans. In 1879 Appleton supplied Brazilian schools with a text on astronomy written by the principal of Public School 12 in New York City. Nor was this all. According to Appleton's own *Catálogo de los Libros publicados en Español,* books adopted by North American schools were also available in more advanced subjects, such as drawing, agricultural chemistry, medicine, gynecology, public education, and American history. All levels of schooling were served: grammar, secondary, collegiate, and even professional. One interesting text dealt with the *Methods of Teaching,* in a volume which tended to standardize teacher training and normal school work in the Americas. This book, which presented a unified program for teachers' colleges in the New World, was written by a superintendent of schools in Pennsylvania.

All good things come to an end, but it is strange to have to find an end of the inter-American book trade after so many Latin American teachers, librarians, educators, and liberal intellectuals had given the highest praise to North American sources of their educational values and literary goals. But we must chronicle the decline of the book trade. By 1890 Appleton and some of the others began to meet real difficulties in the way of payment for their books. Some of these were immediate obstacles, others were due to long-range and chronic handicaps to the sale of books because of widespread illiteracy and reduced educational budgets. Also, the wave of literary "yankeephobia," which set in after 1890, was Latin America's blind and angry retort to *leyenda negra,* Manifest Destiny, and the corollaries of North American expansionism and imperialism of the day. The dwindling profit and activity of the book trade seemed to coincide in time, perhaps by accident, with the oncoming years of economic investment in Latin America, "dollar diplomacy," and the strong Latin American policies of the United States from 1890 to 1914. Yet it will be hard to prove any direct connection between the twilight of inter-American book ties and the Latin American dislike for the diplomatic and economic events of that generation. One thing is certain, however: cultural relations and the ideas circulated in books took a back seat; while the talk turned to reciprocity, tariffs, silver, and sugar, or to arbitration, corollaries, and doctrines.

About the time that Pan-American relations were being discovered by government—from 1890 to 1914—inter-American cultural relations had evolved freely for almost two hundred years without government direction. Of course, ideas and exchanges did not exist in a vacuum; they felt the effect of current events and forces. It is just as much a paradox to point out that, although inter-American relations were free from government, the actions of government in war, hemisphere Americanism, boundary tensions, and monetary policies left their mark upon psychologies and attitudes. On the other hand, the decline of book publishing owed as little to contemporary government action as the rise of cultural relations originally owed to government inaction. The stumbling block was bigger than the Latin American policy of the United States.

The more likely and ever-present reason was the slow, even the re-tarded, development of any large, literate reading public in Latin America. This was Latin America's own internal problem, dating from the two and a half centuries of colonial America before a United States had even come into existence. For all the vast period in which the Church had a monopoly over and in education, reading and book collections were confined to a few. Latin America inherited this problem, and its nineteenth-century *caudillos* perpetuated it. Only in Argentina was there a real effort (Sarmiento's) to establish public libraries and the wider reading habit. But illiteracy injured the book trade directly, while inter-American science and scholarship were more immune to popular apathy.

Poor schooling, small budgets, and the absence of public libraries dashed the optimism of most liberals and educators at first; and after that, of publishers. In most of those countries the age of improvement in education and enlightened reform had come to a temporary stop by 1890. Even where there was both the tradition and practice of sudden change, there was little change in the educational structure. The move-ment to build schools and libraries took little or no hold upon the pro-grams of government, while international proposals to save Latin American culture by means of illiteracy drives were still far in the future. The negative psychology which prevailed was harmful to the inter-American book trade. This situation first challenged Appleton's pa-tience, then wore it thin.

Appleton, for one, paid for this situation in Latin America by having to withdraw from that book market. As usual, Latin American conditions and finances were felt in the United States. Since Latin American governments were devoting larger proportions to public works, army, and other material needs, it became necessary for Appleton to ask for a security of three thousand copies of a book as an advance to assure purchase and payment.[19] Latin American ministries of education found these conditions hard and embarrassing to meet. In fact, they could not meet them. The result was that shortly before 1900 Appleton discon-tinued more than fifty years of active inter-American business. Sales and sales promotion for books in Latin American centers came to a halt.

The aftermath came quickly: for a half-century Daniel Appleton of Manhattan had competed with, and even displaced, such respected European publishing houses as Hachette of Paris and Rivadeneyra of Madrid. These European firms issued books more cheaply, bound in paper, and were now able to catch up with and replace their erstwhile North American rivals. Latin America turned increasingly to these older

European houses for cheaper editions, better arrangements, and credits. Thus a century of book progress came to an end; cultural rift lay ahead. Latin America—its poets, essayists, critics, and book buyers—turned away from hemisphere Americanism and returned to an admiration of European, particularly French, culture. A second *fin de siècle* of admiration for things Gallic overcame the Latin American. The myth of a hard-headed North American Caliban was invented by the poet to contrast with Ariel, Latin America's spirit.

The era of Pan-Hispanism, Pan-Latinism, and Pan-Americanism in 1900 opened upon a propaganda of ideas and values in which North American book publishers were silent and inactive. The inter-American book trade had spent its once great force and thus again looked homeward for its readers. Latin American poets and novelists took to the fray, without an answering voice, since North Americans were too busy to notice. Had they wished to debate, the rebuttal might well have come from North American science and scholarship which could easily refute the charges of Latin poets and essayists. The rich Jeffersonian traditions and living patterns of North American freedom in science and scholarship were the triumph of reason, the cultural companions of a democratic spirit and technological (that is, material) progress. It would have been easy to show this side of North American life to critical Latin Americans.

Not all of the book market was lost. Enough was left to create transition and background for the present. Book exports to Latin America may have declined sharply, but the North American reading public still responded fairly well to novels, articles, and tales of adventure about Latin America. Books in English on Latin America continued to entertain the domestic reader. The pre-Pan American consciousness of the hemisphere entered history; the unilateral, nationalistic-cultural outlook conquered the inter-American spirit, just as in politics the position of the United States government was also unilateral on matters of the hemisphere. In this sense we can say—for both the United States and Latin America—that strengthening cultural nationalism in either region overlooked the inter-American idea.

There was good reason in contemporary Latin American events for the continued vitality of North American interest in politics and for the adequate sale of books. A remarkable series of dramatic crises, such as the republican overthrow of the Brazilian monarchy, tension with Chile, the Cuban crisis, the route through Panama, all helped to stir public interest in the "green continent." Mexico, without crisis under Díaz, also won public attention here. Some few readers were attracted by the lengthy rhetoric in the conferences arising from the new born American States. Special events of the day also summarized years of historical curiosity about Hispanic things and peoples. For one thing, the public celebration of the 400th anniversary of Columbus' discovery of America was widely noticed. Furthermore, Hubert Howe Bancroft's volumes on Spain's contribution to the history of the Southwest and Far West gave permanency to local and regional history.

The romance of Latin America never really ceased to hold readers. Thomas Janvier of New York, like his contemporary Ricardo Palma of Peru, compiled a treasure house of Mexican legend for readers. Janvier spun fantasy together with history for an interested public. Janvier's friend and colleague, Rollo Ogden (later to be more famous as an editor of the *New York Times*), wrote for the better magazines several articles on contemporary Spanish and Spanish American poetry and letters. Ogden, although now a little-known Hispanist, once did a good deal to acquaint North Americans with the worth of nineteenth-century Spanish poetry and literature. Janvier and Ogden joined forces in 1890 when Janvier wrote the introduction to Ogden's translation of the Colombian literary classic *María,* which Jorge Isaacs had recently written. New York City was the place of publication for their translation. Certainly the internal market had not disappeared with the vanishing exports of books. There were even some magazines, published in Spanish in the United States, like *América Científica* and *Ilustración Norteamericana,* which already were set up in Spanish editions here and then sent to Latin America.[20]

It is one thing to trace the historical growth of the experience with cultural ties in this hemisphere; it is quite another to analyze and classify the ideas put into circulation. Between the covers of these books—whether sold at home or abroad—one must probe to see the origins and precedents for present-day ideas about Latin America. Only by leaving title pages and publishers' imprints and entering right into the content of men, books, and culture contact can we understand the ideas that liberated the scientific and learned mind of both Americas. This is the way to establish adequate psychological rapport. The background of the inter-American book trade leads directly to the foreground of active scientific and intellectual researches into Latin American ethnology, natural science, and history. North American societies and scientific leaders were the personnel of the whole process. They continued to give high scientific frequency and regularity to inter-American exchanges.

The strongest ties were still the historic ones of secular and rationalist scholarship, based upon science and investigation. The specialized and learned few had always retained confidence in Latin America, notwithstanding the rise of parallel romantic, exotic, and hostile conceptions obtained by the popular interpreter. Since remote colonial days, an intellectual curiosity had firmly bound the most respectable representatives of North American intelligence to Latin American culture. Consequently, a considerable portion of the interest expressed by North American scientists and scholars went into the books which were being published. This interest led to a magnetic fascination for ancient American man, his origins, and his monuments. Even the missionary impulse of Mather and Sewall yielded before the energy and accuracy of scientific and learned research. The inter-American book trade merely conveyed facts and ideas written by those who knew or studied something. Standing in front of the publishers were North American scientists, historians, ethnologists, and geologists—men of inter-American science and scholarship.

Chapter 3

AMERICAN EARTH SCIENCES

*7*HE FIRST books on the earth sciences to awaken North American curiosity about Latin American geology and geography were those of the Prussian scientist-traveller, Baron Alexander von Humboldt. Before Humboldt's celebrated investigations in Ecuador, Venezuela, Colombia, Mexico, and Cuba, most accounts bearing upon rocks and soils had to do with mountains, mines, and their precious metals. Humboldt's field mission from 1799 to 1804 (he spent a short time in the United States) made use of first-hand observation, study, interviews, and note-taking; his books on Latin America were not published until ten years later. Before 1800, therefore, the geology and geography of Latin America and the descriptions of landscape, rivers, earthquakes, ores, and mountains were incorporated into the general histories, travel accounts, chronicles, and mining studies, which we have noticed. The science of geology did not have much chance to develop before Humboldt's generation, the last before Latin American independence. The great scientific work in Latin American botany was not matched by geology except for the work of Juan and Fausto Elhuyar (before and during Humboldt's time).

Books on Latin America dealt mainly with history, ethnology, and language. For most of the Spanish period almost all scientific thought as reported in books dealt with subjects of this kind—outside of theology, of course. Zoology and botany must be included under the heading of natural history before we can talk of natural science in Latin America. As to physics, we have already seen the inter-American exchanges of interest in Franklin's essays on electricity and optics, and the embryo contact in astronomy. Medicine, related to natural history, took up Dr. Barton's and Samuel Mitchill's work. Once Humboldt,

68

the scientist, had given rational and empirical status to the Latin American earth, the scientific impulses already connected with inter-American thought radiated immediately into geology and geography as fields of interest. Geology moved into the company of history, ethnology, and literature, supplying its own workers.

Unfortunately, Humboldt's work and Mitchill's praises came at a time when Latin American revolution and European war precipitated hindrances, so that any scientific plans for field work were cut off. Books remained the media of communication for ideas, in addition to the direct contacts which the scientific societies had achieved. Even where books on geology were limited, papers, articles, and transactions substituted for them and for the rare field visit. First-hand observation and field travel in Latin America waited almost a full generation after Humboldt's own travels (although no single expedition ever duplicated his extraordinary tour). In general, conditions in Latin America before 1825 left inter-American scientific relations in the earth sciences just about where they were already: an occasional book on the subject, reviews or articles, the nomination of Latin Americans to membership, and the exchanges of scientific transactions, as they have already been described.

One enduring impulse to North American interest in Latin American science came in 1818 from the *American Journal of Science,* edited by Professor Benjamin Silliman at Yale College. Pages of the *Journal* reveal the frequent and extended use of scientific information drawn from, or bearing upon, the achievements of science in Latin America. There is at least one illustration of the *Journal's* success at increasing the scientific community's knowledge—this time about Brazil, a country of subcontinental size about which too little was known. Only a scanty scientific literature was available about Brazil, although the *North American Review* had just published a book review of the botanical classifications and scientific travels which Spix and von Martius, the noted German naturalists, made in Brazil. But there was always room for a greater diffusion of this knowledge among North American scientists.

At least this is what von Martius himself urged. He wrote to Professor Silliman on February 13, 1824, offering through the *American Journal of Science* cultural and scientific ties with North American scientists interested in Brazil who had read his writings. Martius (Karl Friedrich Philip von, 1794-1868) sent to Silliman the account of the famous scientific field trip to Brazil (1817-1820). Like Caldas, the

Colombian astronomer, von Martius, the German botanist, sought to build continuous contact with North American science.

My friend and companion Dr. de Spix and I published some months ago the first volume of our travels from Rio de Janeiro through S. Paulo to the center of the gold mines. . . . You will oblige me very much by acquainting your countrymen with these publications. If you wish to have from time to time literary notes of German books, I shall send you them with great pleasure.[1]*

Martius was not a Humboldt, but he knew *Port Folio*'s formula for "making one country better acquainted with the other." He certainly never received anything like the honors which North American learned societies vied with each other to heap upon Humboldt. Professor Silliman printed the Martius announcement and invitation as he received it, without comment. The year before, 1816, Carey & Lea in Philadelphia published John Mawe's *Travels in Brazil*. These were among the earliest efforts to start up a special interest in Brazilian subjects. This was only the beginning; advances would come later.

From time to time special and pertinent articles dealt with Latin American science. Almost always Silliman published them in the *American Journal*. Very often Silliman received them from North American travellers, medical men, and persons of scientific bent who lived in Latin America. Travellers and correspondents supplied him with the data of mineralogy, geology, technology, botany, and medicine. He gave considerable space to news of Latin American science, but it is meaningless to index the numerous articles.

One of the more fruitful, and certainly very competent, examples of real scientific correspondence came before 1850 from Dr. W. S. W. Ruschenberger, then of the United States Navy in the South Pacific Station, who later became president of the distinguished Academy of Natural Sciences at Philadelphia. Ruschenberger was another important person in the history of North American and inter-American science who contributed frequently to Silliman's *American Journal*. Chilean science was very much on Ruschenberger's mind during the years he served the Navy in those waters, and he undertook to distribute knowledge to North American scientists, using Silliman's *Journal* and his own book which he wrote afterward. One of the lesser known but leading lights of the natural sciences, Ruschenberger translated and

*Notes to this chapter begin on page 172.

made excerpts of the noted French scientific investigator in Chile, Claude Gay. Even while Gay's work was carried on, Ruschenberger reported it serially, before the many-volumed, encyclopedic study was published. Ruschenberger's stay in Chile coincided as well with the intellectual and university reforms of Manuel Montt. From all this he was so convinced of the need to report Chilean scientific activity to Silliman, that he wrote he was willing to volunteer "these notes under the impression that they will be interesting to you; as they at least show that something is doing for science in this part of the world."

The practical connection of science with technology also awakened Silliman's interest in the prospects of Latin American resources. In October, 1841, the *American Journal of Science* published correspondence between the celebrated North American engineer in Latin America, William Wheelwright, and the Yale professor. Written between New Haven and Talcahuano, Chile, where Wheelwright was occupied with the steam navigation and railroading enterprise which made him so famous, their correspondence discussed the possibilities of "Steam Navigation to the Pacific by the Isthmus of Panama and along the Western Coast of South America." The technological side of the Wheelwright-Silliman letters went into the combustible qualities of Valdivia coal, mining operations and methods, Chilean navigation techniques, and some other scientific-technological matters on which Wheelwright was seeking professional advice from Silliman—or perhaps an interest.

William Maclure[2] of Philadelphia was another scientist who contributed frequently to Silliman's *American Journal of Science*. Time has obscured Maclure, like Ruschenberger, from rightful recognition as a scientist of high inter-American stature. Maclure, with Ruschenberger, was a leader of Philadelphia's Academy of Natural Sciences. In fact, William Maclure founded that Academy. He was its chief patron and benefactor for many years. Benjamin Silliman considered and stated that William Maclure founded the science of geology in the United States in the nineteenth century. Maclure was a remarkable figure. He was a rich man, a wealthy philanthropist, who upheld the "moral" Utopian socialism of Robert Owen, another rich man and philanthropist.

Maclure also held a place in that distinctive company of North Americans who travelled and lived in Spain in the first part of the nineteenth century. He kept his love for Spain, combining it with philanthropy and an affection for Mexico. In both countries he cultivated his feeling for science and a deep interest in geology, both of which are revealed in all his considerable correspondence and papers. He sent reports and geologic observations from Spain to Silliman's *American Journal*, 1822, 1823 and 1824. From Spain he went to settle and live in Mexico. He continued his studies of geology and mineralogy in Mexico, where he lived out "the evening of his life." Maclure died at San Angel (a suburb of Mexico City) in 1840. As Joel Poinsett assembled materials for Mexican antiquities and history, William Maclure did the same for Mexican earth history. He forwarded to Philadelphia scientific groups the basic data on Mexican geological formations. Maclure identified himself completely with the traditional pattern of inter-American scientific exchange. He also left a financial endowment to the Philadelphia Academy of Natural Sciences and an incentive for investigations.

Maclure supplied the library of that Academy with many scientific volumes on the natural and geological history of Spain and Mexico—fruit of his residence, his income, and turn of mind. The Catalogue of the Academy for 1837 stated that Maclure donated as much as five-sixths of its materials, chiefly books.[3] He brought back with him from Spain a great many tomes on mineralogy, geology, and agriculture, which he himself had hoped to use in a geological map of Spain but which he never finished. He did leave behind him in Spain the sum of $60,000 which he had invested in land for an industrial, cooperative school along Owenist lines for Spanish boys. Here was his cooperative ideal and his philanthropy, intended to reform education and improve science in schools. But the return of the reactionary Bourbon dynasty in 1823 cost him the land, buildings, and his program—all of which was turned over to the priests. All that he had left from three years' stay in Spain were those volumes on Spanish science which he generously bestowed on his favorite North American scientific society, the Philadelphia Academy of Natural Sciences.

Maclure was a generous man, and inter-American science benefited. He gave the Philadelphia Academy volumes and transactions on biology, geology, and natural history, publications from Barcelona, Madrid, Havana, and Lima. Maclure brought into the United States the treatises of the great Spanish biologists Larreátegui, Gómez Ortega, and Cavanilles. Naturally enough the economic man in Maclure was inseparable from the scientist: he also gave an unusually rich group of items on Spanish banking and economic history before 1822, newspapers, important documents on Mexico, several pieces of classic Spanish literature, and books of a nonscientific character.

The Philadelphia Academy of Natural Sciences—like its neighbor, the American Philosophical Society—quickly picked up the now-established patterns of inter-American intellectual relations and named Latin American scientists as corresponding and honorary members. A rather large number of well-known Latin Americans were nominated between 1818 and 1880:

> Baron de Collins, Cuba, 1818
> Pedro Abadia, Peru, 1821
> Mariano Rivero, Peru, 1821
> José Hipólito Unánue, Peru, 1821
> Ramón de la Sagra, Cuba, 1829
> José Bustamante, Mexico, 1829
> Andrés del Río, Mexico, 1829
> José María Vargas, Venezuela, 1835
> Celedonio Carbonell, Puerto Rico, 1859
> Felipe Poey, Cuba, 1867
> Mariano Roa Bárcena, Mexico, 1874.[4]

Thus the well-tried road of building a community through inter-American memberships continued to go parallel with the equally established work of exchanges. A healthy body of scientific spirit took shape in the Western Hemisphere.

Maclure had a very clear idea of this goal. He also realized fully how to go about achieving it. He did not approach inter-American relations accidently or haphazardly, as we can see by one effort he made in 1835. From his home down in Mexico, Maclure wrote to Dr. Samuel G. Morton, who was then the secretary of the Philadelphia Academy of Natural Sciences. Maclure pressed Dr. Morton to open correspondence with Venezuelan scientists, in order to encourage inter-American cultural relations, especially with the land of Simón Bolívar.[5] Maclure showed the activity of North American science—as compared to religion —in bringing the reforms of reason to the Latin American mind:

Mexico 30 October 1835

Mr. Michelena the Minister from Venezuela here informs me of the real change that has taken place in public opinion there that the influence of the military and the priest is annihilated and that their last President was a civilian a man of science Dr. José María Vargas an able physician has studied in Edinburgh and travelled much over Europe....

It is the first after Jefferson that a man of science has been put at the head of the state on this side of the Atlantic. . . .

In consequence of the above and that the Academy may benefit by an interchange of materials for the diffusion of real knowledge I have to request that you (with the assistance of one of the Academy not so much occupied) would put up the following books. . . .[6]

Neither Maclure nor his Academy colleagues stopped there. In subsequent letters Maclure supplied North Americans with the knowledge they wanted about Mexican and Guatemalan science, adding a premature political optimism about the "young converts to freedom in Mexico." His own "religion" was that of liberty, both for science and progress in America. He asked that Latin Americans be invited into the choice circle of North American science. The century and a quarter in time which separated the efforts of Cotton Mather from William Maclure were even more apart in any standard of measurement of their two intentions: science and religion. Both sought to gain the American half-world, the Western Hemisphere, for their single community of selected ones. Maclure was in the better position to act. He recommended to Dr. Morton that the exchange of scientific transactions with Venezuela at once be followed up by the nomination of Dr. José Vargas as corresponding member of the Academy of Natural Sciences. This took place almost immediately, in 1835. After that, all the publications of the Philadelphia Academy were sent to Caracas in 1836, not only as a repository of knowledge, but in order "to give an idea of the utility of the society to those infant societies [in Latin America]. . . ." Dr. Vargas, others after him, and the small body of Venezuelan scientists entered the fraternity of North American science.[7]

Geology supplied only a single impulse for cultural associations in the Americas. Societies and individuals who were interested in botany and zoology contributed their own incentive. The complexities of geology were easily outdone by the bewildering species of plant and animal life. Classification was the first, probably the hardest, task for both life and earth sciences. The flora and fauna of the Americas may not have had an easy taxonomic relation, but those who studied them did. Scientists engaged in investigating and classifying biological species were brought together by this common interest. Geology and biology, parents of the concept of evolution, were also the pair of subjects which brought forth persons well-fitted for an inter-American task. In North America we return to the respected figure of Dr. Samuel L. Mitchill, who rendered such important service to the hemisphere. Very early in the nineteenth century (1814) in his "Discourse upon the Botany of the Two Americas"—an interesting use of that term—Mitchill exposed his audience of North Americans to the vast and expert literature upon Spanish American botanical science, written by scientists, explorers, and noted travellers.[8]

Dr. Mitchill, within five years, carried out for the Lyceum of Natural History of New York the same inter-American scientific work (exchanges of ideas and memberships) that William Maclure did for the Academy of Natural Sciences and that others did for the American Philosophical Society. Mitchill was always a vigorous and positive friend of hemisphere science. In 1825, at the peak of his reputation, Mitchill had made scientific friends all over Latin America, especially in Peru, Mexico, and Argentina. He had exceptional scientific, educational, and political advantages. He was the New York member of the Buenos Aires Society for the Promotion of the Natural and Physical Sciences. Mitchill lent his initiative and name to the invitations which the Lyceum of Natural History extended to Latin American scientists.[9]

Mitchill acted as a liaison between the American Philosophical Society and Mexico, even though the Philadelphia Society did not really depend upon his assistance. His name was widely known. In 1819 he somehow served to give a clearance to the correspondence of Andrés del Río, the noted Mexican geologist, with the American Philosophical Society. A letter from A. Richards (for the Philosophical Society) to Mitchill, dated February 23, 1819, shows this:

I avail myself of your kind offer to find a conveyance of the package directed to the Philosophical Society and College of Physicians, Philadelphia. . . . It is from the professors [at] Mexico. Should those Gentlemen wish to correspond with the Mexicans, I will with pleasure be the medium of a safe conveyance.[10]

There was already an active correspondence between Andrés del Río and the leaders of science in New York and Philadelphia. The famous Mexican scientist was named to membership in the Lyceum of Natural History, New York, in 1817, when it was founded. He was chosen by Dr. Mitchill's society even before the American Philosophical Society and the Philadelphia Academy of Natural Sciences had selected him. Many Latin Americans followed del Río into membership in the New York Lyceum; they represented almost all of the trans-Caribbean scientific community. Membership in the Lyceum was not automatically given to Latin Americans; the number was select.[11] Latin Americans were given honorary membership, and the by-laws limited these to forty.

At different times the honorary members of the New York Lyceum included Pedro Abadía of Peru (1820), Mariano Caldas of Mexico (1828), Bartolomé Muñóz of Buenos Aires (1823), Francisco de Corroy of Mexico (1823), Juan Ehlers of Mexico (1835), Ramón de la Sagra of Cuba (1835), and Felipe Poey of Cuba (1851), in addition to many others listed in the Appendix. Once again we see from the list that some Latin Americans were members of several societies at the same time; this underscored the inter-American trend. We also see that the Lyceum of Natural History, acting independently of other societies, had followed the same direction toward the choice of Latin Americans as members and the exchange of publications. Here again the intellectual *laisser-faire* spirit, without either joint action or the assistance of United States government, pointed each society's own effort at a common cultural goal.

Latin America's response to these invitations was generally the same. There was a pattern here, also, or perhaps a history was being made. Before, and later in the nineteenth century, Latin Americans were willing and glad to send contributions and library materials in exchange. This was real two-way traffic. They likewise named North Americans to membership in their scientific and learned bodies. In the case of the Lyceum of Natural History, the inter-American process was clearly at work. The early catalogues of the Lyceum are like those of other North American societies. They show a scientific library in formation and growth, enriched by Latin American gifts and donations which were otherwise hard to get. Materials might sometimes be topical, like the *Abeja Argentina,* in fourteen numbers, from Buenos Aires. Much more scientific in character was the gift of *Anales de la Academia de Medicina* (Buenos Aires) sent by Bartolomé Muñóz in 1823, the first year of publication. This reciprocity in scientific and cultural matters had been going on since the eighteenth century.

The Cuban scientist Ramón de la Sagra, a highly reputable botanist and one of that great generation of Hispano-Cuban minds, gave the New York Lyceum his *informe* (report) on the state of botanical science in Cuba and the condition of the botanical gardens there, about which Alexander von Humboldt had written earlier, in his essay on the Island of Cuba. De la Sagra was also pleased to inform Dr. Mitchill and the Lyceum of the establishment of a Chair of Botany at the University of Havana (1825). The exchange and library resources of the Lyceum went far beyond this. One of the treasures of New World botany was donated, probably by way of Dr. Mitchill: the famous *Flora Peruviana et Chilensis* of the Spanish botanists Hipólito Ruíz and José Pavón. These were but two of the scientists of Spain in the era of the Enlightenment who went to Latin America to carry on investigation and classification. The Lyceum soon obtained the volume of Brazilian botany and travels by Spix and von Martius, shelving it alongside of J. B. Sigaud's *O Propagador das Sciencias Medicas,* published at Rio de Janeiro in 1827. There were many similar gifts, invaluable as scientific sources.

Mitchill's great personal activity in intellectual cooperation helped make it more effective, and he remained interested in its achievements and results for a long time. For the whole quarter century from Miranda's frustrated expedition through the struggles for Independence and recognition and into the era of the Monroe Doctrine, Samuel Mitchill had always and unceasingly looked on Latin Americans as the intellectual (and political) equals of North Americans. They were peers in the hemisphere. Mitchill never changed these views. We have seen how they were uttered in 1807, 1810, and 1814. When he addressed the New York Horticultural Society in 1826, this inter-American Jeffersonian again connected science with the political and economic benefits of reason and progress, repeating his opinion that "our intercourse with South America brings to us more of its production than we could possibly have obtained in its provincial state." His politics remained as broad as his scientific horizon, an avowed fellow-traveller of Latin American freedom and cultural liberation. That is why he was continually being sent letters and gifts of plants and seeds, now from Dr. Unánue of Peru, now from Bartolomé Muñóz of Buenos Aires, and again from Ramón de la Sagra of Cuba. One letter of Sagra to Mitchill specifically asked him to develop inter-American exchanges of botanical drawings, of plants and seeds, and of the journals of the North American botanical gardens with those of Havana.

No complete record exists of the activity of Mitchill in the Lyceum of Natural History. The early *Proceedings* seem to have disappeared without much trace, leaving a blank in the history of inter-American science, which luckily is partly filled by the minutes and correspondence which were printed in the *Annals* of the Lyceum. These have not been lost. In addition, Benjamin Silliman rescued much more material from possible oblivion (reports, digests of papers, etc.), which he published in the *American Journal of Science.* The *American Journal* preserved and reproduced many items that were in the lost *Proceedings.* The *American Journal* then gave many pages over to reporting the minutes and discussions of the Lyceum of Natural History. This happy arrangement between New Haven and New York was a blessing. Thus we know from the *Proceedings,* as they are recorded in the *American Journal,* that there was active correspondence with Dr. Hipólito Unánue of Peru and with Mariano Rivero also of Peru, a reprint of the botanical discoveries of José Pavón, and an analysis of the work of Bonpland (Humboldt's famous associate), among many other important articles.

The *American Journal* kept alive the memory of strong links between American scientists. One tragic notice reported the decline and fall of Mexican science from its high eighteenth-century state. The report, written by Andrés del Río, appeared as a contribution to the Lyceum from its Mexican member. It was read "before the New York Lyceum of Natural History 8th May 1826, and ordered to be sent to Professor Silliman for publication in the American Journal of Science." The article was read and printed on the eve of Andrés del Río's own visit to the United States. At this unusual opportunity for the personal communication of ideas by a famous Mexican scientist before his North American colleagues, del Río lectured at the American Philosophical Society in Philadelphia and at the Lyceum of Natural History in New York. It was a precious moment to personalize the whole spirit of inter-American science through free discussion and exchange of ideas. Del Río, better than anyone else, was able to give a picture of current science in New Spain (since Humboldt and Mitchill had described Mexican scientific achievement).

It was a sad picture. Emancipation and the struggles of freedom had treated science in Mexico quite harshly. Del Río scored the neglect and abandon of natural sciences in Mexico. He pointed to the years of decline since 1810, and stressed how his own laboratory had suffered from years of revolution and the ending of royal support. He stressed the contrast between republican attitudes towards science and those of the earlier monarchy. Like the Jeffersonian Dr. Mitchill, Professor del Río was thinking of the enlightened Spanish monarchy of the eighteenth century, not the benighted reactionary regime of their own day. Remembering how fulsomely Dr. Mitchill, the republican, had praised the cultural achievements of New Spain, and what credit he had given to the Crown for its support of science, it must have been painful for Mitchill, Silliman, and others, to learn that Mexican scientific progress had ceased "in consequence of the unfortunate condition of our laboratory, after having been thirty years in charge of a chemist like [Fausto del] Elhuyar. . . . It is true that under the old government he pursued his occupation steadily, through necessity: for he who has once had a taste of the experimental sciences cannot possibly ever abandon them."[12]

Mitchill lived through a great era of emancipated, creole American, scientific growth. If there is one North American scientist who had a dedicated sense of inter-American values, it was Sam Mitchill, who might well have become the real Uncle Sam of inter-American relations to replace the symbolic "Tío Sam" of Latin American anti-Americanism. He enriched North American science by these efforts to expand its cultural horizons. But all of North America's zeal and good will could not restrain these forces in Latin America which interrupted and even prevented progress. Latin American internal upheavals and the return of Church influence, combined with the rise of the *caudillo* in government, cast long and dark shadows upon the early moments of this inter-American day. And with the death of Samuel Mitchill, the one-man incentive behind scientific relations also faded. Individualism had many advantages, but there were also disadvantages. Natural science in both Americas had no better friend than Samuel Mitchill, but he could not overcome or change social, military, and educational handicaps in the rest of the hemisphere. It was too much for one man, even one as Jeffersonian and republican as Mitchill. His personal touch was replaced by the cultural machinery of the learned institutions and the process of organization. For all that he and others accomplished, there was yet a great deal to be done. Fortunately, new and recent North American societies picked up the work of older ones, and the movement for contacts grew into the second half of the century from the start made in the first half.

One change after 1850 was the transfer of interest from botany to geology and geography. Under these auspices we find new groups and associations renewing the inter-American patterns. For example, studies in natural history were helped by exchanges with Brazil in 1849 and 1851, when the Instituto Historico e Geographico at Rio de Janeiro was pleased to receive the *Natural History of the State of New York,* and then sent up to the New York State Library at Albany a complete set of its own Brazilian volumes.[13] Astronomy was a great subject for science, but the study of the skies, although an ancient one in America, played a secondary role in the cultural relations process. The same can be said of mathematics and the more physical sciences. The earth and life sciences exerted a greater force of attraction. Geography and geology took up the work of botany, although contacts in all these subjects never really ceased.

Geography, which made possible the original discovery of America, now contributed to the cultural rediscovery of the other America: the

American Geographical Society joined the movement. Moreover, a generation of United States Navy men began to explore and open the continental Latin American rivers and drainage basins to pilots, merchants, geographers, and government surveys.[14] What mining was to geology in America, navigation and hydrography were to geography. Before the establishment of the American Geographical Society in 1852, the work of exploring, surveying, and mapping Latin America was carried on by officers of the United States Navy—successors to the officers of the Spanish Navy, who had done similar work before them. At about the same time that Commodore Perry went into Japanese waters, Lieutenant Thomas Jefferson Page had sounded the Río de la Plata, Lieutenant Gillis surveyed the South Pacific along the coasts of Chile, and Matthew Maury led his historic expedition into the Amazon Valley, also credited to Lieutenants Herndon, Gibbon, and Lardner. These scientific expeditions were sponsored by Congress and endorsed by leading North American scientific societies.

The American Geographical and Statistical Society was founded in 1852, serving those with a general and a special interest in geography. Included under the term "general" interest were many items whose relevancy was more in the direction of commercial and statistical information about Latin America. At first this had a negative effect upon cultural relations, because the neglect of science in favor of commerce did little to add or contribute to inter-American relations. The Society's interest in Latin America was rather uneven, partly scientific and strongly commercial; it grew slowly. As late as 1870 not one Latin American geographer had been invited to membership. However, published articles in the Society's official periodical supplied information about Latin America. The very first *Bulletin*, describing the opening meeting in January, 1852, surveyed the promise as well as the ever-present resources of the Latin American scene through the eyes of Edward A. Hopkins, recently appointed United States consul to Paraguay. Hopkins was a commercial-minded entrepreneur and promoter as much as he was anything else.[15]

Hopkins knew Paraguay. He had lived and travelled in the River Plate region—he was a business man. He was neither a Humboldt nor a Mitchill nor a Prescott. A practical and experienced businessman, certainly not the formal student, Hopkins prepared for the American Geographical Society a vividly phrased, eye-witness account of the geography and resources of the Parana-Plata River Valley. The Society received his paper, the "Memoir on the Geography, History, Productions and Trade of Paraguay," very well. In fact, the American Geographical Society then declared its support of the project of the United States Navy to explore and navigate the waterways of the Río de la Plata system. At another time—June, 1852—the Geographical Society called upon the one-time president of New Granada, Tomás Mosquera, to give an account of Colombia's geography, environments, landscape, and people. One of the most interesting and practical items for North Americans was a series of population and fiscal figures called *Statistics of American States,* which regularly carried the trade, business, and vital statistics of Ecuador, Chile, Argentina, Peru, New Granada, Uruguay, and the other Latin American republics.

The Society's work was unexciting. In fact it was less than ordinary. Articles and an occasional talk meant very little. But the Society initiated a new procedure, a "next stage" for spreading ideas. The scattered articles in the *Bulletin* and the *Journal* are not the whole story. They scarcely indicate a desire to learn about Latin America, to say nothing of exchanges. Instead, we have to trace the Society's steps towards work with government, to commence efforts to enlist the services of Latin American consuls in New York, or to seek the aid of United States government officials in pursuing objectives for inter-American cooperation.[16] For the first time in the history of cultural relations, government entered the scene. The Geographical Society was the first North American body to ask for such assistance. The only other society to work with the government was the Smithsonian Institution, but the Smithsonian was part of the government, and the Geographical Society was not.

The Geographical Society was different in yet another way. The goal of interchange of knowledge was not quite the same for the Geographical Society as it was for the Smithsonian. Indeed the Society's aims seemed to be different from those of other North American societies, such as the American Philosophical. For both the Smithsonian Institution and the private learned societies the purpose of culture contact with Latin America was evidently and clearly to diffuse knowledge. The Geographical Society, at that early date, was not yet so scientific and intellectual. The Society stated that it followed more material objectives, as an adjunct of cultural relations, seeking rather to obtain "any information, maps, documents, that may be of interest and advantage to the mercantile community." That explains why the Society turned to the United States government and to Latin American consular agents (in New York) for assistance. Geography found government and trade twin supports in winning interest in Latin America. But the Society's bid for government help was original, and up to then unprecedented. It hinted at one inter-American channel which would cut its own way.

In order to obtain the cited "information, maps, documents," the Geographical Society in 1854 asked Governor Horatio Seymour of New York to write to the national Secretary of State for government aid. William Marcy was then Secretary of State. Marcy, himself a former governor of New York and friendly to the purposes of the Geographical Society, was willing to help. As Secretary of State he sent out a circular letter to United States consuls and ministers in Latin America asking them to cooperate with the Society and its agents. If the Geographical Society had hoped for a position as special and prominent as the Smithsonian, this was impossible; the Society was compelled to find and make its own connections with Latin American consuls in New York. At that time United States government support was premature and vague, made by routine letter. The formal results never compared, even faintly, to the assistance given to the Smithsonian for its program in Latin America.

The Society's private initiative produced better and more tangible results—at least in one case. The Society worked out a happy arrangement with the Chilean consul in New York. In fact, the Chilean home government was just as eager and cooperative, giving its full support to the offer made by its consul. The Republic of Chile was quite willing to carry on scientific and cultural relations with this private, geographical society. The government at Santiago, through Foreign Minister Antonio Varas (Manuel Montt was president), sent a letter to the Geographical Society, accompanied by a shipment of government department reports, Chilean financial statistics, papers on the Chilean claims to the Straits of Magellan, together with geographic notes on the rivers of South Chile.[17] The Chilean government stated that it would send other scientific volumes, reports, and studies from time to time and be glad to answer questions presented by the Society. By 1855, therefore, the rise of geography in the Americas moved cultural relations to the point where governments just about began to recognize the subject as a new function and as an area of desirable activity. Nor was the government of Chile the only government to support the exchange of "publications beneficial to the advancement and development of both countries." Governments were expressing interest in technology, international fairs, and geodetic surveys.

The Civil War years in the United States from 1861 to 1865 suspended and then halted most of the Society's work. Other North American societies and institutions were not as seriously affected, but the

Geographical Society almost stopped its activity. As a result, the cultural work of other bodies continued without any change in pattern or policy, while the Geographic Society's program took advantage of the interruption to emerge with a change. The postwar years gave the Geographical Society the chance to reconstruct its practices in inter-American relation, conforming (unconsciously) to the historic and familiar procedures. After 1870 there was a new approach; now the Society moved along the well-trod path of inviting Latin Americans to corresponding and honorary membership. Geography, one of the newer subjects of societal activity, fell into line with history, ethnology, botany, and other academic friends of Latin American thought.

The number of Latin American corresponding members rose from four to seventeen between 1870 and 1872. Most of these were Mexicans and Brazilians, representing countries where organized geographical work had already begun. However, even though these members were called Fellows, their effectiveness was not as great as the term implies. Correspondence with them was infrequent and irregular. Their role was a paper and honorary one, little else. Nor did the Geographical Society get very much in the way of articles, gifts, donations, or exchanges from them. This contact of geographical fellowship was brief. As a matter of fact, it declined between 1880 and 1900, coming to an end by the latter date, after which no more Latin Americans seem to have been named. It is hard to guess why this unhappy ending should have occurred this way, especially when we contrast it to the far greater success of Historical, Antiquarian, Philosophical, Ethnological, and Natural Science societies.

Most of the progress made by the Society, at least in Brazil, owed its gains to the intervention of Charles Hartt. Canadian-born, North American in residence, occupation, and scientific training, Charles Frederick Hartt was a scientist of unusual dimension. His is one of the great names in the history of inter-American science, like Mitchill's or Maclure's. Hartt, who had taught geology at Vassar College in 1868 and then at Cornell University after 1870, was a Brazilian specialist who worked in ethnology, geology, and paleontology. He had originally gone to Brazil in 1868, in the famous expedition of Louis Agassiz, as an assistant. But the Geographical Society called upon Hartt rather than Agassiz to present the facts of both Brazilian geography and geology since his chief "was not usually enrolled among geographers." Hartt contributed greatly to Brazilian geology but put the Geographical Society on the road of cultural relations by nominating his Brazilian associates and friends to membership.[18] They were elected.

If personal fellowship and membership ties were not too impressive, the Geographical Society was at least able to follow other North American societies in nature and extent of institutional ties, as shown through exchanges. From 1879 to the end of that century the Geographical Society obtained a scientific liaison with the chief learned groups of Latin America, Portugal, and Spain. Publications went out from New York to Mexico City, Santiago de Chile, Buenos Aires, Lisbon, Madrid, Guatemala, Costa Rica, and other places, as follows:

Argentina
Buenos Aires: Instituto Geográfico Argentina
Sociedad Científica Argentina
Instituto Histórico-Geográfico
del Río de la Plata

Córdoba: Academia Nacional de Ciencias

Brazil
Rio de Janeiro: Royal Geographical Society
Biblioteca Nacional
Instituto Historico-Geographico
do Brasil
Museu Nacional
Observatorio Nacional
Seccão da Sociedade de Geo-
graphia de Lisboa no Brasil
Sociedade de Geographia

São Paulo: Commissão Geographica e Geo-
logica da Provincia de São
Paulo

Chile
Santiago: Der Wissenschaftliche Verein
Observatorio Astrónómico
Oficina Central de Estadística
Oficina Hidrográfica

Costa Rica
San José: Oficina de depósito y canje de
publicaciones
La Gaceta, Diario Oficial

Guatemala   Dirección Federal de Estadística

Mexico Museo Nacional
Observatorio Meteorológico
Sociedad Científica "Antonio Alzate"
Ministerio de Fomento
Observatorio Astronómico, Tacubaya
Sociedad Mexicana de Geografía
y Estadística[19]

Institutional exchanges such as these were fine, but they did not come to life in the way personal interchanges could. Here again the work of Charles Hartt proved to be effective. Hartt put the sciences of geology and geography ahead of the place where William Maclure and other predecessors left them. Hartt did more for the special field of Brazil-American relations than Maclure, Mitchill, or any other. They had had little contact with the Brazilian Empire. He almost created the field of Brazilian studies for North Americans. Geology and geography were his professional interests although he soon turned to Brazilian ethnology. Hartt's permanent place in inter-American science was equal to that of William H. Prescott in history, John Lloyd Stephens and Ephraim Squier in Indianist work, and Samuel L. Mitchill in inter-American natural science.

Hartt had a unique role in cultural relations. Before his day Brazil, under Emperor Pedro II, had not had very much scientific attention given to geology. Much had been done about botany and ethnology. Until the time of the Agassiz expedition, in which Hartt shared, geology enjoyed slight inter-American prestige. Hartt changed all this. He brought Brazilian students to Cornell University and trained a generation of North American scientists to continue his geologic work in Brazil while developing their own specialties. The Brazilian Empire appointed him to the high government post of Chief of the Geologic Survey (1875), although he was a foreigner. His published work in this field was the *Geology and Physical Geography of Brazil* (Boston, 1870), which is the report of the Thayer-Agassiz expedition. Brazilians republished this work in 1941 as one of their classics.[20]

His letter to Charles Daly, then president of the American Geographical Society, reveals Hartt to be one of the earliest of our Latin American specialists. This letter, asking Judge Daly's support for Hartt's desire to be Geologist to the Brazilian Empire, was dated from Cornell University, Ithaca, New York, June 1, 1872:

My Dear Sir:

I am about making application to the Brazilian government asking for the appointment as Geologist to the Empire to undertake a Geological Survey of the country. I need to send along with my application recommendations from some of our scientific men and societies in the United States. Since you know something of what I have already done in the way of exploring Brazil, would you have the kindness to give me a note which I might use in the way I have spoken of?

I have devoted myself exclusively to South American studies for several years and I long to make them a life work. I hope, however, that in the event of my appointment it will not be necessary for me to sever my connection with Cornell University. . . .

Yours respectfully,
Ch. Fred. Hartt[21]

Hartt did save geologic science in Brazil from decline, charlatanry, and from being overwhelmed by excessive emphasis on mining. In the United States he opened up unusually wide interest in Brazil. Individual benefactors and patrons of science as well as the Peabody Museum at Harvard and Cambridge supported his work. His return to field work in Brazil in 1874 was made possible by financial grants from E. B. Morgan of Aurora, New York, a trustee of Cornell University, and by Dr. J. C. Rodrigues, editor and proprietor of *O Novo Mundo,* a newspaper with Brazilian-American appeal, published in Portuguese in New York City. Rodrigues was another forgotten figure, once very active in inter-American relations. Again Hartt entered the Amazon Valley.

The Amazon Valley was in the focus of empire-building dreams for centuries. After the Herndon-Maury survey, and also in response to domestic and European commercial pressures, the Brazilian Empire opened that internal waterway to world navigation. Then, in 1874, Hartt undertook to add intensive geologic, ethnologic, and archaeological studies of the vast region. Based in the city of Pará, Hartt's expedition entered the valleys of the Tocantins, Xingú, and Tapajós rivers, adding the science of geology to the hydrographic work of the United States Navy men and others who knew the vast Amazon drainage basin. With little financial assistance from either the Brazilian or United States governments, Hartt made much progress with aid from private sources. On the other hand, it is fair to say, if he received too little money from Brazil, he was rewarded with academic and public honors as few have been before or since. He became a member of the important Instituto

Historico e Geographico Brasileiro (1875), Director of Survey as we have seen, and in 1876, Chief of the Sections of Physical Sciences, Mineralogy, Geology, and General Paleontology of the Museu Nacional, Rio de Janeiro.[22]

One of the more important reasons which allowed Hartt to do more for cultural relations than Mitchill, Maclure, or Prescott were able to do was his position which opened Brazilian scientific circles directly to him. As a scientific worker of repute and a scientific official of note, Hartt did more than some institutions or societies could have done to carry out relations personally. But even this does not match his long-run legacy, especially the training of those who succeeded him in Brazil. Hartt's activity has had a continuous influence right down to the present. His students took up where he left, at his premature death, and extended his influence well beyond his own tragically-short lifetime. Among his students were Orville Derby, a distinguished geologist in Brazil in his own right, and John Branner, geologist, Brazilianist, and the founder of Brazilian studies at Leland Stanford University after 1900. Through Branner, Hartt's Brazilianism entered California higher education in the first quarter of the twentieth century. Not until the first decade of the twentieth century, when Bailey Willis of Stanford worked with Francisco Moreno in developing Argentine geological studies and Isaiah Bowman worked the Andes, did the rich heritage of inter-American earth science turn up such first-rate figures.

Almost singlehandedly the individuals of this trio of Hartt, Derby, and Branner gave scientific basis and organization to Brazilian geology. Hartt had died in 1878 at the age of 38, but Derby and Branner's work led into the next century. Each man, within his all-round scientific outlook, had room for special training or interest: Branner took to practical and even economic geology, while Derby, like Hartt, had a bent towards fossil study and paleontology. Hartt—as we shall see in the next chapter —also acquired a permanent fondness for Brazilian ethnology and archaeology. In fact, the aspect of South American studies which Hartt "longed to make a life work" might well have been Brazilian anthropology and prehistory, to such an extent that his students wrote that "so engrossing had these ethnological studies become to Hartt that it is not improbable, had he lived, he would have given his entire attention to South American antiquities. . . . He was a pioneer in this special field." Thus, as the North American scientists Mitchill and Maclure had trained their minds upon Spanish American culture contacts, Charles Hartt had rediscovered Brazil.

By 1870 North American institutions and societies had raised their sights and lifted their eyes above Mexico, Cuba, and the Caribbean towards South America proper—Brazil, Chile, Argentina, and the whole of *tierra firme*. A long and historic cultural effort was crowned with success, whether or not individuals and societies knew of the whole inter-American process (as those with present hindsight can). Some geologists (historians and ethnologists, too) knew little or nothing of what the next man was doing, yet the entire contribution had a unity based on these individual services. Out of this freedom and variety came an association of New World minds, independent of political support and political difference, aloof from government direction as well as the difference between their governments, whose spirit was nourished by the inter-American acceptance of a Jeffersonian ideal. These men were emancipated from inbred religions and from their ancestral ideologies.

Since 1800 scientific and scholarly interest had been stronger towards Mexico than for any other single Latin American country. Mexico's nearness, the treatise of Humboldt, the fascination of the Aztec and Maya civilizations, the glamour of its history, and the wonders of the landscape, awakened more curiosity about Mexican history, nature, and her people than Brazil did. Even Hartt's work and reputation could not shake the prior position of Mexico. Every type of North American society sought and welcomed Mexican members, since that early date when Andrés del Río and José María Bustamante had joined both the American Philosophical Society and the Philadelphia Academy of Natural Sciences.[23] Notwithstanding their country's internal troubles, Mexican scientists and learned societies were highly respected. In fact, putting this in a different way, the community of science and scholarship with Mexico (and the rest of Latin America) flourished in spite of war, boundary disputes, Mexican claims arguments, annexationism, and the Manifest Destiny psychology. The good sense of reason and science was deaf to the fanfare of war trumpets.

When the Sociedad Mexicana de Geografía y Estadística was founded in 1839 (the Society still carries on its work), the basic force in inter-American relations asserted itself. Cultural reciprocity led to many interchanges of membership. For example, the Sociedad Mexicana, like the Brazilian Instituto Historico e Geographico (founded at about the same time), invited North Americans to membership. This was true, two-way interest. Mexico and Brazil were more active in this respect than some other Latin American countries, but such mutual interchange went on all over. A rare scientific award came to a North American in

1872 when the Sociedad Mexicana paid tribute to the science and inventiveness of Samuel F. B. Morse. Only Alexander von Humboldt had been singled out for such honors before this, and no North American has been since. The Mexican Geographical Society called a special session and assembly in honor of Morse. The easy cliché by which Latin American poets of the next generation could denounce North American technique and science as intrinsically evil, in contrast with the Latin American cult of beauty and good, was never accepted by Latin American science, which had only good will for North American ability.

North Americans who were correspondents of the Sociedad Mexicana are the best answer and index to the way in which the inter-American spirit was not poisoned by Manifest Destiny, *leyenda negra,* the sore point of annexationism, and the ill will aroused by the War with Mexico. There was no room for nationalisms or jingoism here. The enduring nature of scientific cooperation and the permanence of enlightenment made up the rational side of North American culture. Friends of Mexico and of Brazil, historians, inventors, ethnologists, engineers, and scientists populated that terrain in the hemisphere, while some of the best names in North American intellectual life entered the roll of members of the Sociedad Mexicana from 1839 to 1890:

Charles Daly	Aaron H. Palmer
Joseph Henry	Nathaniel Shaler
William H. Prescott	Porter C. Bliss
Brantz Mayer	Henry Clay
Pierre Soule	Daniel Webster
Buckingham Smith	Henry Ward Poole
M. F. Maury	William Cullen Bryant
Edward Lee Plumb	Stephen Salisbury[24]

The inter-American work of science was always enriched by individuals, but it did not depend upon them. Institutional cooperation kept pace with personal contacts, and exchange relations always marked these successful efforts. By 1880, for example, the Sociedad Mexicana had already regularized its exchanges with every important North American society, while these in turn sent their transactions regularly to Mexico City. All this went on without government assistance, a part of the impulse of free association which brought them together. It is of course true that the United States government knew what was going on—at least in some cases—since some of the societies did their work close to the seat of government, and a few were in fact part of the government. The United States government thus had to be interested in the exchange of technological, geodetic, and statistical data. The direct role of government in the promotion of science in the Western Hemisphere was limited to the agencies dedicated to science: the National Institution for the Promotion of Science and the Smithsonian Institution, to use a better known example. These served as the "cultural eyes" of the national government.

The National Institution for the Promotion of Science was unfortunately short-lived. It was established at Washington during the first half of the nineteenth century, lasting from 1840 to 1845. Before its name was obscured and erased by the Smithsonian Institution, the National Institution entered enthusiastically and successfully into the general trend of inter-American relations during the brief period of its existence. As the Appendix will show, the National Institution brought many Latin Americans into the scientific fold: Mexicans, Cubans, Chileans. It had both design and purpose in its program; and while the Institution, like other institutions, stirred the efforts of several individuals, we can single out the person and services of Aaron H. Palmer, originally from New York and then an active resident of Washington.

Aaron H. Palmer was another nineteenth-century personality who helped turn the North American mind towards inter-American and even world horizons. Palmer deserves mention on his own, although he should also be grouped among the others. He entered inter-American work for his own reasons and ended by taking the lead in a noteworthy process. In Palmer's case, like Mitchill, Maclure, Hartt, and so many others, each man's parallel lines of action ultimately joined the others, meeting again and again in a common endeavor. Like many of his contemporaries, Palmer was also interested in the Far East and the opening of Japan. But his contribution to inter-American relations was far more important to him—and to New World cultural history. Certainly the National Institution gained from his decision.

Palmer combined the inter-American functions of the book business with the exchange of science and scientific ideas. He owned and operated the "American and Foreign Agency," which was a sort of international shipping and forwarding agency for books, transactions, and other types of publication. He had his own cultural exchange organization and a system of book connections with Latin America, Europe, the Far East, and the Philippines. He could be, and was, very helpful to the National Institution in its efforts to promote exchanges with the Real Sociedad de Filipinas at Manila. Working in this individual way, in the generation before Appleton entered the inter-American book trade, Aaron Palmer was a one-man institutional middleman. He entered into a regular correspondence with Francis Markoe, Jr., on scientific matters. Markoe, then secretary of the National Institution, undertook to establish cultural ties with the Instituto Historico e Geographico Brasileiro in 1842, as well as with other Latin American societies. The greatest interest of the National Institution lay in the natural sciences, and although all knowledge was on its agenda, greatest emphasis was put on the natural sciences.[25]

The time came soon enough when the Smithsonian Institution took over and displaced the National Institution, in both domestic and inter-American leadership. Before its demise, however, the Institution had made progress in effecting exchanges with the best agencies in Old Spain: the Museo de Ciencias Naturales, the Real Academia Española, the Real Academia de la Historia, and the Academia de Ciencias Naturales. Part of this was parallel and contemporary with the literary interest in Old Spain; but because science in Spain was connected with science in Latin America, and had been since the sixteenth century, Spain also paid respects to the science of North America.

Science was both the touchstone and the lodestone of the nineteenth century. When Latin Americans heard the phrase "diffusion of knowledge," they opened their minds to the true voice of North America. The idea of cultural relations may have had meaning only for a few North and South Americans, but the leaders of Latin American thought responded favorably just the same. Whenever North Americans acted with something to say, Latin Americans listened. There is no better example of this than the profitable experience of that other famous North American man of science, Professor Joseph Henry, once he became secretary of the Smithsonian Institution. All Professor Henry had to do was to mention what he wanted to the secretaries of Latin American learned societies, and his request was instantly granted. Never did they turn down his proposals. Witness the reply sent in 1873 by the secretary of the Sociedad Mexicana de Geografía y Estadística. Notice also Professor Henry's concept of an inter-American, all-American cultural community:

[Correspondence] from the secretary of the Smithsonian Institute of Washington, saying that it was being proposed to publish a weekly journal of the work being done in the leading literary and scientific societies of America.

He wished that ours would be willing to send him everything it had on the production of its members, as well as all those scientific publications appearing in Mexico, so that he might give the intellectual world an idea of the high culture which America had attained.

Answered, sending the works which he requests and which the Society could obtain, and offering to continue to send this kind of work, together with other publications to appear in the future in Mexico.[26]

Professor Henry's opinion of Mexican science was as high as Dr. Mitchill's!

A long time before, in 1808 to be exact, the famous Colombian scientist Francisco de Caldas appealed to the American Philosophical Society for greater correspondence between the astronomers of the hemisphere. He headed the observatory at Bogotá. There were two other conservatories in Latin America: one at Puebla in Mexico, and one at Córdoba, in Argentina. Little came of Caldas' request; it was dormant for half a century. After that a familiar parallel took form: what Charles Hartt did for Brazilian geology Benjamin Apthorp Gould did for Argentine astronomy, meteorological science, and the inter-American cooperation of astronomers. In the sense that the resources of North American science by the time of Joseph Henry gave real fulfillment to the early promise of Samuel Mitchill, so the great service of Benjamin Gould provided a satisfactory answer to the premature request of Dr. Caldas. The observatory at Córdoba, one of the best in the Southern Hemisphere, was practically reborn under Gould's earnest direction. As director of the observatory, Gould remained in Argentina for almost fifteen years. He was the only North American of that day to be elected a member of the Sociedad Científica Argentina, to which he gave many books and publications. It was easier to forge a basis for astronomers' unity at the end of the century, than it had been at the beginning. He also left a generation of students to carry on his work.[27]

Of all the North American institutions engaged in inter-American work, the Smithsonian was able to catch up and even pass some of them. If we combine the Smithsonian's prestige with that of the learned and scientific societies, we can bring out more clearly the real assets of North American scientific culture. For all the publicized—and justified—leadership of the Smithsonian, the fact is that the Smithsonian did not add anything to the technique and methods of inter-American cooperation; it followed a well-worn trail to the south. The model of inter-American action, begun long before by the American Philosophical Society, was the exchange of transactions with scientific societies. Since the Smithsonian was charged with the diffusion of knowledge, this program was welcome. On the other hand, the Smithsonian never nominated Latin American individual scientists to membership. There was neither provision nor procedure for doing this. In this respect, the North American scientific societies were unique and independent. The Smithsonian did very well with the role of go-between in the exchanges between North American science and Latin American bodies. By 1850 the Smithsonian had effectively (and perhaps unknowingly) adopted the precedent of the Philosophical Society and contributed to the permanent exchanges of scientific work in the Americas. At that time the Philosophical Society sent out its own *Transactions* to the Sociedad de Naturalistas Neo-Granadina (Bogotá), the University of Chile, and the Academia de Medicina in Mexico City. The Smithsonian not only sent out its own work but also distributed the transactions of many societies; the Philosophical Society mailed only its own publications.

The Smithsonian had obvious advantages over the private societies and over individual scientists. It was the intermediary of exchanges for a great many other societies and institutions, and it was as well an agency for government and government publications. The Smithsonian made use of government consuls and foreign officers. With these resources the Smithsonian could transmit to Latin America a fairly complete scientific index of North American knowledge and publications. In cultural terms, the Smithsonian was a single, nationalizing mirror which could shine the light of all North American science fully into the mind's eye of Latin America. The combination of its private endowment with public funds seems to have ensured success. The Smithsonian did not have the financial burden of mailing its transactions and exchanges to all parts of the hemisphere. This could have been costly, because the Institution was especially charged with the "diffusion of knowledge," in the form of publications, papers, books, transactions, articles, and newspapers.

The Smithsonian departed from the well-set pattern in one respect. Because it was an agency of government, the Smithsonian did not, or could not, nominate Latin Americans to membership, as the private learned societies did so frequently. It was committed by law and choice to the promotion of research and the distribution of knowledge. This dual emphasis was outlined as early as 1847, with the specific purpose of "enrichment of South American collections," although a definite procedure for this work did not develop until much later.[28] For over a generation the Smithsonian did help North American societies distribute their papers in Latin America. After 1880 it agreed to go a step further and act similarly in Latin America for the scientific and statistical papers of the United States government. At that time the international exchange of scientific publications, particularly those issued by the government, became an early cultural relations function of the State Department. But the State Department accepted and then appointed the Smithsonian Institution as its chief cultural relations officer, especially for Latin America.

The Smithsonian broadened the definition of science, and therefore its own work, to include ethnology and anthropology as well as the natural and earth sciences. Our emphasis here will be with the natural sciences, partly because of the Institution's charter and partly because of the interest of the first secretary, Professor Joseph Henry. The circulation of the Smithsonian papers soon became hemispheric. By 1850, the distribution of its volumes, known as the "Contributions," began to reach Havana, Caracas, Bogotá, and Rio de Janeiro. This had always stimulated a reciprocal exchange; and by the same token, the societies of Havana, Mexico, Yucatan, Buenos Aires, Rio de Janeiro, and other Latin American centers sent their papers up to Washington.

Cuban contributions included published papers, some of which had appeared in the *Observatorio* of the Real Colegio de Belén, or the transactions of the Real Academia de Ciencias Médicas, Físicas y Naturales de Habana. The Cubans were very active, but so were Mexicans, Colombians, and Chileans. The Smithsonian received a file of Latin American scientific periodicals coming from the Mexican Academy of Medicine, and a great many journals from the Museo Nacional, the famous historic School of Mines, the Colegio Palafoxiano, as well as the Mexican Geographical Society. Dr. Felipe Poey, a noted Cuban member of a family which included several scientists, was correspondent of a few North American societies. He reciprocated the earlier relations of the American Philosophical Society and Cuba by exchanging publications with the Smithsonian. Dr. Poey was glad to send the *Repertorio Físico-Natural* to the Smithsonian; similar exchanges took place with Brazil, Chile, Colombia, and Argentina.

Even Argentina gave high place to the Smithsonian in Latin America. It is a pleasant matter to record that in 1854, when Bartolomé Mitre of Argentina and the Uruguayan Andrés Lamas organized the Instituto Histórico-Geográfico del Río de la Plata, they wrote their admiration for North American cultural and scientific institutions into the very constitution of their faraway Instituto. A long time before this,

Dr. Samuel Mitchill of New York had brought Buenos Aires science into contact with the Lyceum of Natural History, through the personal agency of Bartolomé Muñóz of Buenos Aires. North American societies had followed suit and established additional relations. Now, in 1854, as Argentina rid itself of dictatorship and entered her long era of liberal and progressive growth, Article VI of the Instituto's by-laws provided especially for Argentine cultural relations with the American Philosophical Society at Philadelphia, and with the Smithsonian Institution in Washington.[29] Further dipping at random into the ample evidence for the reception given to the Smithsonian in Latin America, we come up with another example. On February 6, 1868, Professor Lucien Pratt of the rather isolated University of San José in Costa Rica expressed his great enthusiasm and gratitude for the books, transactions, and the magnificent collection of physical and chemical materials which the Smithsonian donated to his laboratory and library. There was no *anti-yanqui* feeling here; nobody objected to cultural imperialism and Jeffersonian expansionism.

It may be of some interest to see how the Smithsonian also organized business support for scientific and cultural exchange. In addition to enlisting the aid of North American government agencies and officers the Smithsonian got help from private business and companies. The shipping lines and the Panama Railroad carried scientific matter into Latin America free. "The line of sailing vessels between New York and the West Coast of South America, belonging to Mr. Bartlett, 110 Wall Street, also engaged to carry all the Chilean exchange free of charge." This saved money, gave the Smithsonian an experienced carrier, and set up efficient machinery of distribution. This work was also successful. The next step made the Smithsonian still more hemispheric, by the appointment of official agencies in Latin America to help carry out the task of diffusion of knowledge.

As Appleton & Company gave continental and inter-American organization to its book trade, so did the Smithsonian for its scientific material. Agencies actually gave Latin Americans the share and responsibility for spreading knowledge. The agencies which Smithsonian first set up in Latin America included the following:

Argentina:	Museo Público, Buenos Aires
Brazil:	Commission of International Exchange, Rio de Janeiro

Chile:	Universidad de Chile, Santiago de Chile
Costa Rica:	Universidad de San José
Ecuador:	Observatorio, Quito
Guatemala:	Sociedad Ecónomica de Amigos del País, Guatemala City
Mexico:	Museo Nacional
Colombia:	Central Office of Exchanges National Library, Bogotá
Venezuela:	University, Caracas

With this mention of the "Central Office of Exchanges" of the Colombian National Library at Bogotá we come nearer to the role of government in these cultural processes. This new-born appearance of government at first renewed the work of consular assistance to science, backed by official blessing and approval but without any participation. In 1869 progressing cultural relations and technical studies brought government bureaus and departments closer to the scientific work of geology, topography, geodetic and coastal surveys, census accounts, scientific agriculture, and ethnologic accounts of the Indian tribes. The combined energies of learned bodies, government agencies, and individuals lifted intellectual cooperation to a still higher level.

At first the official correspondence of governments dealt with the scientific reports of different departments and bureaus. Publications of the United States government were sent to Latin America, and Latin American government studies went to the United States. In response to a request from William R. Seward, then Secretary of State, and from Professor Joseph Henry for the Smithsonian, arrangements for exchange with Latin America reached a new solution with some striking proposals. The republic of Colombia accepted and acted on them in 1869.

To carry out the recommendations the president of Colombia, by executive order, set up the Biblioteca Nacional at Bogotá as the Central Office "for the exchange of publications with those of other countries of America." The Latin American country presented its own vigorous case for inter-American cultural relations, and the Colombian president resolved:

1st, That the literary and scientific works of the nation are very little known and circulated outside of the country, on account of the lack of relations established for this purpose;

2nd, That the republics of the United States of America, Bolivia and Chili have already initiated the establishment of such relations with the Colombian Union, and it is not doubted that the other American nations will gladly welcome the organization of exchange of publications, which may make us better known to each other; and

3rd, That no means can more efficaciously contribute to the cause of enlightenment and towards the fraternity of the nations of America, than the establishment of a literary and scientific correspondence among the different peoples, which would be the result of such exchanges,

DECREE.

Article I. There is established in the National Library, under the charge of the Librarian a central office for the exchange of official publications, and of such literary and scientific works as the national government, the government of the states of the Union, and private individuals, authors or publishers may designate to be sent to other American countries in exchange for their publications.

Article II. The National Librarian shall enter directly into such negotiation or correspondence with the librarians of the other countries of America as may be necessary to establish the regular exchanges and literary relations. . . .

Other proposals in the decree repeated the purpose of the proposals, and essentially the Colombian intention to favor inter-American cultural exchange was abundantly clear.[30]

It is a valuable digression to show that the interest of Colombia in cultural relations conveys a special tribute to North American science and Anglo-American thought. New Granada, so proud of Castilian speech and the purity of Spanish language, and so self-conscious of the Hispanic element in her culture, found much that was attractive in North American civilization. Her men of science had already been made members of North American scholarly bodies. Colombia was ready to turn to North America for fulfillment of common ideas and values in the generation before the Panama imbroglio. The cited decree was not a dead letter. The Colombians were well aware of what they were doing. In that day of Liberal reform of schools and the establishment of the University, the Colombian National librarian, writing to Professor Henry, held high hopes for inter-American cultural identity:

It remains to be mentioned that a case with like contents is remitted at the same date with the above for the National Library at Washington: so that the one in question is expressly destined for the Institution over which you preside as Secretary.

I am led to hope that the remittances will promptly be augmented, both in number and in importance; but the honor will still inure to me of having exchanged with you the first note on the inception of these literary relations.[31]

Señor Otava, the New Granadan librarian, was conscious of helping to make inter-American history. He was right, but in that day of individualist, unorganized relations many persons were misled into thinking that their acts were quite original. He could not have had the hindsight to know that "literary relations" were already older and firmer than he thought.

From the private institutional program for inter-American connections which the American Philosophical Society launched a century before, we have arrived at a scientific and cultural function of government. This function was very important to the Smithsonian, which refused to give it up. There had been formerly much public and congressional debate over whether the Smithsonian Institution ought to have been a library instead an agency of acquiring and diffusing knowledge. The Smithsonian retained the "library" function of exchange, a routine of collecting and mailing, which led to honor, *sui generis*. In 1879, the secretary of the Smithsonian, in a letter to a government official, stated:

It is to be noted in this connection that the Smithsonian Institution discharges its function of intermediary of exchange, not merely between the institutions of the United States, but also of all America; and that it is the established agent of exchange for the societies of Canada, as well as of Mexico, of Chili, and other Central and South American States. This policy it is entirely willing to continue.[32]

The Smithsonian now wove a network of communication that bound a scientific community in the Western Hemisphere. Brazilians repeated in 1880 what the Colombians started in 1869. As a result, inter-American cultural reciprocity was as effective as tariff reciprocity, even if much less publicized. Nevertheless, the Secretary of State in 1880, James Blaine, was far more concerned with commercial relations with Latin America. The emerging Pan-American idea and the first Conference of American States showed this clearly. Cultural relations moved to the rear, and government and business moved to the front.

By 1881 history was made. The products of science and scholarship, supported by organized intstitutional effort, settled on a permanent, deep foundation. One needs only to look at the Smithsonian's exchange list in 1882—tremendously expanded over an earlier list of 1854—to see how Latin American science and learning welcomed the chance to join in voluntary cultural federation with the United States:

Venezuela
    Caracas: La Unión Médica; órgano del Gremio Médico de Venezuela

Mexico
    Chapultepec: Observatorio Astronómico Nacional
    Guadalajara: Sociedad Médica de Guadalajara
    Guanajuato: Colegio de Guanajuato
    Mérida: Sociedad Médica Farmacéutica
    Mexico: Academia de Medicina
                       Asociación Médico-quirúrgico Larrey
                       Colegio de Minería
                       Escuela de Agricultura
                       Escuela de Medicina
                       Museo Nacional
                       Escuela Nacional Preparatoria
                       Government of Mexico
                       Ministro de Fomento
                       Observatorio Meteorológico Central
                       Sociedad Andrés del Río
                       Sociedad de Alumnos de la Escuela de Medicina
                       Sociedad Humboldt
                       Sociedad Médica
                       Sociedad Mexicana de Geografía y Estadística
                       Sociedad Mexicana de Historia Natural
                       Sociedad Minera Mexicana
                       City Council
                       Revista Científica Mexicana
                       Board of Public Works
    San Luis Potosí: Instituto Cientifico y Literario
                       Sociedad Médica
    Toluca: Instituto Literario del Estado de Mexico

Cuba
    Habana: Academia de Ciencias Médicas, Físicas y Naturales

Instituto de Segunda Enseñanza
Revista General de Comunicaciones
Inspección General de Telégrafos
Administración General de Correos
Observatorio Magnetico y Meteorológico del
　　Real Colegio de Belén
Real Observatorio Físico-Meteorológico de la
　　Habana
Sociedad Económica de la Habana
Universidad de la Habana
Sociedad Antropológica

Argentina
　　Buenos Aires:　Instituto Histórico-Geográfico del Río
　　　　　　　　　de la Plata
　　　　　　　　Ministry of the Interior
　　　　　　　　Buenos Aires [Province] Statistical
　　　　　　　　　Office
　　　　　　　　National Office
　　　　　　　　Academia de Ciencias
　　　　　　　　Asociación Médica Bonaerense
　　　　　　　　Biblioteca Nacional
　　　　　　　　Biblioteca Pública
　　　　　　　　Instituto Geográfico Argentino
　　　　　　　　Museo Público de Buenos Aires
　　　　　　　　Sociedad Científica Argentina
　　　　　　　　Sociedad Rural Argentina
　　　　　　　　Sociedad Zoológica Argentina
　　　　　　　　Sociedad Paleontológica Argentina
　　　　　　　　Statistical Bureau
　　　　　　　　Universidad de Buenos Aires
　　Córdoba:　　Academia Nacional de Ciencias Exactas
　　　　　　　　Oficina Meteorológica Argentina
　　　　　　　　Periódico Zoológico

Bolivia
　　　　　　　　Universidad de Chuquisaca

Brazil
　　Rio de Janeiro: Emperor of Brazil
　　　　　　　　Bibliotheca Nacional
　　　　　　　　British Library
　　　　　　　　Government of Brazil
　　　　　　　　Instituto Historico, Geographico e
　　　　　　　　　Ethnographico do Brasil

Museu Nacional
Naval Observatory
Municipal Council
Escola de Minas de Ouro Preto
Gaceta Medica
Ministry of Public Works
Palaestra Scientific Society
Royal Geographical Society
Sociedade Auxiliadora da Industria
    Nacional

Chile
    Santiago: Ministry of Interior
                      Academia Militar
                      Bureau of Statistics
                      El Plano Topográfico
                      Government of Chile
                      Ministro de Instrucción Pública
                      Museo Nacional
                      Observatorio Nacional
                      Oficina Hidrográfica de Chile
                      Sociedad de Historia Natural
                      Sociedad Médica
                      Universidad de Chile

Guatemala
                      Meteorological Observatory
                      Instituto Nacional de Guatemala
                      [Heir to books and library of the
                        Sociedad Económica de Amigos del Pais]

Colombia
    Bogotá: Government of Colombia
                      Sociedad de Naturalistas
                      Biblioteca Nacional
                      Observatorio Astronómico Nacional
                      Observatorio Astronómico Flammarion
                      Society of Public Works
                      Sociedad de Estadística y Geografía
    Medellín: Universidad de Antioquia

These Latin American societies included in the Smithsonian list are as
good a cross section of New World science as can be found. This is an

institutional guide to organized knowledge in the Americas. A clear history and a legible process made possible this cooperation in the sciences.

The study of man in America came next. Ethnology and archaeology added another important chapter to the evolution of history in the New World. High up on the page of knowledge were those studies which found in Latin American Indians not only material for investigation but also the means for further exchanges of transactions and members. Man-in-nature and the aboriginal civilizations of America stood logically close to natural habitat and the earth sciences. Whether anthropology was one of the natural sciences or whether it lay closer to history and social evolution need not be answered here. The contributions of anthropologists and ethnological research certainly had vast importance for inter-American scholarly connections. Once again, success came from individuals and societies who worked out their own ways of getting in touch with Latin America.

Chapter 4

THE STUDY OF MAN

*7*HE FASCINATION with Indian origins added American man to the list of inter-American studies, compelling a rediscovery of the pre-Spanish history of the New World. Anthropology, archaeology, and ethnology came into their own as strong pillars of the cultural relations structure. Latin American anthropology and archaeology—background of today's race relations topic—became a permanent part of North American scholarship, research, and patronage. Because of the need for field work, it would be right to say that anthropology's contact with living Indian peoples was to be expected rather than dependence upon written history, since both subjects had their own special *modus operandi*. Nevertheless, Latin American history was never too far away from Latin American anthropology, ethnology, and archaeology. In fact, Latin American history was close to Indianist study and had been since the European Discovery of America and the earliest historiography of the sixteenth century. Without daring to call that common content and treatment interdisciplinary, since the word is premature and too modern for a Renaissance broadness, the affinity of history for anthropology was a fact.

The fond feeling between these two subjects was also due to the further fact that in the formative years of inter-American relations— before 1820—the Indian cultures of Latin America could best be known by reading books and articles about them. There was little travel and less field work, at least until Latin America was emancipated from Spain. The reasons for this were obvious: permission to travel was nearly impossible to get, Latin America was politically (not culturally) in another world. Also, the fashion of culture at the time was to read and to speculate upon what others had seen and recorded. Dependence

103

upon books was increased still more, because those Indian civilizations of greatest advance and interest were still known chiefly as they had been described centuries before (1500 to 1800), by contemporary chroniclers, historians, notaries, and explorers. Only through these reports, books, and narratives could those ancient peoples of America be known again. American archaeological knowledge was not born until shortly before 1800; investigation for the next generation still depended upon written sources which revealed much as well as little about the Inca, Aztec, Toltec, Chibcha, Maya, and less advanced men of America.

Since the eighteenth century North American students and societies had sought ever greater knowledge about the Latin American Indian cultures. It followed from this that the inter-American role of anthropology resembled and repeated that of science and history: printed books on the subject, exchange relations between societies, and the nomination of Latin Americans to membership in these bodies. Again cooperation was free and reciprocal, successful without any direction from government. The free association of minds was all that was needed. The first North American students of Latin American ethnology were motivated by curiosity. Some of these were "part-time" students; historians like Jeremy Belknap and Ebenezer Hazard, or the medical figure of Benjamin Smith Barton, probably read and learned about Indian culture in America as a by-product of their main interests. Nevertheless, individuals and societies already known for their inter-American work in the sciences, such as the Lyceum of Natural History in New York and the American Philosophical Society in Philadelphia, also responded to the Indian as a topic. It can be said that the standard portrait of the Latin American aboriginal (as he looked in the books about him) was almost as familiar an image to the North American mind, as to the Mexican, Central American, and South American.[1]*

After Latin American independence from Spain and Portugal, in the first quarter of the nineteenth century, the monumental ruins of the Maya, Aztec, and Inca came under direct inspection. The famous codices were found and described. Field travel, experience, and observation of the architecture vindicated the memories contained in books and codices and proved the historical memoir. The field opinions of archaeology equalled the opinions of the earliest writers on Indian antiquities. North and Latin Americans made common intellectual and scientific cause in their joint rediscovery of pre-Columbian man in

*Notes to this chapter begin on page 174.

America. However, before this could really mean anything, Indianist studies had to break free from armchair literary authority that was so bookish in method. Book knowledge and the extensive library collections were a sort of carry-over of humanistic, Renaissance influences; and the historian, literary chronicler, or antiquary held higher honors than the archaeologist or ethnologist. This was difficult to overcome, but just the same it did change with time. The archaeological finds in Egypt, Persia, and Yucatan gave both impetus and respectability to that subject. Archaeology and then ethnology grew up in an inter-American world of their own, increasingly free from library materials. They were able to combine a familiarity with historical, written sources with eyewitness, empirical field methods. And the magnificent ruins were of great help to their pride and confidence in the subject.

A surprising number of North Americans were well-read in the literature of the long-departed Indian civilizations, while their curiosity about the ethnology of the living Latin American Indian lagged. With increasing attention directed towards Indian America, book materials were no longer the last word, even though individual titles and well-known collections on Indian themes were fairly plentiful. To be sure, much of this echoed the romantic era of philosophical notions about "the noble savage," passed down from the eighteenth century, but the fact still remained that a large number of basic treatises that Spaniards and Latin Americans had written were the only sources of knowledge, before the era of field expeditions and archaeological travels. But written literature and book sources were not the only causes of unbalance between methods and collections. There was another inhibiting factor: because most books in English and Spanish on the Indian preferred to deal with the more exciting native cultures of Peru and Mexico, the general reader and even the scholar could do little on their own but follow this lead. As a result, the cultures of the Aztec, Inca, and Maya, being more advanced, "colorful," and architecturally impressive, received most attention. The other Indian cultures of South America (Brazil, Cuba, Chile, Argentina) were neglected.

No one should belittle this book learning. Its two most important achievements were the high level of interest and the concrete advances in inter-American connections. Extending the range of the natural sciences to the "life sciences," it became more and more usual for societies and individuals, eager to appreciate Latin America, to turn southward to study Indian society and culture. Book knowledge first created and stabilized the literary and scientific interest which preceded the era of field work, and it also supplied a needed check against too much field technique. Historically, the reading of books, chronicles, and articles came first. These originated our inter-American cultural relations and the exchanges of knowledge and memberships. The process was the same for ethnology as it was for other subjects. Once more the American Philosophical Society led the way for other North American societies to follow. For all the individualism of subject matter and groups doing this work, there still was a uniform result, notwithstanding variation and freedom in the approach.

The American Philosophical Society included American Indian studies from the beginning. The Philosophical Society fondly supported research and gathered book materials on Indian grammar, philology, and linguistics. As always, another profitable way of carrying on this work was to nominate those Latin Americans as members who would, and did, contribute to the Society's transactions and help its researches as well as the library. We have already seen that the first Latin American member of any North American society was Alejandro Ramírez, member since 1801 of the Philosophical Society. In turning its attention to Guatemala so early the Society of course did not know that the Central American region actually contained one of the great cradles of archaeological and ethnological history in the New World. It soon found out that book references to Yucatan were based upon evidence drawn from the monumental ruins.

Thirty-five years later, in 1836, the Philosophical Society again followed up its interest in Middle America. The Society and its associates were ahead of more publicized Americans in this respect. Five years before John Lloyd Stephens began the nineteenth-century's archaeological rush toward the rich Maya discovery, and even before Ephraim Squier dug into the prehistoric earth and the living ethnology of Central America, the American Philosophical Society had already dipped into the enormous bowl of Guatemalan Indian antiquities. Individuals and societies unknowingly sustained and fed a historical process. It is instructive to reread the letter of Manuel Galvez, corresponding member of the Philadelphia Society, president of Guatemala, and a friendly co-worker of that Juan Galindo who himself was a member of North American societies and a contributor of several articles to their publications:

Guatemala 31st May 1836

Sir:

I have had the honor of receiving your esteemed letter of the 21st of July of last year. I regret very much the delay that it has experienced on its way hither, as well because I would not wish that my Silence should be considered as a want of attention on my part, as on account of the interesting nature of the subjects to which your letter refers.

It is advantageous to a Country like ours, that wants only to be better known abroad, to hold a correspondence with an Officer of learned Societies, and we consider it an object of importance, while at the same time, it will contribute to enrich your fund of knowledge, by the information which your members will receive of our antiquities, statistics, natural history &c.

I am preparing a Collection of printed Documents which I shall transmit to you by the first opportunity. I have already written to the Academy of Sciences, established here in 1832, in consequence of a decree issued by me as governor of this State, not only that they should transmit to you the Ms grammars of Indian languages which are, no doubt, in their public library, but also that conferring upon you the title of their Corresponding Member, agreeably to their Statutes, they may carry on with you a Correspondence which, no doubt, will prove advantageous to this Country.[2]

The Guatemalan gave as clear a statement of the aim and theme of inter-American cultural relations as those already found. With Latin American leadership and this sort of encouragement, Guatemalan Indian grammars, dictionaries, and vocabularies went up to Philadelphia to enrich the Philosophical Society's book collections on Central and South American Indian languages, and to set the stage for strong and eager cultural friendships.

In this way "ethnological panamericanism" stirred a supposed North American parochialism and materialism toward a broad and well-received inter-Americanism of outlook. It enlarged the exchange of knowledge with small, as well as with large, Latin American nations, spreading fertile seeds of contact in a receptive soil. The same happened with the American Ethnological Society as soon as it was founded. The New York Lyceum of Natural History, the New-York Historical Society, the American Philosophical Society, the Massachusetts Historical Society, and the Philadelphia Academy of Natural Sciences—where they were interested in ethnology—had all aimed a scientific message to Latin Americans in the same way.

The American Ethnological Society held its first meeting in 1842, and within the next twenty years (by 1863) counted at least seventeen Latin Americans as members. In this brief, first epoch of its existence, the Ethnological Society moved quickly to find a place in the picture of inter-American mindedness which was becoming clear. The best way to search out the possible unity of American origins was first to get a concerted effort among scholars who did the research. In spite of the variations encountered among the original inhabitants of the New World, and no matter what differences of culture, speech, and nation existed among the investigators who came afterwards, it is evident that a common inter-American scholarship came into being.

One of the better results of the rise of ethnology was the decentralization of both history and archaeology from too great an emphasis upon Peru and Mexico. A cross section of all the Latin American members of the American Ethnological Society showed a more balanced geographical distribution of membership as the other Indian areas of Latin America came under notice. This did not mean—nor has it ever meant —that Mexican studies lost first place. The Society simply added Latin American members from Cuba, Guatemala, Ecuador, and Colombia to supplement those from Peru and Mexico. In some respects the list of associates, like the articles dealing with Cuban and Colombian antiquities in the Society's *Transactions*, made possible the first aboriginal studies of the Caribbean region. On the other hand, some time had yet to pass before Brazilian ethnology was given proper attention in North American circles.

The Latin American members of the American Ethnological Society show the widened geographical range of interest and the dates of admission show how sustained it was for that time.

José de la Luz (Cuba), 1861
Andrés Poey (Cuba), 1861
José Barrundia (Central America), 1852
Modesto Flores (Central America), 1861
Colonel Codazzi (New Granada), 1857
A. P. Herran (New Granada), 1845
José Obaldia (New Granada), 1861
Tomás C. Mosquera (New Granada), 1861
Ezequiel Uricoechea (New Granada), 1861
F. Villavicencio (Ecuador), 1861
Vicente Rocafuerte (Ecuador), 1845
Tomas E. Carrillo (Yucatan), 1845
Juan Pío Perez (Yucatan), 1845
José Pacheco (Mexico), 1845
José F. Ramirez (Mexico), 1845

Pascual Gayangos (Spain), 1845
Manuel Gomez Pedraza (Mexico), 1845
Mariano Rivero (Peru), 1845

This pattern showed that real effort brought evident success. It was helped by the connection between ethnology and history in those days. If an ethnological society did not gain Latin American members, a historical society did. There were some Latin American Indianists, for example, who did not join North American ethnological societies. Instead, they became members of historical societies. This was the case with Juan Galindo, ethnological investigator of great contemporary repute, who readily accepted membership in the Massachusetts and New-York Historical societies and contributed frequently to the American Philosophical Society. He was not a member of the Ethnological Society, although he was widely known in Guatemala and Central America for his work on Maya antiquities.[3]

As a matter of fact, it would be hard to say which was pushing the study of the American Indian more zealously, the historical or the ethnological society. Historical studies certainly rounded out the interest in Indian culture. Before the atomizing age of specialization, history and ethnology attracted a related kind of mind. Moreover, most persons and societies which worked, or were interested in, these subjects were in touch with one another. One very good example of this was John Russell Bartlett, whose active positions combined ethnology and history. Bartlett was secretary of the American Ethnological Society and of the New-York Historical Society. He was also a member of the Mexican Boundary Commission in 1846-1848 and, much later, became librarian of the famous John Carter Brown Library at Providence, Rhode Island, that major center for Latin American history and sources. Bartlett's promotion of inter-American scholarly relations certainly should be better known. His two strategic offices at the head of the historical and ethnological societies put him in close touch with studies of the New World Indian.

Himself no scholar and not inclined towards investigation, Bartlett gave generous time and attention to Dr. Carl Behrendt, an early specialist in Maya history and culture. He also gave managerial direction to other activity in this field. Bartlett was probably the first prominent North American to count Brazil in the work of inter-American culture and intellectual exchanges. It would be impossible to say at what point Bartlett ceased his ethnological job to take up the historian's; he brought many Latin American archaeologists, ethnologists, as well as historians into his New-York Historical Society. In administering his sort of mutual assistance pact between history and ethnology in behalf of Latin American studies, Bartlett was very much like his friend and contemporary, George Gibbs. Gibbs, who belonged to the same learned societies as Bartlett and who was to become a special friend and benefactor of the Smithsonian Institution's work, was a remarkably persistent architect of inter-American intellectual cooperation.

The rediscovery of the Maya monuments in Yucatan stimulated the historians of the New-York Historical Society to greater interest in archaeology and ethnology. The usual way of expressing scholarly interest was first to get Latin Americans to become members of North American societies. And so it was done in this case. Nomination of the noted Maya investigator Manuel Alonso Peón—one among the many Historical Society members—illuminated the eagerness of historical society to include Indian culture history as part of its work. History seized its fine chance to take part in the first phase of Middle American research. George Gibbs had already received in New York from Manuel Alonso Peón a shipment of archaeological "curiosities" for the New-York Historical Society. A letter from Gibbs to John Russell Bartlett showed how inter-American cultural kinship grew, in spite of the current vogues of Manifest Destiny arising from contemporary patriotism in the War with Mexico. The New-York Historical Society shared with North American scholarship in general the rewards of a more friendly approach to the Latin America mind than the derivative of an ancient *leyenda negra,* now revived in an atmosphere of war and anti-Mexicanism:

[prob. 1847.]

Dear Bartlett:

Enclose these resolutions in a letter to Don Manuel Alonso Peon of Merida Yucatan, stating that you have been informed by Mr. Jas. R. Hitchcock that he is the proper person to whom to convey the respects of the [New-York Historical] Society. Also have a diploma ready for Peon as corresponding member, and mention that in your letter that we shall be glad to receive from him any documents or antiquities, and any information as to the country, particularly works on the *Maya. . . .*

Tell Peon that at a suitable opportunity when peace comes you will send him our collections.

Geo. Gibbs[4]

For many people the New World Indian had a past just as interest-

ing as the white man's; and probably only in classical and ancient archaeology was the tie between history and prehistory as close as it was in
Latin America. There was a thin line between history and Indianist
studies and, as we can see, it was easy to move from one to the other.
Nor was the contact between the two subjects confined only (or ac-
cidentally) to the work of Bartlett, Gibbs, and the New-York Historical
Society. The American Antiquarian Society, for example, carrying out
recommendations of its by-laws of 1814, made progress in the field of
ethnology by choosing Juan Galindo in 1836, and by adding Mexicans
and Yucatecans in time. After 1910 this Society brought in the Argentines Juan Ambrosetti and Samuel A. Lafone Quevedo. Over and over
again, the use of memberships as the agency of cooperation, first tested
by the American Philosophical Society, proved to be a permanent way of
satisfying almost every kind of society.

Books as well as men made it possible to get the best results from the
whole machinery of cultural contact, rather than from just one part.
Corresponding members in Latin America made much easier the exchange of books and transactions, gifts of "curiosities," museum pieces,
transactions, and volumes of high and low interest. Undoubtedly the
role of books in the hemisphere had an importance of its own. As stated,
books made up for the lack of field opportunities and travel. The wealth
of printed materials available in the United States was put to good use.
The publications of missionaries, travellers, chroniclers, historians, and
ethnologists grew in numbers. Library technique gave a secondary in-
sight, even a perspective, to ethnology and archaeology. Indeed, the great
number of printed materials on the Latin American Indian made it
both possible and necessary to summarize and draw some conclusions
from the existing state of knowledge. One of the best-known résumés
was the "Notes on the Semi-Civilized Nations of Mexico, Yucatan and
Central America," written by Albert Gallatin for the American Ethnological Society's *Transactions* and then separately printed. Gallatin,
president, chief benefactor, and patron of the Ethnological Society, did
little else than bring together in one place the views of Prescott, some
judgments of Spanish historians, and the more recent discoveries of
John Lloyd Stephens. The article was not too profound.[5]

An emphasis upon literature and language underscored Gallatin's
interpretation. The pairing of language (grammar) and ethnology was
widely favored at that time. In fact, some considered ethnology as a
branch of philology and grammar; later, the same linguistics heading
would include folklore, legend, and myth. Language and grammar domi-

nated Gallatin's generation. His "Notes" reviewed the Mexican number system, calendar, and other inventions of that society; but he gave most of his attention to the philology and grammar of the Aztec language. He also confined his study to those parts of central Mexico which had always been better known. Gallatin showed little interest in, or knowledge of, the Indian cultures of northern, western, eastern, and southern Mexico. Now it can be seen how vocabularies, Indian language grammars, and dictionaries, such as those sent from Guatemala to the American Philosophical Society, were samples of an ethnological method which had wide appeal, were produced by-products of influence, and had evolved out of book collections and library work. Counting on authorities in books and other secondary sources, Latin American ethnology, like history, absorbed the humanistic tradition until both were parts of literature and the descriptive essay. Letters and history, letters and ethnology, were the opposite sides of the same coin.

There were also those somewhat less literary-minded who felt that the study of grammar might help the Church and missionary both to understand and convert the South American Indian. No doubt the missionary need for such grammars, which dated from the sixteenth century, created that bibliographical and library search for grammars which was so strong in the nineteenth century. The missionary impulse provided great energy to get to the native. Missionaries, historically, proved to be productive grammarians and even courageous field workers, but these achievements did not improve the level of linguistic knowledge. It simply meant that missionary use of language was mainly practical, from Spanish colonial times down to the Protestant missionary of the nineteenth century.

The inter-American search for Indian grammars and word lists suggests the revival of classical languages in western Europe after 1400. Grammars also became collectors' items. This quest after the "one world" of American man through language and linguistics left a characterizing tradition upon inter-American ethnological studies, which borrowed from the humanist, bookish spirit of the Renaissance on the one hand, and the laboriously compiled grammars and dictionaries of the religious on the other. The trustees of the Astor Library in New York were very self-conscious about the importance of their Indian grammars. In their report to the New York State Assembly (1853) they made a good deal of the scarcity and high price of the grammars, which soon were to become part of the New York Public Library. Their collection, they said,

. . . has also the best of the vocabularies of the different dialects of the Mexican and South American Indians, which were collected and published by the early Spanish missionary priests.

Books of this last class have become excessively rare and consequently dear. A perfect copy of Molina's *Arte de la Lengua Mexicana* cannot be had for less than fifty dollars; and Rincon's *Grammar* of the same language, a mean little duodecimo, bound, or rather done up in a limp vellum, which few would accept as a gift, costs much more than its weight in gold.[6]

Over a period of fifty years, by gifts, donations, and purchases, most of the major North American societies and libraries mentioned here had already obtained good collections of Indian language materials. In fact, the American Philosophical Society, the New-York Historical Society, and the Massachusetts Historical Society, had richer ethnological materials, in English and Spanish, than the Ethnological Society.

However, at the time that interest in Indian linguistics reached its height, some critics began to assert that architecture and artistic monuments of the advanced aboriginal civilizations offered a truer index of the mind and spirit of American man. Disagreement arose over ethnological method. Those working in Indian ethnology at first hand held different opinions and misgivings about relying exclusively upon grammar and language in evaluating Indian culture. Some felt that language was but a means to the end; others found that visible architecture was a far truer guide than a library of written sources. A few others began to feel that neither books nor monuments, but rather the new physical anthropology, could throw the most brilliant light upon the dark recesses of American antiquity. Among the latter was Dr. Samuel George Morton, who was widely known in Latin America and who was active as a physician and as a member of the Philadelphia Academy of Natural Sciences. Morton, of course, belonged more to the science people than to grammar and linguistics.

Dr. Morton studied and analyzed physical measurements, especially of crania, and his opinions led him far away from the linguist's. In fact, in his letter of 1847 to John Russell Bartlett of the American Ethnological Society, Dr. Morton declared flatly: "You may rely upon it, philology, however important in Ethnology, is not infrequently a broken reed."[7] He was sure of the weakness of linguistics as a key to Indian structures and had less confidence in language in building the road to inter-American relations. Morton was a medical man, an anatomist, and a leading officer of the Academy of Natural Sciences, where he and

William Maclure had set up hemisphere cultural relations. However, his criticism of linguistics as a dependable tool did not mark any great advances by physical anthropology. True, his search for physical-anatomical evidence, specimens, and crania brought him colleagues in South America; but physical anthropology did not displace linguistics. However, the general attack upon language did happen to coincide with the rise of archaeology as a Latin American subject. Archaeology grew into a vigorous, appealing, and impressive body of knowledge of antiquities and culture about man in America. Although no Rosetta Stone was found to make Indian languages (glyphs, codices) readable, American archaeology was about ready to have its say on the subject of man.

Philology, in spite of Dr. Morton or the rivalry with archaeology, was not ready to surrender to either biologic anthropology or to architectural history. Language continued to win societies, institutions, and individuals to the study of the Indian. Those white, Anglo-American and Latin American cultures of North and South America, which differed from each other in their Hispanic and English cultural background, were nevertheless agreed that the search for a single *Urmensch* and *Urkultur* in America should be in the foreground of their work. At the same time, both linguistics and archaeology gave parallel support to Latin American studies. Latin American archaeology and language study used the printed books, library materials, and existing vocabularies and grammars—to varying degree. Physical anthropology did not—also to different degree. There is something else to be said for the direct experience which archaeology required; field observation prevented investigation from becoming a supplement to library and desk study. Physical anthropology became an adjunct of museum collection, off to one side of the major Latin American subjects.

After the independence of Latin America, travel permitted North Americans and Europeans to become more familiar with the other America through first-hand experience, long residence, and immediate research. There was no doubt that field archaeology, together with ethnology and cultural relations, gained considerably from the advantages of working *in situ*. At the time when Albert Gallatin in New York summed up the philological contributions of the Nahuatl Aztec in Mexico, John Lloyd Stephens lived with the descendants of the Maya in the light and shadow of ancient Maya buildings in Yucatan, while Brantz Mayer went out many times to study the monuments of Aztec architecture in the Valley of Mexico. The fairly sudden encounter of the Yucatan Maya coincided with the rediscovery of Mexico City's archaeology, and with awakening interest in the Inca of Peru. Guatemalan Indianist riches were already placed at the disposal of the scholars of the American Philosophical Society. The lure of American prehistory, probing areas and problems far removed in time from the written accounts, came under the eye of a serious and increasingly well-trained archaeology, which found new sources of knowledge, opened a scientific debate, and pushed inter-American cultural cooperation still further.

One odd result was that Indianist archaeology (as well as history) preferred to deal with remoter origins and the far past, turning almost completely away from ethnology of the living Indian and the descendant of the near past. There was a general as well as an intellectual feeling that the Latin American Indian in his nineteenth-century setting was only a poor and dull copy of that original and remarkable American who had been so brilliantly and excitingly described by Spanish historians and chroniclers two centuries before. In contrast, current Indian affairs and contemporary ethnology had far fewer followers. If we take as examples of this preference for the distant past the data and observations of Joel R. Poinsett in his *Notes of Mexico* or those of Dr. William Keating, another North American resident in Mexico, we see that both these observers showed far greater excitement in the visible remains of pre-Cortesian monuments than in the living Indians all around them. Brantz Mayer did the same. Mayer, who stressed the accuracy of architecture and the dating of events according to monumental ruins rather than the opinion of books and sources, made out an excellent argument for the validity of the ancient era. He turned his mind to the problems of early Indian civilizations, with little to say about the Indian of his own day. Even symbolically, the remote Indian was heroic, stalwart in courage, republican in virtue; living aboriginals were either the enemy, the scorned, or the unnoticed.

Ethnology, even more than archaeology, came closer to the time of history and to the scope of the historical societies, because historical, documented sources were constantly used. Just because the study of the contemporary Indian tended to lag, with the exception of Ephraim Squier's pioneering work in Nicaragua and Peru and the work of those German and European scientists in Brazil, it became easier for historical and ethnological research to use the same technique and to study the Indian's customs through books and manuscripts. A good deal of gain came from this, although too great a reliance upon older sources tended to substitute for field residence and direct ethnographic reporting. There was another method of work, which did avoid the charge of excessive dependence upon books. This was to use the very respectable device of selecting Latin American authorities as members of North American ethnological societies. Where field travel and residence in Indian society was difficult or impossible, this proved to be a roundabout way of getting information, data, and specimens direct from the locale.

For example, the archaeological discoveries of the Yucatan Maya lifted both public excitement and scholarly curiosity. They also impelled the New-York Historical Society and the American Ethnological Society (among others) to nominate to membership those early Maya specialists, Juan Pío Pérez, Tomás Carrillo, and Manuel Alonso Peón of Yucatan. This brought results, gifts, donations, museum pieces, and exchanges. The discovery of the Maya swept away the barriers of the War with Mexico, replacing Manifest Destiny with the appeal of cultural relations. It combined great gains to archaeology as a subject, with advancing inter-American scientific fellowship. Moreover, many North American contemporaries were eager to find and prove the advanced accomplishments of an American Indian civilization which would be equal to the Mediterranean and classical lands and would justify the greater heritage of America compared to Europe. We can call this cultural Americanism, cultural nationalism; it was part of an older trans-Atlantic debate over American and European superiority, begun in the 1700's.

In the general revival of learning about the Maya, the first North American name we meet is, of course, that of John Lloyd Stephens.[8] Names carry great authority. Just as the strong prestige of Mexico and Peru clouded the sight of other archaeological regions in Latin America, so the name of Stephens obscured the initiative of other contemporaries, now forgotten. In every department of science and learning which formed the whole subject matter of Latin American studies, the permanent gain was always greater than the activity of any man, no matter how much he did. Neither William H. Prescott in history, nor John Lloyd Stephens in Mexican archaeology, nor Charles Hartt in geology was the creator of inter-American interest. It arose as a product of the North American mind, freely associating with the minds and ideas of Latin America. The silence that now covers other workers in that vineyard is both misleading and distorting. Big names have unjustly jostled offstage those others who had their moment and opportunity. In the case of Mayan studies, for example, larger mention than ever before goes to a forgotten North American of the generation of Prescott, Stephens, Ticknor, Irving, Squier: Benjamin Moore Norman of New Orleans.

While Norman was "rambling," as he called it, through Yucatan and the Maya country, he visited the celebrated ruins and set down on paper some clear field descriptions of the monuments which then remained at Chichen Itzá and Uxmal. Norman's work was more extensive than Stephens, since Norman also wrote several books on the archaeology of southeastern Mexico. His work on Yucatan appeared as *Rambles in Yucatan; or Notes of Travel through the Peninsula, including a visit to the Remarkable Ruins of Chichen, Kabah, Zayi and Uxmal,* published in 1842, the year when the American Ethnological Society began its work. Stephens' first book had come out the year before, 1841. Some years later, in an exchange between the American Ethnological Society and the Brazilian Instituto Historico e Geographico, John Russell Bartlett thought enough of Norman's work to send it to the Brazilian society as a sample of the best in North American ethnological research. Norman looked for, and thought he had found, a patron who might bring the support of wealthy, private institutions. He got in touch with Dr. Francis Hawks of New York.

In that small but shining galaxy of North Americans who admired Spanish culture as well as inter-American cooperation, Dr. Francis Hawks was a bright star, now much dimmed by time. Hawks was also one of those few North Americans who had visited and lived in Old Spain. He was versatile and had many facets to show his generation: he was a student of Spanish literature, a historian, a geographer, and an ethnologist.[9] He collected the documentary sources for the history of the Protestant Episcopal Church in the United States. Hawks was owner of one of the most representative Hispanic libraries which could then be found, containing valuable manuscripts, books, and Spanish newspapers. He translated into English from Spanish the very useful Rivero-Tschudi account of the Indians of Peru. He was an influential official of the American Ethnological, New-York Historical, and American Geographical societies. In these capacities Hawks made ready to aid the work of inter-American relations. Benjamin Norman therefore picked a good man when he wrote to Dr. Hawks and sent him the archaeological specimens from Yucatan. The "idols" and statuary that he shipped were probably of the same type as the collection of "idols" and objects that Joel Poinsett, earlier, had shipped to Philadelphia from the Valley of Mexico. Could Dr. Hawks have added these pieces to those which Manuel Alonso Peón of Yucatan sent to the New-York Historical Society for its collection? Or were they lost?

Norman's full service to us remains obscure, although some scholarly societies of his day picked up his trail. Removed as he was from the world of societies and institutions, all he could do was to give Hawks and others a first-hand sketch, plan, and survey of some of his work, including the architectural drawing of the ruins of Chi-chen. Historical and ethnological societies took up their role in the field. Norman found himself in a company where the names of Stephens, Squier, and the officers of the societies overshadowed his. He knew this. That is why he turned to Dr. Hawks for prestige and support, as he wrote the former from New Orleans, April 25, 1850:

I have shipped my collection of Idols etc., to New York, but I have not yet fully decided what to do with them; this will be a matter requiring your action which I shall avail myself of when I have the pleasure of meeting you again. The arrival of the Idols in New York will afford a good opportunity to revive the subject of American Antiquities.[10]

Norman then enclosed some articles on Amerindian antiquities which he hoped Dr. Hawks would recommend for publication to Evarts Duykinck, then editor of the influential *Literary World,* raising the question, "Do you not think it possible to prove the people of this continent—indigenous—those who built the splendid structures I allude to? Is there any proof to the contrary? I am quite impatient waiting to see your works on American Antiquities." But Hawks did little or nothing for Norman. He had many other chores, including the preparation of children's books on Latin America. His was a managerial rather than an investigator's interest in Latin America. Hawks did not do anything himself on American antiquities. Although he read and collected books on Hispanic civilization in the Old World and the New (his library in the New-York Historical Society has many invaluable titles) and in spite of his institutional connections with ethnology, Hawks had other matters on his mind. Norman's knock on the door was not heard; John Stephens was admitted and well received.

Several others entered the inter-American stage at about this time. Brantz Mayer, archaeologist, diplomat, and historian, was one of them. Unlike William H. Prescott, who was better known and stood in the spotlight, Brantz Mayer knew Mexico at first hand, lived, travelled, and studied there. In his own way, without the name to match Prescott, Mayer contributed to the brand-new subject of early Latin America. He was one of those few North Americans chosen for membership in the Sociedad Mexicana de Geografía y Estadística. Brantz Mayer came from Baltimore, a city of many ties with Latin America—economic, journalistic, and political. There he had received some of his education at St. Mary's College, one of the most active academies in the teaching of Spanish. When he reached Mexico later, Mayer contributed to the record of literary and intellectual traditions of the American Embassy (Legation) there. He arrived several years after Poinsett's departure and several years before the coming of Buckingham Smith, another inter-Americanist and Hispanist of major rank.

Brantz Mayer's books about Mexico stemmed from his long residence. He never lost his interest in Mexico even after his removal to San Francisco, California. The Mexican past was his specialty. He contributed to Mexican archaeology and history because he seriously read about the country to which he had been sent for diplomatic service. Mayer was one of the first North Americans to describe the contribution of the prehistoric Aztec society to the national history of Mexico, but his conclusions about those Indians differed widely from those of historians and ethnologists.[11] Mayer, in short, argued that the written evidence of history on the one hand and the ethnography of the living Indian descendant on the other meant far less to culture history in America than did archaeology. Art and the architecture of monumental remains told him a more vivid story; they were the most revealing cultural and even chronological clues to pre-Cortesian Mexico. He had greater self-confidence and better connections that Benjamin Norman, and he took up cudgels as strongly for his archaeology as Albert Gallatin did for grammar and language.

As far as Mayer was concerned—and he backed his field trips with historical research—both the language-minded ethnologist and the bookish historian were pale shadows alongside of the dazzling materials visible on the monuments. He felt that the source manuscript and linguistics were both brittle compared to the solid, almost eternal duration of architecture as cultural evidence. His point of view, however, tended to fall upon unwilling ears because he went to an extreme. He went so far as to say, as a historian and an archaeologist, that the much-lamented loss of Mexican and Maya books (that is, the vanished codices) really had little or no effect upon our knowledge of Mexican antiquities. He was convinced that the so-called pictograph codices and the "hieroglyph" vestiges were not at all true historical sources and records but rather merely aide-mémoires, useful only to the degree that they once hinted to native experts the dates, rulers, and place-names of their past. He went still further: Mayer would have substituted archaeology for linguistics, hinting strongly that the love for grammar and language in ethnology was but an intellectual echo of nineteenth-century romantic attention to ballads, folklore, grammar, and supernatural tales. This meant that linguistics lacked a stable and reliable method; and while linguistics and literature might (and did) awaken interest in American Indian myth, legend, and magic, Mayer insisted that archaeology alone caught the true theme of the Americas, because it captured the expression, the narrative, and the cultural-historical meaning of American art and architecture.

North Americans like Brantz Mayer, Benjamin Moore Norman, John Lloyd Stephens, and Ephraim Squier[12] gave their own useful contributions to the archaeological record of the Amerindian past. At the same time, ethnology continued to hold its own and to grow. The American Ethnological Society recorded the rise of interest in the living Latin American Indian—his customs, culture, and society. The Ethnological Society clung to its hard task, especially in the less attractive regions, where investigators had to compete with more striking research and findings in Mexico and Peru. A clear-cut expansion took place, carrying the ethnology of Latin America beyond the advanced cultures of Mexico and Peru into the tribes of the rest of the continent. This was the most difficult problem. Of course progress was slow. The Ethnological Society followed a whole inter-American perspective, giving attention to the Caribbean, to Brazil, and even to Chile.

John Russell Bartlett, secretary of the American Ethnological Society, reviewing the progress of ethnology in 1843, captured the sense of the broadened viewpoint. Bartlett reported the ethnological investigations currently taking place in Latin America. He directed attention to the Indianist work carried on in Chile, Peru, Argentina, Venezuela, and Brazil. He opened the eyes of North Americans to the performance of the Castelnau scientific expedition, which was then crossing the Mato Grosso of Brazil, en route to Bolivia from São Paulo. Although Bartlett himself never saw or visited Latin America (except northern Mexico) he did make it possible for North American ethnology and the American Ethnological Society to commence official, institutional relations with Brazilian ethnology. Bartlett led the American Ethnological Society away from the overemphasis upon Mexico and Peru into Latin America proper, bringing to his efforts the collateral search for Latin American members, correspondence, articles, exchanges, and other tested measures of cooperation.[13]

The Ethnological Society did not abandon interest in the "diversity of languages, the remains of ancient art, and traces of ancient civilizations in Mexico, Central America, and Peru." That would have been an ill wind, doing no one any good. It might have destroyed both archaeology and ethnology. Just the same, there was no intrinsically sound scientific reason why a specialization in Mexican and Peruvian antiquities at that time should have centralized the geographic nature and location of Indianist work, while lowland and woodland peoples of America were overlooked. There was no convincing argument why the Indian peoples in other ethnological and archaeological zones should have roamed (in several senses) unnoticed, far from the highland centers of aboriginal research and along the remote border of American Indian investigation.

Any effort, no matter how small, accumulated some gain in the process which tried to de-emphasize the "big three" regions of advanced Indian culture. Brazilian contributors to the *Transactions* sent up from Rio de Janeiro different articles, such as:

1.   An Account of certain Antiquities, chiefly stone Implements found in Brazil. . . . By Virgil von Helmreichen of Rio de Janeiro.
2.   On a collection of Peruvian Antiquities in the Cabinet of Senhor Bartoza of Rio de Janeiro. By Thomas Ewbank.

Ewbank's article, although really pertaining to Peru rather than to Brazil, at least revealed the help of that nineteenth-century author. Considering the bewildering number and variety of the peoples and cultures known as the "Latin American Indian," still another surprisingly good step forward took the form of articles and reports about Nicaragua, Colombia, the Caribbean, and Brazil. Ephraim Squier of New York, much more the ethnologist than either John Lloyd Stephens or Benjamin Moore Norman, dealt with the Central American Indian in his "Archaeology and Ethnology of Nicaragua," published in the Ethnological Society's *Transactions,* third volume. For the first time (1845), North Americans interested in Central American ethnology had clear field information about the customs, native industries, house architecture, language, social organization, and culture of Nicaraguan tribes.

Cuban and Colombian ethnology came next. In addition to choosing their Latin American members from those countries, ethnologists printed informative articles about Cuba and Colombia. In one of its early *Proceedings,* the Ethnological Society published, in translation, the description which the distinguished Colombian José Vergara y Vergara gave of the lands and peoples of his native country. One of the most famous Cuban scholars and scientists of the nineteenth century,

Andrés Poey, already a participant in several North American learned societies, presented the difficult topic of "Cuban Antiquities" to North American ethnologists. The rest of the Caribbean-Central American area was surveyed, if not analyzed, by Berthold Seeman in his account of the "Aborigines of the Isthmus of Panama." These men raised the curtain on what is now called the "Circum-Caribbean Culture."

Inter-American cultural and scientific relations did not develop in a vacuum. It was perfectly natural that the contemporary economic and territorial expansionism into the Caribbean and central and northern South America should have coincided with scientific and cultural interest in the same regions. Moreover, there were advantages to following the flag. The steps away from Mexico and Yucatan into the Caribbean had much to offer. These intellectual and institutional ties were an expression of the North American cultural whole. The many-sided expansion and inter-Americanism of the generation of the Mexican War contained cultural dynamics, imperialism, Manifest Destiny, trade ambition, canal interest, and Anglo-American Caribbean interest—all in one. The historic trend towards cultural ties with Latin America took its own tack, leading towards scientific community in America, not to aggrandizement. Inter-American relations grew up with the rest of North American history, but it came of age according to its own constitution and heredity.

Across the Caribbean was Brazil. That vast area of Portuguese America cried out for rational study. It is known that some European and several North American travellers and visitors had observed Brazilian history and society at different times in the nineteenth century. North Americans, and Brazilians themselves, had learned a good deal about the geography, flora, fauna, mineral resources, and ethnology of the Brazilian Empire. Now the American Ethnological Society struck off on its own path. Again, John Russell Bartlett, acting under the joint instructions of the New-York Historical and American Ethnological societies, opened the way for initial and permanent cultural relations with Brazil. He started his preparation many years before the more famous reports of the United States Navy men in Brazil. He also preceded the activity of Agassiz and Hartt in Brazil. These Navy men—Herndon and Maury—and the scientists Agassiz and Hartt have found their recognized place in history; but Bartlett pioneered without any honor in his day. His contact was made with the Instituto Geographico e Historico of Rio de Janeiro.

The "year of decision" and the War with Mexico in 1846, in spite of the release of Manifest Destiny psychology, did not stop the expansive good will of American scholarship toward Latin America. The War with Mexico bred anti-Latin attitudes on one side and anti-Yankee antagonisms on the other; but the democracy and equality of cultural relations compensated by finding friends in Latin America. Long before the Mexican War and the threats to Spanish-speaking territories in Cuba, Mexico, and Central America, the American Philosophical Society—the prototype of societies created a short while later—had made friends in Latin America. Individuals, first in Spanish Latin America, then in Portuguese Brazil, were pleased to join North American societies. War did not stop the scientific process of reciprocal, two-way connection. Still, it was notable for societies to plan out and give an administrative character to their relations. As we shall see, ethnology was the newest tie to bind.

Let the Revista Trimensal of the Brazilian Instituto Geographico e Historico use its own words about the birth of Brazilian-American cultural relations:

> 146th meeting, March 18, 1846.
> Letter from Mr. John Russell Bartlett, secretary of the American Ethnological Society, in New York, inviting this Institute, with the compliments of that Society, to initiate a fraternal and literary correspondence which will surely be of no small benefit to both societies, and in general to the promotion of science on the American continent.
> Together with his letter, Mr. Bartlett sends for the Library of this Institute, the first volume of the *Transactions* of the Ethnological Society, along with the following works offered by their authors.[14]

This invitation, quickly followed by the Brazilian Instituto's return exchange of materials for the American Ethnological Society and other North American institutions, began the continuous process of gifts and exchanges between Brazil and the United States.

The books which went down to Rio de Janeiro deserve to be listed as examples of North American ethnological and scientific work. They include:

1. Samuel George Morton, *A Memoir of William Maclure Esq., late President of the Academy of Natural Sciences of Philadelphia.* Philadelphia: 1844.
2. Samuel George Morton, *An Inquiry into the Distinctive Characteristics of the Aboriginal Race of America.* Philadelphia: 1844.
3. Benjamin M. Norman, *Rambles in Yucatan; or Notes of Travel*

*through the Peninsula, including a visit to the Remarkable Ruins of
Chichen, Kabah, Zayi and Uxmal.* New York: 1842.

4.   Alexander W. Bradford, *American Antiquities and Researches
into the Origin and History of the Red Race.* New York: 1844.

5.   William H. Hodgson, *Notes on Northern Africa, the Sahara and
Soudan in relation to Ethnography, Languages, History, Political and
Social Condition of those Countries.* New York: 1844.

The Hodgson book, one of the earliest on Africa and the Negro
continent, had special value to Brazil because of African population and
influences in that nation. Dr. Morton's biographical sketch of William
Maclure usefully suggested to Brazilians how a Jeffersonian and philanthropist had found the way for science to unite the Americas in the
pursuit of reason and natural philosophy.

The Brazilian Instituto, at its March meeting, replied to these over-
tures. It granted corresponding membership to the North American
authors of these books. With its appetite for North American thought
aroused, the Brazilian society sent up to New York for additional copies
and also asked specifically for copies of John Stephens' now-famous
Incidents of Travel in Central America, Chiapas and Yucatan. Nor was
this all. The Institute formally established institutional and cultural relations and correspondence with the Ethnological Society which lasted
many years. Finally, the Instituto Historico e Geographico Brasileiro
chose Albert Gallatin and John Bartlett, chief officers of the Ethnological
Society, as North American members. Thus Brazil returned the two-
way understanding by enlarging the membership roster. The institutional liaison behind research into American man began to extend to the
rest of the hemisphere in "fraternal" cultural relations.

The success of "ethnological panamericanism" was still more marked.
October 29, 1846, the Brazilian Instituto received a North American
request which may well be a historical landmark. It came to Brazil
together with a note stressing again the value of North American
scholarship:

Letter from our corresponding member, Mr. John Russell Bartlett,
secretary of the New-York Historical Society, offering the Instituto,
in the name of that Society, the collection of its *Transactions* during
the year 1845, and declaring it would greatly prize a correspondence
with this Instituto, whose publications it will always receive with great
satisfaction. . . .

Another from the same gentleman, in his capacity as secretary of
the American Ethnological Society, in whose name he offers to the

Instituto the first volume of its *Transactions*. He similarly expresses
the desire of the Ethnological Society to enter into fraternal correspondence with the Instituto Brasileiro, reciprocating the exchange of
publications.

This communication in itself was not too unusual, since by now the
Brazilian society had also regularized its literary exchanges, adding the
Historical Society of Pennsylvania. What was important was the optimistic state of mind which was ready to put inter-American relations
upon an organized, permanent basis by proposing a hemisphere Congress
of scholars. In the clear and bright noon of inter-American cooperation
a sign of extraordinary interest appeared.

In one of Bartlett's several notes to Brazil, he included a note from
Herman Ludewig, a colleague of his. It was dated August 25, 1846,
and went out under the auspices and letterhead of the New-York Historical Society, addressed to the same Brazilian Institute. Although the
subject of the letter is for a Congress of North and South American societies on matters of inter-American cultural interest, there is no evidence that similar letters went to Latin American countries other than
Brazil. Perhaps Brazil was the trial balloon. Maybe the failure to get
an acceptance was discouraging, in spite of the relations with Brazil.
At any rate there was no follow-up with other Latin American countries.
It may also have been that Brazil was the most important country to
which the invitation could have been sent, because its government was
monarchical, and the rest of America was republican. It is hard to know.

The letter is given here because ethnology and history in Latin
American studies were still so closely allied, and also because the name
of the American Ethnological Society together with the New-York Historical Society stood behind the invitation. Because of its length only
the most pertinent extracts follow. The request for a Congress is striking
in tone. As to its importance, the minutes of the Instituto Brasileiro show
that serious attention was given to the unprecedented invitation, and it
was read to the full membership.

August 25, 1846.

Gentlemen:

. . . A Congress of all the historical societies of the American continent towards this important end [the history and ethnology of the
New World] could not fail to have the happiest results. Even if these
societies would only communicate to each other the fruits of their
respective researches, we will already have advanced a third of the
way.

Up to now there has been no concern about this, and Europe has continued to centralise toward itself the efforts of even the most national-minded of New World scholars.

It is a consequence of the pronounced individualism of the Anglo-Saxon race, that up to very recently, there were some societies in the United States which even doubted their own existence. And as for this Instituto to whose members I have the honor of addressing these words, I could barely get any information because its *Revista Trimensal* cannot be found in any of our historical libraries.

We know almost nothing of the literary and scientific efforts of South America; and even as to the literature of past centuries we lack a critical journal dealing with the treasures which Barcía mentions in his edition of the Bibliotheca Oriental y Occidental of León Pinelo. In the United States, at Boston, only the Massachusetts Historical Society has in its library the collection by Pedro de Angelis dealing with the provinces of the Río de la Plata.

May not the students of New World history hope that a fraternal and scientific association, that a mutual exchange of each other's publications will replace this reciprocal silence? that North and South Americans can assist each other's researches, whose results from now on will benefit both? that all Americans, finally, will make common cause in the exploration of the historic treasures of their continent?

The immense advantages of association supply us with an undoubted guarantee that these hopes, these desires are not far from accomplishment, and because of this conviction, the Ethnological Society and Historical Society of New-York are the first to extend a friendly hand in close scientific and fraternal relations. . . . [15]

So far has inter-American joint cooperation progressed in the hundred years since 1846, especially in the cited subjects, that it is easy to forget the significance of this early suggestion and to lose sight of so important a precedent.

It is ironic that the excessive "particularism" which marked the "individualism of the Anglo-Saxon race" prevented both Bartlett and Ludewig themselves from knowing and appreciating how far inter-American cultural relations had actually developed. It should be clear by now that far more was known before 1850 about Latin America and about the "literary and scientific" efforts of South America than Bartlett, Ludewig, or any other single North American could know or keep up with. The *laisser-faire* spirit of North American government was so free from direction, control, and over-all supervision, that the total progress of inter-American relations was hidden from each society or individual. None knew the work of the other; the right hand did not know what the left was doing. The North American individualism to which Ludewig's letter referred had mixed blessing: it had the energy and initiative to create relations while it wasted energy by specialized and decentralized efforts, unique and different for each society. Yet the complete result was the same, and it was successful.

Foreign cultural relations with Latin America were free and responsible but were at the same time, unintegrated and uncoordinated. It was too early to hold a congress of that sort: a proposed panamerican institute of history and ethnology, or a congress of Americanists. First it was necessary to tie the societies together in a more common, North American cultural federation. The Bartlett-Ludewig correspondence with Brazil proves how strong was the impulse for hemisphere cultural organization. The silence about it, on the other hand, revealed the prior need for getting North American societies together in some way before any inter-American organization could result. But this was as difficult as getting Latin American societies together. However, a substitute agency could help. The Smithsonian Institution became the scientific centralizing agency which at least served the purpose of exchange.

Individual societies did little or nothing to integrate these relations; their own efforts were enough. Nor could the Smithsonian bring an inter-American congress about, possibly because of financial problems and the lack of widespread support. The remarkable proposal of Bartlett-Ludewig fell upon deaf ears, both in Latin America and in the United States, but not before the Instituto Brasileiro's minutes noted tersely that the "Instituto voted that the First Secretary, with the customary form, reply suitably to the cited letters." The time was not yet ripe for such a congress.

At this time—about 1846 to 1850—a much-needed liaison agency came into existence, providing a single, integrated channel for the whole of inter-American cultural work, and making possible a diffusion of North American culture into Latin America. After 1846 the Smithsonian Institution followed the precedents of well-established patterns of inter-American exchange. The Smithsonian promoted exchanges through a centralized basis, using methods and arrangements developed by the private societies. The failure of the inter-American Congress, or of any other nonpolitical assembly, did not stop the Smithsonian from organizing cultural communication. The Smithsonian acted in Latin America on behalf of North American learned societies and the government of the United States as well as for itself. The Smithsonian's unusual advantage in this respect was that it combined the work of a private learned society, concerned with the promotion of science, with the role of a chartered instrument of government. The agency, however, had another point of major difference with the privately established societies. The inter-American work of the Smithsonian did not include the nomination of members from Latin America.

The Smithsonian Institution, like the American Philosophical Society, won unusually high esteem from Latin American scientists, scholars, and learned institutions. In fact, no other North American institution, except the American Philosophical Society, matched the prestige of the Smithsonian in the eyes of the other America. This was an original and high tribute for a newcomer on the scene. The fame of the Institution made it possible to choose the Smithsonian as the integrating agency. Then the Smithsonian both supplemented and represented the privately supported societies, giving them assistance of an organizational sort while adding continuously to its own leadership and reputation throughout Latin America. Because it was associated with inter-American science and scholarship the Smithsonian was not hurt by being an agency of North American government.

The Smithsonian took up the study of American Indian ethnology in addition to the already cited work in science. Neither in its program nor in its technique of exchange procedures did the Smithsonian create or innovate topics of investigation or plans of exchange. These were much older than the Smithsonian. What the Smithsonian did was to dig energetically into the known soils, pushing a little more successfully than the others could. The Smithsonian neither changed nor challenged the dominating North American identification of ethnology with linguistics; it merely improved the study of Indianist philology and grammar. As Indianism continued to search through language and grammar for the traces of man in the Americas and for any unity of language stock between the Indians of English and Spanish North America, that is, Mexico, the Smithsonian also accepted this emphasis. However, the Smithsonian was in a better position than the societies to initiate original field studies and special publications. Linguistics also pointed to Brazil and continental Latin America, although to a somewhat lesser degree. The Smithsonian had its hands full with language studies, language maps, and its special language interest in Mexico. The direct program of work focussed upon Mexico, while Latin America seemed a reflected glory. Smithsonian news and findings were published in the *Contri-*

butions to Knowledge and the *Transactions,* which were exchanged and circulated all over Latin America. The echo of Smithsonian cultural activity in Mexico resounded in Bogotá, Caracas, Santiago, Buenos Aires, and Rio de Janeiro.

The biggest project was the *Handbook of the North American Indian,* which brought Mexican and North American scholars into working connection. It took another eighty years before the Smithsonian issued its *Handbook of the South American Indian* (also based upon inter-American contributions). At the earlier date, however, the Smithsonian confined its attention to the Mexican Indian, perhaps because in ethnology, as in geology, Mexico was considered to be a part of North rather than of South or Central America. Professor Joseph Henry was then secretary of the Institution. We have seen what he was able to do with its program for Latin America.

We need not review Dr. Henry's success in expanding cooperation in the Americas in the natural sciences. His success in ethnology was as great. There are many examples of his initiative and leadership. For one thing, one of the most personal of his many helpful and well-directed acts won from A. J. de Irisarri, the famous Guatemalan-Chilean poet (then minister to the United States from his native Guatemala), the letters of introduction necessary to continue the research among the Maya Indians in Guatemala. Dr. Henry helped Dr. Behrendt, the specialist on the Maya (and an assiduous correspondent of John Russell Bartlett), to carry on field investigations at La Paz and Peten. Implementing the interest in the Maya begun by Manuel Gálvez with the American Philosophical Society and carried out by Norman, Stephens, and the New-York Historical Society, the Smithsonian in fact gave Dr. Behrendt a grant for Maya research.

Aztec and Maya cultures were the chief attraction. Here Dr. Henry led the Smithsonian along the well-worn route to Mexico and Yucatan. No doubt these regions were unparalleled in archaeology and historiography, both for brilliance of achievement and for opportunity for study. But fullest knowledge of pre-Cortesian aboriginal society and culture lay outside of Central Mexico's plateau-valley and the Yucatan peninsula. It was important to find out something about the many other Mexican tribes and widely distributed native subgroups. There was a profusion of dialects and culture habits in Mexico. It was just as necessary to get some knowledge and a descriptive ethnology of the living and existing Indians as it was to study the ancient prehistory. Dr. Henry then called upon Buckingham Smith, who knew Mexico and had lived there. Smith studied in the Spanish Archives. He had written on Spanish exploration and conquest and had also published on the Indianist philology, especially of the Sonoran and Northwestern Mexican tribes. Smith did his best work as a Hispanist, historian, and inter-Americanist; but he also made some mark as an ethnologist. He helped the Smithsonian in both capacities.

Smith suggested the name of his good Mexican friend José Fernando Ramírez as the competent director of the Mexican portion of the proposed *Handbook*. Ramírez was a good choice for anything so cooperative in nature. He was already well known in the United States since he was a corresponding member of the American Ethnological Society, the New-York Historical Society, and the American Antiquarian Society. He was a leading historian of Mexico, of the generation which included Joaquín García Icazbalceta (also a friend and colleague of Buckingham Smith). Also, Ramírez was the Spanish translator of William H. Prescott's *Conquest of Mexico*, in the edition published in Mexico City. Like many historians of the nineteenth century, Ramírez knew the related fields of Indian languages, distribution of tribes, and the cultural geography of the Indians. Like many other North American scholars, Smith was not concerned about Ramírez' politics (which were conservative and even monarchical). He and Ramírez were good friends.

The contact of the North American Buckingham Smith with the Mexican José Ramírez was but a small radius which touched the hemisphere around them. The sphere ranged out beyond them to include Dr. Joseph Henry and George Gibbs, secretary of the New-York Historical Society, whose interest in Mayan archaeology and prehistory has already been described. Gibbs wrote a letter to Dr. Henry about the proposed *Handbook of the North American Indian* which shows both the current linguistic emphasis of ethnology and the way in which that subject attracted and organized the strongest inter-American ideas:

January 21, 1863

Mr. Buckingham Smith called on me today and showed me a letter from Don José Fernando Ramírez, of which I enclose an abstract.

"There exist no vocabularies of the languages nor have the grammars ever been preserved, written by the early missionaries. It is almost impossible to bring together those that have been printed. On this subject a work has been commenced entitled *Cuadro Descriptivo y Comparativo de las Lenguas Indígenas de Mexico*, by Don Fernando [*sic* for Francisco] Pimentel. The first volume only has been printed which comprehends the analysis of twelve languages. Unfortunately, material is wanting. Those contained in the first volume are the Huaxteco, Mixteco, Mame, Othomi, Zapoteco, Tarahumar, Tarasco, Totonaco, Opata or Teguema, Cahila and Matlaznica. If you have succeeded in publishing the grammars about which you informed me [Buckingham Smith published a Pima and Esleve grammar in collaboration with John Gilmary Shea], and they should arrive in time, they will be examined in the work.

"I have not seen and am unacquainted with the *Archaeology of the United States,* by Samuel F. Haven, about which you write me. Of the Smithsonian *Contributions* I have only the second, third and fourth volumes, unless the first volume should be the *Ancient Monuments of the Mississippi Valley* [by Ephraim Squier] which I possess. At present there is no way of sending books into Mexico unless the Department of State will take charge of them."

Mr. Smith has handed me the above with the view that I might ask of you to send to Señor Ramírez such other papers of the *Contributions* as belong to archaeology. That gentlemen is well known as one of the most distinguished scholars in that department in Mexico, and one whom it would be desirable for the Institution to number among its correspondents. I am, however, astonished at the account he gives of the paucity of works on the indigenous languages of that country, so opposite to our general belief here. Under any circumstances Pimentel's work should be procured, if possible.[16]

The Smithsonian's support of this project never ceased until it finally emerged as the *Handbook of the North American Indian.*

Another point was clear: efforts to "decentralize" Indian studies and turn greater attention to Brazil and the less developed cultures now had less chance of success. The Smithsonian's project underscored the prevalent interest in Mexico, perpetuated it, and raised it to a higher level than before, securing a firm basis for the future excellence of work in this area. It meant a longer time before the rest of Latin America could catch up. Descriptions of Indian civilization were still concerned with the advanced cultures of Peru and Mexico, and the belief in diffusion within America stemmed from this emphasis. In addition, behind the linguistics lay the assumption inspired by the Bible and the Judaeo-Christian tradition: originally there had been one language among men. This same language once united now-different peoples. The theory of social evolution, having assumed progress from the simple to the complex, also looked for a primitive simplicity of speech and grammar, reflecting the level of ideas. Very few thought to turn to the geography

and paleontology of Latin America in the search for human origins. It
was hard to associate progress with simple folk. Nothing in Brazil, Chile,
Colombia, or Cuba was as impressive and grand as in Mexico and Peru.
Also, source materials and evidence in Mexico and Peru were very rich,
both in documents and monuments. Consequently, the golden suns of
Cuzco and Tenochtitlán threw deep shadow and eclipse on other Latin
American Indian societies. The Smithsonian agreed with the trends
of archaeology and ethnology.

We have, however, seen how John Bartlett of the American Ethnological Society tried to end the monopoly of Mexican, Maya, and Peruvian
studies. In addition to those institutional ties with Brazil, which have
already been described, Bartlett also encouraged correspondence—published later—from Virgil von Helmreichen of Rio de Janeiro, who had
spent some time among the Brazilian Indians of the Serra do Espinhaço
in the Valley of the Rio São Francisco. Von Helmreichen supplied the
Ethnological Society with his field observations (and his own drawings)
of Brazilian Indian artifacts, shells, rock paintings, idols, pottery, and
other objects. Even more important than his collections was his education of North American ethnologists to the viewpoint, soon to be diffused by Charles Hartt, that an older, aboriginal civilization had first
inhabited the historic places of Brazil. These aborigines had been driven
away by late-comers—whom the Portuguese found in Brazil in the sixteenth century. Here too we see the search for the *Urmensch* and the
primitive unity of man and speech in America.

American ethnology in Brazil found its strongest worker in the person
of Charles Hartt. He was a specialist, as we have said, in the century
before specialization. Hartt realized many of the aims for United States-
Brazilian cultural relations which John Russell Bartlett and Herman
Ludewig had tried to secure with, and through, the Instituto Geographico e Historico Brasileiro. The permanent worth of Brazilian ethnology in the rank of Latin American anthropological studies owes more
to Charles Hartt than to either Bartlett or Ludewig. As we have seen
in another connection, Hartt had other scientific interests in Brazil. We
must now look at his ethnological contributions, because he went on to
specialize in Brazilian Indianist antiquities.

Hartt's former students wrote of him that he "busied himself studying Munducuru and Maue dialects of the modern Tupi language of
the Amazonas, and in bringing together for the first time the stories
and myths which are current in the tribes. He had prepared a large
volume on the grammar, vocabularies and stories of this language which

yet (1878) remains unpublished."[17] Hartt's grammar and dictionary
of the Tupi (still unpublished) was given by his wife to the Brazilian
Museu Nacional after his death. Fresh from the faculties of Cornell
University and Vassar College, Hartt advanced further in Brazil than
any other foreigner, before or after him. He was the first North American
to become assistant director of the Museu, because no Brazilian could
match his scientific knowledge and training. We have seen him apply
for the post of director of the Geodetic Survey under the Empire. He
mixed his ample knowledge of Brazilian geology and paleontology with
substantial ethnological work, and as the fashion was, he also "busied
himself" with grammar and language. At least for Hartt, language instead of resting upon books depended upon as sound a geographic and
environmental base as he could see for himself by his own field trips into
the regions of Brazil.

Hartt had the best training for combining geology with paleontology,
using both of these sciences for studying the ethnology of the Brazilian
Indian. He did his great work in those river valleys of Brazil which had
the greatest historical importance as well: the Amazon and the São
Francisco. In both basins Hartt separated the study of geology from
mineralogy. Then he dug more deeply than others into earth strata and
rock history. Finally he realized it was necessary to take man into the
whole account of Brazilian and New World prehistory. He seems to
have been well aware both of the influence of geography upon man and
his works and of the return contribution of man to nature. Hartt had
the feeling that the Amazon and São Francisco valleys held the traces
of the original ancient culture of Brazil, far removed from the highland
cultures to the west in Peru. He studied the remains of early cultures
where he found them. He understood that Brazilian natural history as
well as human history would be read more easily with the aid of geology,
paleontology, and ethnology.

In spite of his distinctive contributions to Brazilian ethnological
work, Hartt's manuscript notes, so rich in the observed data from
Amazon tribes and archaeological sites at Bahia and Pará, have never
been published. Neither have his proposals for scientific study of Brazilian antiquities and Indian mythology. Fortunately, some of his other
work was printed. His papers on the topics of Indian pottery, Brazilian
rock inscriptions, myth, folklore, and native cemeteries have appeared.
These were published in both North American and Brazilian scientific
journals, which were pleased to print his essays. Hartt published very
frequently in the *American Naturalist*, as well as the *Archivo do Museu*

Nacional at Rio de Janeiro. Some of his papers were booklets and some were books. Hartt's great Indianist work on the Botocudo Indians came to life again in Brazil about a decade ago when his best-known scientific treatise, *Geology and Physical Geography of Brazil* (first published in the United States), was reprinted under Brazilian government blessing. It is still a loss both to Brazilian ethnology and to the complete inter-American cultural record that his manuscript materials, letters, and reports have never been published.

Death cut off his work but not his contribution. However, since his ethnological work, based upon field visits, was overlooked because so much of it was then in manuscript, some people concluded hastily that Hartt was chiefly a geologist who had taught at Cornell and Vassar and who had trained some students to succeed him. Only his associates, and particularly his colleagues in science, knew and appreciated Hartt as one of the first students of Brazilian ethnology, who improved the knowledge of that subject a great deal. His integrity as a field worker, his influence as a director of the Brazilian Museu, and his scholarly connections with North American institutions gave Brazilian ethnology a lift, especially in the eyes of North Americans.

Hartt also obtained important financial grants for his Brazilian studies. Had he lived longer he surely would have received greater support. As it was, the Peabody Museum of Archaeology and Ethnology at Cambridge assisted his researches. (The Peabody Museum in 1870 was already launched on its original and active support of American research. It had given grants of $352 in 1860 to Dr. Behrendt for Central American and Yucatecan investigation and the sum of $250 to Porter C. Bliss in 1871. These men and the Mexican zone in which they chose to work were already well known to the public, to museum people, and to institutions.) The first North American grants given for study in Brazil were given to Hartt in 1872 and 1875. They reflect the strong expectation of inter-American achievement as well as the special interest being focussed on Brazil. The Peabody directors gave Hartt $500 at first and $600 again. Hartt thus received the first North American grants-in-aid for research in Brazilian studies.[18] He thereby supplied a personal assistance to the correspondence which Bartlett instituted.

By this time Brazilian work acquired the foundation for its future growth, and contemporaries already held Hartt in great esteem. He helped the organizational work of ethnological students as he did in geology, by recommending his Brazilian colleagues for membership in North American societies. It was here, without knowing it, that he personally gave real meaning to Bartlett's expectations. In addition, he wrote many articles which he hoped and intended would heighten scientific interest in Brazil as the place to study. In order to do this he replaced the literary and speculative approaches with more scientific method. He made his argument for Brazilian ethnology very clear in this respect in his report on the "ancient Indian Pottery of Marajo, Brazil," where he described his findings of pottery and mortuary urns on Marajo Island, at the mouth of the Amazon River:

We have no historical records of the tribe that built the Marajo mounds. . . . We have no record of the existence of any tribe in the Lower Amazonas that buried its dead in jars.

I do not feel like coinciding with von Martius in the supposition that the Marajo mounds were made by Indians of Tupi descent. There are many resemblances between the pottery of Marajo and that of Peru and North America that will be worth study.

I hope that future explorations will enable me to clear up much of the doubts expressed in this paper, and cast much needed light on the ancient races of the Amazonas Valley.[19]

Hartt read the rock inscriptions of the Serra do Erere on the Tocantins and examined those of the Rio São Francisco against the descriptive literature written in the eighteenth century. His historical ethnology confirmed his conviction that the Brazilian Tupi, encountered by Portuguese soldiers, missionaries, and settlers in the sixteenth-century Conquest, had themselves displaced an earlier people of Brazil. The culture of the mounds, urns, and rock markings antedated those of the historic era.

Hartt's sense of cultural relations and an inter-American science was just as challenging. His own words give spirit to his plea to stimulate Brazilian studies and de-emphasize Peru and Mexican leadership:

It is a great shame that the antiquities of Brazil have so far received little or no attention, yet the country is one whose ethnology is extremely interesting, and it is desirable that the history of its many tribes should be traced out.

The neglect of Brazilian antiquities has arisen, no doubt, from the comparative rarity of the relics and the difficulty of exploring the country. Stone implements are found all over the Empire, ancient pottery occurs in many localities, especially burial stations, and Kjokkenmoddings (*sambaquies*) exist on the coast as at Santa Cruz in the Province of Espiritu Santo, on the Bay of Rio de Janeiro, at Santos, and elsewhere.[20]

Tragically, Hartt's ethnology depended largely upon himself. No North American ethnologists came into Brazil in the next generation to take up directly from where he left. Only geologists followed him. It took at least two generations for a posterity in Brazilian ethnology to succeed him. On the whole, it seems, there can be no question but that North American dedication to Mexico won out. After that came the swift and steady rise of attention given to the Indian of the American Southwest.

Before 1900, also, the surviving interest in linguistics, and the bookish approach to Latin American antiquity remained very strong among those who carried great weight. Field work, whether in Brazil or in the Southwest, was less rewarding than language, grammar, and historical sources. Years of effort and labor on dictionaries, Indian grammars, and philologies found new literary dignity in collections of Indian myth, aboriginal legend, and traditional literature. At the University of Pennsylvania, a Chair in American Archaeology reiterated the name and aim of the Peabody Museum at Cambridge. North American universities supplemented the pioneer work of the societies and began to teach courses on the American Indian, Latin American archaeology, and the origins of man in the Americas.

Daniel G. Brinton held the Chair of American Archaeology at the University of Pennsylvania, towards the end of the nineteenth century. Brinton's emphasis upon myth, literature, and linguistics was even more exclusive than that of the neighboring American Philosophical Society. Brinton would have liked to synthesize languages. He tried to integrate grammatical and philological systems of the Latin American and Mexican Indian into one cohesive, literary communication that would effectively open up the history of hemisphere prehistory. For him, as for so many others before him, language was literature, going hand in hand ahead of archaeology and far in front of field ethnology and physical anthropology. Brinton's concern for myth—and he certainly lacked the social and psychocultural insights used today—won a reputation for him, but it also brought him much professional criticism for ignoring field work and direct observation. Perhaps the establishment of the Chair of Archaeology at the University of Pennsylvania does add to Philadelphia's prestige in the Latin American field, but Brinton himself made no better progress than Barton, Mitchill, and others who, in the first quarter of the nineteenth century, had to depend upon books and written accounts. Those of the pioneer generation from 1800 to 1825 at least found it hard or impossible to visit Indian regions of Mexico and Latin

America. Brinton, on the other hand, had every opportunity. Yet, like William H. Prescott in history, he never visited the land and peoples about whom he expounded. In spite of this, his views were positive and firm, probably because his confidence came from being read in the literature of early Spanish and native authors. He was most at home in Mexican antiquities, although he did draw up maps of Chaco and South American language groupings.[21]

By that time (1882) other North American ethnologists were equally active and at work in the Latin American field, using literary sources as an aid rather than as an end. In the general air of that day, the method of Boas had not yet invigorated field research, while the particular field studies of Adolphe Bandelier among Latin American Indians and those under Spanish influence in the American Southwest were almost ceaseless. Bandelier was an energetic student of Spanish sixteenth-century literary sources. He also had travelled and lived in the Spanish Southwest, Mexico, South America, and Spain; but he had not been in Brazil. He was as much at home in aboriginal society and ethnological field work as he was among the printed and manuscript sources. Indeed, in his work he combined the two. Bandelier opposed the damaging influence of Brinton and other bookish ethnologists upon Indian anthropology. He thought and felt keenly about it. Here, in his own words, is one summary of an approach to "anthropological panamericanism" which was kept off balance by too many books:

> Santa Fe, New Mexico,
> Jan. 1885.
>
> . . . What Dr. Brinton has to say . . . has not much to signify. He is a very worthy, active and industrious man, but only a reader and writer. American aboriginal history has never entered into his flesh and bone through practical experience.
>
> So it is the case with many; they gaze at things from an easy chair, cite the nation before them into an elegant study, and when he is seated (after they have washed, combed and perfumed him), they question him, carefully noting what he has to say. In this manner they study Ethnology!
>
> Archaeology is gathered from specimens only, and not a moment's attention is devoted to the condition under which they are found as well as to their relations to the country where they have been used.[22]

While the temper, methods, and sometimes the conclusions of Bandelier are open to question, this is not the place for their discussion. The Swiss-

American Bandelier, like the Canadian-American Charles Hartt, was a field worker who also knew the value of literary sources and the worth of historical literature. After his time the techniques of inquiry were to be made even more scientific, more detailed, and more certain.

The major fact which belongs here is that after 1890 North American interest in the Latin American Indian had become permanent, no matter what method was used in research. For well over a century, inter-American scientific communication, strongly based upon curiosity and a desire to know, took form in ethnology and anthropology, two of the oldest and most rewarding subjects for inter-American ideas and associations. The renaissance of learning about the origins and nature of the Aztec, Maya, and Inca cultures in the eighteenth century was part of the common Enlightenment which drew both Americas together. The nineteenth century added societies, methods, individual achievements, and a body of knowledge to the subject. The debate over methodology did not stop progress. Whether emphasis rested upon grammar and linguistics, archaeology, or field ethnology, the recognition of the great works of Latin America, taken from these examples of cultural cooperation did create a scientific fellowship, distributed among the different intellectual bodies.

A broader American history revealed an even fuller story and won still more solidarity. History, anthropology, and archaeology, by probing far back into the American past for an explanation of man and his culture in the Western Hemisphere, preceded and paved the way for the expanded concept of the history of the Americas. We will see that the history of the white man had much to contribute, and that the history of Western European civilization in Latin America was as fascinating as that of the red man. Remembering how much early history slipped under the name of ethnology, and how the New-York Historical Society rounded out its share of cultural relations together with the American Ethnological Society, we can now review the record of history in the hemisphere.

Chapter 5

THE HEMISPHERE MAKES HISTORY

*H*ISTORY MADE the hemisphere turn on the same cultural axis as ethnology, science, and the book trade. There were certain differences, to be sure, since the historian's scope pointed to a past which was not so far back on the time horizon. The historian's limits were the Discovery and Conquest, raised to capital letters because of the capital importance these themes held. He satisfied his aims with written sources which told of voyages, explorations, travels, *entradas,* and conquests. Knowledge of these sources inevitably led him to missionary reports and eyewitness chronicles which knew the Indian cultures at first hand; so that historical ethnology and history were paired in this respect. Because of the rich Spanish and Portuguese sources and the extended written literature on the colonial era of Latin America, the eye-filling parade of conquistadors and viceroys dominated and even replaced the interest in nineteenth-century Latin America. Although many writers swelled the sum of books on current events in Latin America, very few seriously undertook the history of modern times in that continent. The historian fixed his location in the three hundred years between the pre-Columbian antiquity used by the archaeologist and the peoples still living in the nineteenth century. Most historians trained their sight upon the sixteenth century, where the known sources lay and where the official Spanish historians of the Council of the Indies had learned to concentrate their attention. Spanish and North American historians lived with the Conquest. They ignored the progress, reforms, and growth-changes of the three hundred years, by-passing the glories of Latin American Independence, the epics of Precursors and Liberators, and the rationalist talent of the eighteenth-century Enlightenment.

As we have seen in ethnology and the sciences, colonial and early

139

national libraries in the United States owned a fine sampling of the treatises, chronicles, and histories dealing with Spanish American colonial birth. After 1900, North American books and writers began to deal with the topics and men of modern and contemporary Latin America. All the time, however, there was, and is, one important exception. The North American public, newspapers, and officials of government have an understandable concern for contemporary Latin America. During the years of the Wars of Independence, North American journalists, propagandists, publicists, travellers, and diplomats wrote their books, tracts, and arguments to inform North American public opinion, to communicate their points of view, and to set up the debate upon issues of public policy.[1*]

During the generation of the bitter struggles in Latin America, from 1810 to 1830, popular and general accounts of the day supplied the North American reading public with some of the current history of Mexico, Argentina, Brazil, and other new nations. Almost all these books emphasized the events around them, probably because the colonial story was fairly well known by then, but especially because the crises in Western Europe and the Western Hemisphere over the "Holy Alliance," Spanish reaction, British mediation, and Latin American recognition by the United States were pressing and even urgent. These called for information and a position. Speeches, editorials, and pamphlets were regular weapons in the struggle over these ideas.

Wartime conditions have often quickened North American interest in the growing pains of Latin America. With peace and the declining danger from Europe, the pendulum has swung back from the present to the past, returning to colonial history and Indian origins. As peace assured the independence of Latin America and her entrance into the system of nations, the tensions, the fears, and the excitement over national safety declined. Opportunity knocked for the calmer study of history. The American past was again opened to investigation and research. The timely moment may have arrived with freedom from Spain, but there was a great lack of methods and of thoughtful historians. Resources and archives were still closed. It took another century before those North American historians who were interested in Latin America worked up to the levels of method, treatment, evidence, organization of materials, and interpretation which are so clear today. Nevertheless, the first steps were taken. The United States, which replaced Spain in the

*Notes to this chapter begin on page 175.

Southwest and the Caribbean, filled the vacuum with historical studies, joining with Latin American historians in studying and grasping the history of the hemisphere.

In 1800 little was really known about Spanish institutions, culture, and development in America. Nor was too much known of the European Spaniard and the Indian. True, archaeology as a subject had just risen to its own feet. But, generally speaking, the nineteenth-century scholar-observer knew little more than his conquistador-counterpart of the sixteenth century. History had better opportunity, because history accompanied the great Europeanizing civilization into Latin America and lived with Spanish institutional development for three hundred years. Moreover, history as a subject had prestige in the government of Old Spain and the New World. Spanish chroniclers and historians held official position in overseas administration. They assembled the sources and did the writing of the Discovery and Conquest. Besides the official historian, many thoughtful narrators wrote history which lasted. The history of the Indies and the Laws of the Indies were favored and favorite themes in Spanish historiography. We have already seen the standard works which North Americans owned. The vast Spanish sources and materials were better preserved (and more numerous) than Indian remains. They were brought together under royal order.

Since the eighteenth century, Indies papers had swelled the archives at Seville and Simancas. When William H. Prescott, the most famous of North American historians on Latin America, organized his work in the nineteenth century, he was already confronted by the paper riches of early Latin American history, the fullness of printed and manuscript materials, and the Spanish good will and assistance which greeted his request for research help. Prescott, however, never went to Spain; nor did he ever get to Mexico and Peru, about which he wrote. Others sent him the boxes of papers and books which he needed. If anything, Prescott was a Hispanist, not an Americanist. He contributed little to either the promotion or exchange of inter-American intellectual ties, except, perhaps, as Latin Americans translated his books into Spanish. He was a fine writer and an unusually gifted historian in the mode of that day; but in this study of the history of the search for intellectual identifications in the New World and in the creation of scholarly inter-American connections, Prescott was, oddly enough, a historian who overlooked or ignored the flow of fertile contact between North and South America. His scholarship, in addition, concentrated upon the older, Hispanic origins of Latin America. The historian has to move past Prescott to reach living, national Latin America. Prescott's two histories which concern us (*Conquest of Mexico, Conquest of Peru*) are stirring accounts of military campfires, darkened by hard and bold Spanish soldiers, ready for battle with courageous but futile Indian chiefs. It is Europe versus America, but his accounts come to an end when Latin American history really begins. In a history whose rich evolution down to his own day took three hundred years, Prescott dealt with events which took place in two years (New Spain) and three years (Peru).

The new nations of the Latin American independence era did not interest him. Although they also emerged in hand-to-hand struggle, with *próceres* equal in stature to the *conquistadores,* modern Latin America is scarcely mentioned in his published letters and correspondence and not at all in his historical works. Granted his views, this is understandable. The recent Independence movement and the embrace of inter-American relations and the cultural rediscovery of a New World were all outside his notice, because they were the history of America, not of Spain.[2] Prescott was able to see very clearly from Boston the bright ensigns and banners of Catholic Castille, and he lingered lovingly in the sixteenth century. He had great influence upon later historians— and vogue—partly because of his method and style, but chiefly because he tied future historical studies firmly to the era of Spanish conquest, the earliest colonial period, in which he was personally interested. Since his day, the Conquest is almost alive in the attraction which it continues to have for the historians of all countries.

Cooperation with contemporary Latin American culture must have implied a *simpático* attitude toward their nationality and the cultural character which he did not seek to cultivate. Therefore, intellectual exchange in America fell to others. Still, Prescott signalled clearly to many others to accompany or follow him into the Conquest. If Washington Irving gave the classical picture of one man—Columbus—a leader in the Age of Discovery, Prescott featured two stars in the great tragedy of culture conflict in his *dramatis personae*. His cast set off Cortes and Pizarro in the highest relief; dramatic action, heroes and villains make his histories vivid and readable. Here the parallel ends. Washington Irving lived in Spain and loved it; Prescott also loved Spain but did not know the country personally. It was easier for him as a historian to turn back to sources for the past eras of Spain. He then worked Discovery, or rather Conquest, as though at the surface of a rich mine. Historians after him have pushed the vein deeper and deeper. Because of this, the spotlight of history—as in archaeology—was once again directed to Mexico and Peru, leaving the rest of Latin America in half-shadow or, at most, in reflected glow.

Unaware of the gains made by the clear-cut inter-American liaison that their entire generation had already achieved in science, in publishing, in the book trade, in ethnology, and even in history, Washington Irving and William Prescott stood with their individuality. They gave the bounds for colonial Latin American history, which, in turn, they had inherited from the great Spanish chroniclers and historians. The three hundred years of Latin American life were left blank, with their universities, internal and frontier expansion, religious growth, commercial expansion, and city life. The history of interest in these additional aspects of Latin America, as well as the desire to do something in an inter-American structure, had to await others who would add their chapters to the Post-Conquest. Building upon the accumulated assets of learned societies, the energies of book publishing, libraries, and the free association of individuals, the study of the history of the Western Hemisphere rose to new floors, holding together the community of minds. The cultural process was also at work here, even though, once again, most actions were free, independent, separate, and unconnected. These individual steps had clear cultural meaning for historians. History was made.

Notwithstanding the rich material on the Indies, there was still little on the subject of the Laws of the Indies in 1800, in spite of books. The Laws of the Indies, the royal rules for Spanish Empire in America, had little or no appeal for North Americans. Most shelf titles covered literature, history, ethnology, and natural science. The close nineteenth-century connection between politics and legal institutions did not altogether remove history from its cultural partnership with philosophy and letters. Interest in Spanish laws, and the ruling principles of Indies colonial government, were dimmed by the personal accomplishments of amazing explorers, discoverers, and conquerors. Even the great viceroys, as personalities, loomed larger than impersonal laws. Inter-American commercial profits, and United States trade later on, did reveal the need for knowledge of the Spanish navigation and commercial laws, but it was not until 1802, when the Louisiana Territory was purchased, that North American attention was directed at Spanish laws of land and real estate. James Workman of New Orleans wrote a book on the Laws of the Indies to explain the background of Spanish influence and legacy in North America.[3]

The land and government problems of the Louisiana Purchase, even more than the attractive, extralegal trade with South America, gave North Americans a new experience with Spanish land law, mining rights, water rights, town settlements, and Indian relations. Workman's book on the Spanish laws in America should have had many readers. There was a lot to learn about Spanish law. James Workman was an Englishman by birth. He had plans for himself in Latin America before he came to the New World and the young United States. He was part of the generation of Englishmen at that time (1800-25) who had hopes and dreams of profitable penetration of the Spanish Empire. He was one of those who had proposed and written about the migration of Englishmen to Argentina. He was probably not associated with Francisco de Miranda. Workman had left London for Louisiana before the wave of optimism which was released by the British invasions of Buenos Aires and Montevideo (1806-7). In Louisiana, Workman rose to be Judge of the Territorial Probate Court at New Orleans (1807), in a region almost intense with propaganda activity and plans affecting the Spanish borderlands of West Florida, Texas, Cuba, and even Mexico.

Workman rose quickly. He was associated with Edward Livingston in the codification of Spanish and French laws in Louisiana. How he came to write on the Spanish laws in the Indies is not known. He drew some inter-American prestige from his connection with Livingston—years later—when the government of Guatemala requested copies of their code as a guide for the organization of that nation. All that is available is Workman's prospectus, since he never completed the work. There, he wrote that he proposed to translate into book form the Laws of the Indies and the principles of Castilian jurisprudence, thus providing the legal and political framework which affected Southwestern property and possessions.

His book was to be published in New York, although it was written in New Orleans. His publisher was I. Riley, already noted for several books on Latin American history which appeared under his imprint. Workman's prospectus was widely circulated and aroused evident interest, especially in those Middle Atlantic places, such as Philadelphia and New York, which were already known for their devotion to inter-American and Hispanic sympathies. For example, in Philadelphia, the literary magazine *Port Folio* welcomed Workman's idea for the book as providing "a close connexion and extensive intercourse which at no distant period we are likely to carry on with the Spanish Provinces. . . . " These are almost the same words which Dr. Samuel Mitchill used to greet another book on Latin America. Apparently interest and expectation ran as high in the promise of cultural relations as they did in the affairs of state and commerce. Certainly the level of North American opinion, so sympathetic in general to new-born Latin America, was ready for such a book. Even a History of the Americas, which we credit to historians of the twentieth century, was already announced: Edward Everett's prospectus of 1817 for a hemisphere history included the history of Spanish America as well as of English and French America. Everett, then editor of the *North American Review*, had far more influence than the editor of *Port Folio*. But Workman's book did not appear at all in spite of the welcome given to his prospectus, although other books on or about Latin America were then receiving enough subscriptions in advance to justify being printed. All we can now say is that James Workman adds another obscure name and one phantom contribution to the roll of inter-American activity.

Up to this time almost all the literature of history, and other books about Latin America then existing in the United States, were translations. Most of them were from Spanish originals, a few from French, an occasional one from Portuguese. This held true almost to the time of William H. Prescott, and James Workman was no exception. His project did not pretend to be original, consisting chiefly of translations from the printed Laws of the Indies, commentaries, and other adjuncts. During the changing generation from 1810 to 1830, several journalistic accounts of Latin America were printed, much spiced with propaganda, and hardly deserving the name history. These books supplied news and information of passing events. They gave little or no background or history from which to understand current events. Not until after Latin American Independence was gained, between 1822 and 1825, did any semisolid books appear. These are sound to the degree that they were written by North American observers who had at least lived for years in Latin America. They did not attempt to be scholarly, philosophical, or thorough. The best-known were those written by Joel R. Poinsett (1822) and by Brantz Mayer (1844), two North Americans who combined both knowledge and long residence.[4]

Brantz Mayer and Joel Poinsett were the leading writers of the "Prescott Era" to bring Latin American history up to contemporary times. Competing with the epics of Discovery and Conquest narrated by Irving and Prescott was hard; Mayer and Poinsett took an even harder path: explaining the Latin America of their own day. Even today few emerge unscratched from this experience. They did not stop here. Although both were North American diplomats, neither cared to write about laws or institutions. Mayer, we have seen, was historian and archaeologist. Unlike Prescott, the two made efforts to help the separate, but related, cause of inter-American cultural relations by their active work in the societies where they were members. While Poinsett's political reputation derived from his services to the Latin American policy of the United States during several diplomatic missions, he had a more scholarly side. Poinsett gave the American Philosophical Society at Philadelphia several manuscripts on Latin American history and other papers of a bibliographical, scientific, and historical nature.

For the North American public, Joel Poinsett published in 1822 a book which he called *Notes on Mexico*, which preceded by many years the books of Brantz Mayer and William H. Prescott on Mexico. For our present purpose, the chief virtues of his book are that they give an idea of Mexico in Poinsett's day as well as Cortes'. The same can be said about Brantz Mayer. Mayer lived in Mexico even longer than Poinsett. Born in 1809, Mayer's feeling for Mexican history matured after 1841, when he joined the United States Legation in Mexico as secretary. His historical articles and publications are plentiful. His books included *Mexico as it was and is* (1844), *Mexico: Aztec, Spanish, Republican* (1851), *Observations on Mexican History and Archaeology* (1857), *Outline of Mexican Antiquities* (1858).

It is in his history of the "white man's period" (of colonial and early modern Mexico) that Mayer tried to lengthen the chronology of Mexican history, bringing it down to his generation. Brantz Mayer appreciated that Prescott had done all that then could be done on the Conquest. Mayer declared that he was leaving the first century of New Spain's history to Solís, Robertson, and Prescott, "the classic historians of Spain, England, and America." Judged from any modern critique, Mayer's history is faulty in structure and content. Successions of brief and dull recitation, as in a medieval chronicle of bare events, substitute for narrative. Still, it is an outline (not a story) which covers the whole three centuries of Mexican history, and not the handful or less of brilliant military years. In Mayer's history, the Conquest of the Aztecs is deliberately reduced by the larger time perspective and longer sequence of events. His reign-by-reign summary of the many Viceroys carried Mayer over the entire political span of Mexican historical evolution; only 83 pages of the first volume deal with Cortés and the Conquest.

Unlike the contemporary description, *Life in Mexico*, written by Madame Calderón de la Barca, the friend of Prescott, wife of the Spanish ambassador, and a New Englander by birth, Mayer's several books em-

braced Mexican economy, geography, resources and mines, state organization, agricultural production, and recent political history. While
Fanny Calderón's book was, and still is, widely popular because of its
humanity and insights, Mayer gave factual information and a view of
the social and historical picture behind quaint Mexican customs and
respected creole traditions. Being a historian, Mayer worked from his
own books as well as his own field observations. In fact, both Mayer's
library and his published books provide another index to his knowledge
about Latin American history. His library, publications, and experience
were outstanding.

As a matter of fact, the early writings on Latin American history in
the United States follow closely the growth of intelligent collections
of the nineteenth century. Prescott seems to have been the major exception: he was able to get materials sent to him from Spain. While
Brantz Mayer's library on Latin America and Mexico does not compare
with the contemporary ones of Obadiah Rich, Henry Harrisse, John
Carter Brown, and Hubert H. Bancroft, which became publicly used
collections, Mayer's was a private library for his own use. Like Buckingham Smith, another North American historian of Latin America, Mayer
used his books for his historical writing. His library was broken up and
sold after his death. His was not a great collection, but after it was sold
it provided North Americans with such Mexican historians as Andrés
Cavo, Carlos Maria Bustamante, Lucas Alamán, León y Gama, Lerdo
de Tejada, Prescott, Poinsett, Zavala, and many others.[5] The Latin
American library collections were closely connected with the successful
rise of historical studies and narratives. Even if, after 1900, North
Americans went more and more frequently to Spain and Latin America
for archival research, the libraries continued to fulfill the promise of the
eighteenth century that books would be a major ally of Latin American history. In connection with Brantz Mayer, it is interesting not only
to see him as a historian and collector of books but also to recall that
years later when he had settled in San Francisco, he supported Hubert
H. Bancroft's efforts to get the famous Bancroft histories favorably reviewed and received in the Middle Atlantic cities and New England,
where he (Mayer) had many friends.

The study or writing of Latin American history was not necessarily
the same as promoting cultural relations. It can therefore be said that
Mayer, although he lived in Mexico, did almost as little as Prescott, in
Boston, to organize permanent friendships, arrange exchanges, or institute nominations to membership in historical societies. Neither his-

torian used the personal touch for institutional ties. For some reason they did not move in waters stirred by the societies, and as individuals, remained outside the main currents of inter-American thought. Prescott, it is true, had some personal and intellectual correspondence with the Mexican historians Lucas Alamán and José Ramírez (mainly in connection with the translation of his *Conquest of Mexico*). Mayer and Prescott are remembered for their books not their efforts. Fortunately, no individual nor any amount of individualism could stop the inter-American historical process. Others appeared to help the societies attain the necessary cooperation. Among these are Buckingham Smith, Jared Sparks, historian and president of Harvard College, and Francis Hawks of New York.

As we have seen, Francis Hawks was more the patron of Latin American studies than a worker in the historical field. Yet he did a good deal for the subject. Hawks was at the head of strategic learned societies, located in New York. He had an evident lifelong affection for Spanish letters. His own library and Hispanic books showed this. For all his interest and his journey to Spain, he wrote no literary or historical work on Spain or Latin America. Neither Jared Sparks nor Francis Hawks contributed to Latin American history as historians or authors, but they did give help and encouragement to historians. Hawks was a cultivated man, with an affinity and sympathy for Spain and Spain-in-America which surely place him among the unsung pantheon of Hispanists and Latin Americanists of the nineteenth century. His lengthy library catalogued Spanish, Portuguese, and Latin American poets, dramatists, and histories. Francis Hawks may be presented as a silent companion of Washington Irving, Brantz Mayer, William Prescott, George Ticknor, Buckingham Smith, William Maclure, Samuel L. Mitchill, *Port Folio,* the *North American Review,* and the predecessor of so many others. He had enough room left in his spirit for Latin American ethnology and geography.

But it is not as a book man that we return to Dr. Hawks. His best activity, where inter-American relations are concerned, was his support of Buckingham Smith. Hawks did for Smith what he did not do for Benjamin Moore Norman, in the latter's Maya finds. Hawks supported John Russell Bartlett's aims for Latin American ethnology; he also aided Buckingham Smith to extend inter-American cultural cooperation among historians. Hawks was even more the patron of the arts than he was a bibliophile. He joined his efforts with those of the New-York Historical Society to promote history in the hemisphere. In history, as in natural science, ethnology, and the book trade, the sense of inter-American community took hold.

Buckingham Smith, more studious and creative than his friend Francis Hawks, blended an interest in the Spanish borderland of North America, the history of Old Spain, the literature of the Indies, and his specialized pleasure at historical ties among historians.[6] A native of formerly Spanish Florida and a New Yorker by adoption, Buckingham Smith, down to his untimely and accidental death in 1871, possessed an inquiring, research mind for the history of Spain in America.[7] At the same time he kept his eye on an expanded role for the New-York Historical Society, bringing into membership Spanish peninsular historians as well as Latin Americans. He made that Society considerably more inter-American in its connections. Having humanistic tastes, Smith included literature and adventure in his history, and, in keeping with the best spirit of the day, he could combine ethnology, history, and geography in his Latin American studies. Like Brantz Mayer and William Prescott, Buckingham Smith wrote history for the public and the scholarly. Like Brantz Mayer, Smith had also served in the United States Legation in Mexico. Unlike Mayer and Prescott, Smith made it his fundamental business to study and use historical archives in Old Spain. He was interested in early, sixteenth-century history.

Some of Smith's feeling for the Hispanic came to him from his family. His father, Josiah Smith, was the first North American to visit and describe Mexico during the critical years of Mexican independence.[8] It is revealing to digress here for a moment, to show how personal ties of friendship and helpfulness are helped by a historic force making contact with receptive human beings. Josiah Smith set down his narrative of Mexico in the years 1815 and 1816. In this manuscript, which has not yet been published, the elder Smith awakened the memory of an earlier atmosphere. He refers to the guidance and aid given him in the city of Puebla by the Intendant, Francisco Rendón, "who speaks English [and who] resided in Philadelphia in 1777." Through this courtesy, Rendón, who had warm memories of patriotic men and women friends of the American Revolution, recalled the days of the Continental Congress. Josiah Smith was given every courtesy, and visited the textile and glass factories of Puebla—still famous—for whose craftsmanship he expressed great admiration, as he did for Mexico in general. Buckingham Smith experienced this friendly feeling for Mexico, and behind that, for Old Spain.

His father returned to Mexico in 1824 as the North American consul, where the son lived with him. At his father's death in 1825, Buckingham Smith returned to the United States for upbringing and education, which included Harvard College. He did not go back to Mexico until 1851, when he was named secretary of the Legation there, some years after Brantz Mayer. He did very well in the routine of his office but, in addition, unofficially, went out of his way to energize and stimulate the liaison between Mexican and North American science and scholarship. He gave much time and effort to intellectual cooperation, acting as his own clearing house and agent. In fact, Buckingham Smith was a cultural relations attaché, a century before that office existed.

For one example, he sent up to the United States large numbers of books and documents about Mexican history for the order and use of Peter Force, the noted historian and collector. Force, who collected the tracts on the American Revolution, was also becoming interested in Mexican history at the time. In July, 1851, writing to Force, who was then in Washington, Smith told him he had shipped the historical works of the contemporary Mexican Carlos Maria Bustamante, "to the extent I have been able to collect them."[9] For Smith, this was no isolated incident, but a regular part of his inter-American work. All that summer he supplied Peter Force with cases of books and documents on Mexican history, although Smith complained more than once that Force was too lax in acknowledging the safe arrival in the United States of irreplaceable volumes and manuscripts.

Smith rendered valuable service for the newly-founded Sociedad Mexicana de Geografía y Estadística, winning friends and arranging cultural exchanges when most Mexicans had bitter memories of the Mexican War and the North American gains. Smith managed to tie his legation duties to the politically neutral and culturally partisan work of intellectual relations. He steered his position and purpose to make the exchange of publications easier, which meant that here he was acting outside the government and in a private capacity, for the profit of knowledge, for a learned society, and for himself. He arranged with the North American archaeologist Ephraim Squier to present the latter's treatise to the Sociedad Mexicana, and for the Sociedad, in exchange, to send its publications to Squier. Smith sent books to George Gibbs at the Smithsonian Institution and to the New-York Historical Society. He was so eager to add to cultural relations that he even suggested the use of the consular staff to facilitate the shipment of books through Veracruz. In 1852, when Smith was elected to membership in the Mexican Geographical Society, he at once arranged for that Society to obtain

copies of the works of Squier, Schoolcraft, the reports of General Fré-
mont, and—what attests the progress of inter-American exchanges—
the famous historical collection of Peter Force on the American Revolution. It is possible that Smith already had great aims for cultural
connections even before he went to Mexico. In this individual way he
supplemented the activity of the societies.

He knew his work and worth in this respect, and since it was not accidental, he was justly proud. The Mexican government gave him
distinct recognition for his services in promoting relations between the
Smithsonian Institution and Mexican scientific groups. Smith himself
referred to this in a letter which he sent to Spencer Baird, then assistant
secretary of the Smithsonian under Joseph Henry. Smith told Baird
about the particular praise which the Mexican Secretary for Foreign
Relations had given him. He added, "I deem it not a little thing that in
the depths of his business he had found time to write to me himself an
earnest of the interest he takes in American history and archaeology, in
which he stands eminent in this country."

Unruffled by Manifest Destiny, annexationism, and other dangers
to hemisphere good will, inter-American cultural life went on. How
much in contrast with the silent creation of scholars and societies was
the war cry of the expansionists! Yet both are parts of the North American spirit. Manifest Destiny and cultural relations are children of the
same parent. They are twin psychologies. Fortunately, they are not
identical and show a different face to the Latin American observer.
Those were years of Mexican War, Manifest Destiny, William Walker
and the filibusters in Central America, Ostend Manifesto, early Cuban
crisis, and other North American expressions of aggression toward Latin
America. Confronting these tendencies was the figure of friendship,
organizing a community of scholars, based upon reason, history, and
the fellowship of study. In that day the appreciation of Latin America
had little influence upon North American government policy or people.
Nevertheless, the future structure, so energetically sought and cultivated
in the twentieth century, rested upon the hard rock of history; cultural
relations solidified precedent upon precedent. In that immediate present,
however, "popular" opinion and pressure forces governed events. Conflict, and the haste to expand, blinded the people of the Southwest and
the politicos of the country from seeing what fine work was being done
by the Middle Atlantic and New England regions.

Buckingham Smith, in addition to what has been said, also had the
driving intellectual aim of making the southern states, from Texas to

Florida, conscious and friendly to the Spanish influence in their original
settlement and later history. He ran into sharp hostility towards this
part of his work. It made no difference that Smith himself had southern,
Florida origins. The vigorous old Elizabethan and "leyenda negra" conception of Spain, Mexicans, and those of Hispanic race was very alive
in these southern states, as if it were more intense in order to cover up
their basic Spanish background. In a letter to Buckingham Smith from
one J. W. Phelps of Brownsville, Texas, dated June 20, 1854, the writer
described to Smith the nature of President Fillmore's speeches in his
tour of the Southwest and the President's statements on the theme of
Manifest Destiny. Here is the attitude of a Texan, whose state had
gained what it wanted, but opposed more Manifest Destiny for others.
Phelps condemned "lawless filibustering attacks upon Hispanic America.
We have among us already more foreign elements than can be properly
assimilated or Americanized; but of all the ingredients to enter our body
politic we should dread those of Hispanic America the most. Every
morsel of it that in our gluttonous cupidity we swallow down will prove
an indigestible mass that may end in fever, change of constitution,
emasculation, and death."[10]

None of this disturbed Smith. Nor did it interfere with his determined historicism to make the American South conscious of its American Spanish start. He worked, and succeeded in getting some state
historical societies to enlarge their perspective. As we will see shortly,
Smith was one of our earliest North American historians to be aware
of the rich contribution of Spain and Spanish America to North American history. He preceded the Californian Hubert H. Bancroft in the
task of appreciating the work of Spain. He had real success here. At least
one influential member of the Georgia Historical Society was willing to
admit to him that, in 1854, Georgia was more deficient in memories, accounts, and records of her Spanish period than any other southern state.
He had much less trouble with Florida history. His own research, following his history of the remarkable travels of Cabeza de Vaca through
most of these southern states, certainly helped convince him how deep
were the layers of Spanish history and influence there. But Smith's interest in what became called the "Spanish Borderlands" never matched
the romantic appeal and the dramatic literary quality which William
H. Prescott gave to Spain in Latin America and which Francis Parkman
won for France in North America.

His published work on aspects of Latin American history is less
pertinent here than his unpublished project. One of his most worth-while

ideas was his plan to assemble original documents in a broad perspective of American history, intended to include the formerly Spanish territories in the United States. The idea was to publish original documents, chiefly in Spanish, dealing with the Spanish conquest, colonization, and settlement of the "borderlands." Fully a generation before Hubert H. Bancroft did the same thing, Smith excited the interest of North American historians, scholars, and historical societies. Had Smith lived long enough to convince North Americans of the valuable Spanish content of American history, or had he been wealthy enough to buy his source materials from all over, or were he as publishing-wise as Bancroft, Buckingham Smith might have gained the fame which slipped through his fingers. Bancroft had drive, money, and manpower; Smith had none of them. Smith did have the library resources in his vicinity—the fruits of research in Spain and residence in Mexico. As a historian of Latin America he is secondary to Prescott; as the historical editor of original Spanish documents he paved the way for Bancroft.

Yet he did have advantages. He had the support of Francis Parkman, George Bancroft, Dr. Francis Hawks, George Folsom, Jared Sparks, and an impressive initial list of leading individual and institutional subscribers, including the great William H. Prescott. These historians welcomed Smith's project which was "proposed to publish a contribution to the Documentary History of that part of the United States once under Spanish domination. The work will be issued in numbers of about 40 pages each, and will probably embrace about 16 of these numbers, making a volume of not less than 500 pages."[11] Some of the mighty names of North American historical writing and historical patronage lay behind it and supported the plan. The Californian worked hard to gain the backing which came easily for the Floridian. The influence of both the historical society and the great names probably explains why. The proposed "Documentary History" had large vision and would have worked out the History of the Americas idea. From internal evidence the public announcement and prospectus appears to date at 1850, or before Smith took up government assignment in Mexico.

A vast new territory of Spanish history, speech, and customs was now permanently part of the United States, and a few North American scholars were interested in that fact. New England, New York, and Pennsylvania had at least a century of historical experience in things Hispanic. Their scholars, libraries, and institutions supported Smith's grand design. The foremost figures of historical scholarship agreed with Smith's conception of American history. William Prescott was still alive and he ordered four copies; Jared Sparks ơ. Harvard College also took four; George Bancroft, the historian, took ten copies. A good deal of institutional support came from Boston and New York. The New-York Historical Society, where Smith was closely connected, endorsed and patronized his project. Francis Parkman wrote to George Moore of the New-York Historical Society to say that Boston would also support Smith's "Documentary History." But there was a strange lack of backing at Philadelphia, considering that city's strong record of Hispanic activity and interest.

In fact, the failure of Smith's entire *Documentary History* was both puzzling and regrettable. All that came of it was a first volume, obviously important for what was in it but pregnant with the promise of what was to be. The stillborn plans, however, reveal a broad historical spirit, providing for maps, diaries, documents, logs, chronicles, and histories. Nevertheless, dealing with what we have, this one volume helped rescue Smith's whole idea from oblivion, and it proved historically the existence of Spanish North America. Smith edited the first volume (in Spanish) which he called *Colección de Varios Documentos para la Historia de Florida y Tierras Adjacientes*. Actually, we will see that it included more than Florida, taking in Spanish Louisiana and Spanish California. Fortunately, Smith was then beginning his career. He calmed his disappointment at failure by going into history, into Mexico, and into research. But the chief mourner was Francis Parkman, who pleaded for more subscriptions, writing to George Moore of the New-York Historical Society, "Can't you get a few more? The thing ought to go on. It would be scandalous if it failed for want of encouragement. I hope to get 50 copies engaged in Boston. New York is able to do a great deal better if she will."[12] To no avail. His project died and from the ashes arose that phoenix of Hispanic historiography in the United States, Hubert Howe Bancroft, patron and founder of California's famous Bancroft Library.

Scholarly inter-American historical writing was evidently still on a high level, too high apparently for public interest and unattractive in output for readers in regions of Hispanic origin. Smith paid a high price for the individuality of North American historical societies who might have been interested but who could not get together. It may have been from this experience that he determined to get southern historical societies to cultivate more Spanish history. Or, perhaps, his theme of the Spanish in North America was too hybrid, too *mestizo*: not Castilian Spanish, only remotely Latin American, and possibly too new to be North American.

However, before apathy veiled Smith's *Documentary History* from later historians, a small but tantalizing part did see light in time to stir greater interest. What there was, was good, because Smith used original Spanish, and in manuscript. The three documents with which be began the project dealt with:

1. California. 1541.
   Instrucción que debía conservar el Capitán Hernando de Alarcón en la Expedición á la California que iba a emprender al Orden del virey D. Antonio de Mendoza.
   [El original en la Biblioteca Escurialense. . . . Copia sacada por el señor D. José Amador de los Ríos.]
2. Luisiana y Florida Occidental. 1794.
   Oficio del Baron de Carondelet, gobernador etc al Duque de la Alcudia, manifestando el estado de aquellas provincias y las dificultades que á su Tranquilidad suscitaban los ingleses y los de Estados Unidos.
   [Del original que posee el Sr. Pascual de Gayangos.]
3. Indios. 1516-1518.
   Papel sobre los abusos que se cometían en las Indias, en contravencion de las ordenanzas que para su Gobierno hizo el Rey Catholico.
   [Copia en la Colección Muñoz en la Real Academia de la Historia. Tomo LXXVI.]

As the first volume slipped into the archives and among the forgotten forerunners of Latin American history, Smith moved away from the project, taking up the narrative of Cabeza de Vaca, the intrepid traveller of the Southwest. When he finished with this and the Legation in Mexico, Spain beckoned. In 1856, aided by another government assignment, this time to the Legation in Madrid, Smith could again study, write, comprehend, and correspond. He enjoyed, on the spot, opportunities at Seville, Simancas, Madrid—even France—needing none of the intermediary readers, clerks, and research aides who carried the best fruits of the Iberian archives to William Prescott. Smith could indulge his historical sense in the archives. There, he filled himself to the brim with the wealth of materials, the memoirs, chronicles, reports, and documents, loading his notes with copies of the Spanish originals. A vast number of Indies historians, diarists, explorers, and chroniclers thus passed over into the pages of his diary, note, letter, and copy books. Later on, in his second stay in Spain, in 1868, he again copied large portions of Torquemada, Oviedo, especially the *Cronica de las Indias,* and the *Historia*

General. The Archivo de Simancas, the Columbian Library in Seville, even the venerable Torre do Tombo archives in Lisbon saw him frequently.

Historian and Hispanist, Smith's equally lasting work was the creation of cultural ties with the Spanish-speaking world. This is where he differs from so many of the other North Americans who were also studying or writing about Hispanic things, who overshadowed him, and whom he never met.[13] The Spanish Empire in America was indeed a huge terrain for Smith and Prescott to have lost each other on their separate ways. Even in Spain Smith was a different student, combining his love for history with ethnology and the study of New World Indian languages. His connection with the Smithsonian, as we have seen, accomplished what he wanted in that field. He also brought into corresponding membership several outstanding Spanish and Latin American historians, one of whom was a close friend and companion in Iberian research: José Fernando Ramírez, the Mexican historian.

In another instance Smith wrote from Madrid (1855) to George H. Moore, secretary of the New-York Historical Society:

I wish you w^d have José Amador de los Ríos made Honorary Member of the New-York Historical Society. He is the learned editor of the recent edition of Oviedo [Gonzalo Hernandez de Oviedo y Valdés, *Historia General y Natural de las Indias.* Madrid: 1851-1856, 4 vols.] and the author of several works of merit besides. Send the diploma to me. . . . I am having a fine time among the MSS. Mr. Ramirez is in France, and I expect him here shortly, when we shall have a grand hunt together.[14]

And so it was. The "grand hunt" into the Spanish archives brought its rewards. He never stopped nominating or recommending Spaniards and Latin Americans to the New-York Historical Society. He urged the Society to arrange exchanges with Spain's Real Academia de la Historia, in connection with material on Verrazzano. His insistence upon inter-American cultural relations and the exchange of correspondence among historians again singles out the great difference from Prescott, Ticknor, Longfellow, and Irving. In this respect he was more like William Maclure and Sam Mitchill: he did things. A little more luck, and a little longer life, and he would have promoted a historian's guild in Hispanic studies. In 1865 he wrote to his *simpático,* George Moore, nominating the scientist-historian Andrés Poey. Poey, already a member of the American Ethnological Society and the Lyceum of Natural History of New York, was both historian and antiquarian in addition to his scientific pursuits. Smith recommended him warmly because Poey was "given to reading old things as much as I am."

His tone was not always that gentle. Smith had the booklover's touchiness at the dreaded loss of a valued book. In his brief professional acquaintance with a fellow bibliographer, Henry Harrisse, then working on his life of Columbus, Smith struck a sour note, which made him appear all the more lifelike. Smith had, as usual, ordered for the New-York Historical Society Library a number of Spanish American books which Harrisse was to deliver. One book was missing—Bernaldez' useful history of Ferdinand and Isabella. Smith then rebuked Harrisse, who replied:

N. Y. University
October 12, 1865

Dr Sir:

Allow me to say in reply to yr letter of this day just received that when you first wrote me in regard to Bernaldez, I immediately brought the book myself properly packed up and directed to the [New-York] Historical Society, and remitted it myself to the Librarian in charge, according to yr instructions.

With deep regrets, I remain Dr. Sir,
Yr obedt servt.
Henry Harrisse

Some of Smith's other correspondence had still another flavor. He had the opportunity, more than any other nineteenth-century North American historian, to know personally and professionally the most eminent Mexican historians of the day, José F. Ramírez, Joaquín Icazbalceta, and Francisco Pimentel. Icazbalceta was a most erudite historian, and Smith turned to him for advice and research assistance in history. Just before his accidental death, Smith received a letter which illuminates the common interest in early Mexican history which he shared with Icazbalceta:

Mexico, September 3, 1870

Señor don B. Smith,
New York.
My Dear Sir:

I am ashamed of my delay in replying to your letter of August a year ago, which came together with valuable notes which I will use in a new edition of "Apuntes," but I do not know how my duties will allow me to carry that out. I trust in your indulgence to forgive my slowness, which I excuse for reasons of overwork, and grave family misfortunes which I suffered after that letter arrived.

Unfortunately I did not nor do I have any data which might be useful to you for your English edition of the "Naufragios" of Cabeza de Vaca, because you have made use of everything. Nor is it yet possible to obtain here any autograph of such early missionaries as Fr. Juan Xuarez and Fr. Juan de Palos: documents of this sort went out of the country some time back, and if any were left they disappeared in the destruction of the monasteries in 1861. We have nothing left!

Some months ago I published the *Historia Eclesiastica Indiana* of F. Gerónimo de Mendieta, in a volume equal (but thicker) to those in the *Coleccion de Documentos* (which I suppose you to have received). I have a copy for you, which I was to send with others but the loss of a letter held up the shipment. I will take care of that soon. Please accept a copy and give it a place among your books.

Joaqn García Ycazbalceta[15]

Possibly the pace and level of inter-American relations could have continued at its own historical momentum without such dedicated individuals as Buckingham Smith, but that is unlikely. True, we have seen how societies, institutions, colonial libraries, and nineteenth-century collections—Rich, Prescott, Ticknor, Irving, Maclure, Hawks, Smith, Stevens, Harrisse, Bartlett, Force, Mayer, Brown, Astor, Bancroft, and others[16]—the inter-American book trade, and Latin American studies wove the hemisphere web before and after Buckingham Smith came on the scene. Nevertheless, Smith, resembling Mitchill before him, personalized and animated these relations. Individuals like Buckingham Smith gave life to these historic processes, which went on much as they had before, and left a clear pattern for individuals in the next generation to follow—if they had been aware of it. Since so many societies and men began to take increased part in the growth of inter-American communications, one thing at least is clear: Smith practically led one supposedly "local" body—the New-York Historical Society—out into the wider hemisphere connection with Latin America and along the transatlantic cultural cables to Old Spain.

Before 1890 the New-York Historical Society, like the others, learned to open its memberships to Latin Americans, Spaniards, and Portuguese of distinction and repute. On the rolls were Latin American historians from Brazil, Venezuela, Mexico (including Yucatan), Cuba, San Salvador, Guatemala, Ecuador, Peru, and from the homelands of Latin

American history: Spain a nd Portugal. The Society's library also gained in the usual results, grov/ing rapidly with gifts and donations from friendly Hispanists, such as Hawks and Smith, and from the correspondents. With hands outstretched to Spain and Spanish historians the New York Society rejected the *leyenda negra* towards Spain, while it helped to write an enlarged concept of the hemisphere mind towards the larger American history idea. The inter-American list mirrored the living writers of that history. The archives of the New-York Historical Society show how far pilots, such as Mitchill, Bartlett, Ludewig, Gibbs, Hawks, and Smith, had steered that Society's inter-American work: [17]

Vicente Pazos	Ecuador		1819	
Mariano Arista	Mexico		1842	(?)
Tomas Carrillo	"	[Yucatan]	1843	
Juan Pío Perez	"	"	1843	
Alonso Manuel Peon	"	"	1847	
Francisco de Arrangoiz	"		1850	
José F. Ramírez	Mexico		1854	(1863?)
Miguel Lerdo de Tejada	"		1856	
Eugenio M. Aguirre	"		1863	
Francisco Pimentel	"		1863	
José Ramón Pacheco	"		1863	
Antonio Bachiller y Morales	Cuba		1847	
José Silverio Joirin (?)	"		1884	
José Barrundía	San Salvador		1850	
Miguel A. Carreño	Venezuela		1855	
Juan de la C. Carreño	"		1855	
Vicente Coronado	"		1890	
Jacinto Pactiano	"		1890	
José García y García	Colombia (Peru?)		1866	
Joseph Bento	Brazil		1849	
Emperor Pedro II	"		1856	
Dr. Pacheco da Silva	"		1856	

The Appendix completes the list of these members, but several Iberian historians, not included in the foregoing list, were Martín Fernandez de Navï rrete (1844), outstanding historian of the maritime expansion of Spain and the friendly correspondent of William H. Prescott. Nominated by Buckingham Smith was José Amador de los Ríos (1856). From Portugal came two distinguished historians, Alexandre Herculano and Jose Maria Casal Ribeiro. Other Spanish members were César Fernández Duro, historian of the Spanish navy (1884), Jayme Salvá, noted Catalan bibliographer, and the Conde de Tureno, historian of the Spanish constitutional convention of Cadiz (1811). The eighteenth-century action of the Real Academia de la Historia, in choosing Benjamin Franklin as the first of its many North American corresponding members, was now fully reciprocated.

Moreover, this was one way in which the proposal of John Russell Bartlett and Herman Ludewig, acting for the New-York Historical Society (and North American historians) in 1846, might have brought Latin American historians together without any such formal congress. Of course, had all these individual members ever been able to meet, it surely would have been a distinguished congress. But we know how individualist these constituents of the inter-American community really were. They contributed to wide perspective, to be sure, but functioned entirely within their own locality and nation. The failure of that congress was the very strength which brought it into existence as a proposal. Each society and each individual historian went a separate way, energized from within with a sense of cultural *laisser-faire,* unconcerned with outside, collective efforts. This individualism and unilateralism of the nineteenth century pervade the text of the letter urging that historical congress.

Since the idea for a congress originated in an invitation to Brazilian historians, it is pertinent to examine United States-Brazilian cultural relations at this time. History provided no individual counterpart in Brazil to match Charles Hartt in stature. In history, relations between the United States and Brazil developed from institutional and societal actions, in the absence of personal go-betweens. Nevertheless, Portuguese America learned to look northward to the United States just as Spanish America did, and Brazil fitted into the whole, hemispheric account of history, its study and bibliography. The Brazilian Instituto Historico e Geographico, founded in 1837, began almost at once to tie the strands of cooperation together. By 1840 the Instituto had already—on its own —chosen two models of North American cultural life as members. One of these was Washington Irving, "autor bem conhecido e membro de varias sociedades scientificas"; the other was the Harvard historian Jared Sparks, "autor da Vida de Washington, de Franklin, e de varias outras obras."[18] These appointments were made several years before Bartlett and Ludewig rediscovered Brazilian history and ethnology.

Some may think the Brazilian honor small, since both Irving and Sparks had won recognition from leading North American and European intellectual circles, but the fact also is that Irving and Sparks considered this nomination as a distinctive honor. Irving accepted his diploma of membership in a letter which he sent out promptly. Jared Sparks answered in less than two weeks after he had received the nomination, telling of his appreciation and pleasure at the honor accorded him. Sparks went further. He sent to Brazil, for the library of the Instituto, copies of those books which he had published on the history of the United States, joining willingly in the pattern of exchanges and gifts, which made members repay the societies and institutions which named them.

In the early days, one of the most active persons in inter-American exchanges on the Brazilian side was Jose Silvestre Rebello, formerly the first minister of the independent Brazilian Empire to the United States, and later, chairman of the Instituto's Committee on geography. Rebello was also the Brazilian corresponding member of the American Philosophical Society, and he regularly turned over to the Instituto his copies of the proceedings of the Philosophical Society. Rebello was probably one of the prime movers in initiating and consolidating the ties between the Historical Society of Pennsylvania and the Brazilian Instituto. Actually the Historical Society of Pennsylvania awakened to the literary and scholarly existence of Brazilian culture before the New-York Historical Society did. In 1841 the Pennsylvania Society undertook to send its publications, and in that year the Brazilian Instituto Historico acknowledged that it had received "a letter from Philadelphia by the Historical Society of Pennsylvania, which offered to the Library of the Institute the complete collection of its Memoirs up to the year 1840."[19] Although there was no Buckingham Smith or William Prescott in Brazil-American relations and history, there was considerable cultural acquaintance. The Brazilian society gladly accepted reciprocal exchange with the Philadelphia historical society, as it had with New York and other historical societies. The result was a regular exchange of historical materials and their flow from Philadelphia to Rio de Janeiro, to the Instituto. The Brazilian Instituto, very pleased at the idea of cooperation, quietly announced this memorable association of two historical societies in the Americas with these words: "The Historical Society of Pennsylvania has accepted the invitation of the Instituto for a mutual correspondence, and has given us a collection of memoirs." In addition to this now-established mode of institutional bond we can also recognize another familiar phase: the nomination of members. The Brazilian Instituto Historico chose many more North Americans as corresponding members in addition to Sparks and Irving. Among them were the leading writers of history, including William H. Prescott, Edward Everett, George Bancroft (1864), George Ticknor, and friends of history in the historical societies, such as Robert C. Winthrop of the Massachusetts Historical Society and Luther Bradish of the New-York Historical Society.[20]

From New York, Philadelphia, and Boston arose strong impulses for cooperation which charged the New World with cultural energy. There were innumerable instances, too many to be included here, when Latin Americans, very much aware of the real sincerity of the cultural feeling towards them, looked upon North Americans as partners in science and knowledge. What Brazilians did, so did Mexicans. Guatemalans not only sought to be better known in the United States by working with Philadelphia's American Philosophical Society; they did the same with New York societies. In 1834, for example, Juan Galindo, the able Guatemalan historian, archaeologist, and ethnologist, found the same type of scholarly association with the New York Literary and Philosophical Society that he was to get from the American Philosophical Society in 1840. Galindo was already a corresponding member of the Massachusetts Historical Society (1836). Although not a member of the New-York Historical Society—their records may, however, not be complete—he must have given them some valuable works on Latin America, since many titles in its library carry the name of Juan Galindo on the flyleaf. One of the rarest and most valuable of these books was the *Mercurio Peruano,* of which only the American Philosophical Society previously recorded a copy (bought in 1803).

Galindo's letter of 1834, written to Frederic de Peyster, secretary of that short-lived and little-known New York Literary Society, is a sample of how relations flourished among many groups and individuals, not otherwise included here:

National Palace
Guatemala March 15, 1834

Sir:

I have the honor to enclose the necrology of Citizen José Cecilio del Valle, the most distinguished literary character Central America can boast of since her Independence. I also enclose a specimen of his handwriting and signature.

Citizen Valle was born in Choluteca on the 22nd of November 1779 and was much distinguished for his talents even by the royal authorities; on the annexation of these provinces to Mexico Citizen

Valle proceeded as a deputy from hence to that city, and though at first hostile to the Emperor [Iturbide] he afterwards became his Minister of State.

Subsequently Citizen Valle was elected a member of the Triumvirate that first governed Central America after our Independence— and during the last two presidential elections has been second on our list of candidates. He now had the great majority of votes for President and would undoubtedly have been elected when he most unfortunately died . . . on his return in a litter from his estate near the Pacific to this City. . . .

I shall be honored by your reply to the care of the United States Legation in this city, and shall always be happy to correspond with your enlightened society on any subjects that may be considered interesting.

I am Sir, your very obedient humble servant,

Juan Galindo, Colonel of the Federal Army.[21]

Guatemalans, Mexicans, Brazilians, Cubans, and notable Argentines like Bartolomé Mitre wanted to develop associations which were already made and to get to know the United States in those instances where they were not yet begun.

The very famous Hispanism (justly so) of George Ticknor, William H. Prescott, Henry W. Longfellow, Howells, Irving, and so many individuals and groups already mentioned here had a special character. Their preference for the Spanish-European spirit became an end in itself. Inter-American history, ethnology, and science made use of its Hispanophile background to search out and establish the broad Americanism which arose out of Spanish culture in America. This was the chief difference between the historic inter-Americanism and the historic Hispanism of New England. Ludewig expressed this very well in 1846 in his letter to Brazil on behalf of his proposed historical congress: "Europe has continued to centralize toward itself the efforts of even the most national-minded of New World scholars." All through the nineteenth century, in poetry, prose, politics, and inter-American relations, runs this theme of independence and emancipation from European culture and the search for the American and inter-American system. Part of it is nationalism, another part is romanticism. The isolated hemisphere found identification by turning inward upon common New World origins and history, a mutual sense of scientific and scholarly community.

This was a positive force in the Americas between 1800 and 1900.

The later Latin American attack on the "materialism" of Yankee cul-ture, or the famous poet's imagined division of the hemisphere into the half-worlds of Ariel the good and Caliban the bad, had not yet been asserted. None of the good will recorded in this history was imposed by the "strong over the weak"; they were spontaneous, voluntary, and natural attractions. Stronger than the forces which hold them together, the law of gravitation explains their mutual attraction. Since the eight-eenth century, these cultural relations were independent of economics, diplomacy, and strategic interest; they were based upon nonmaterial, Jeffersonian values of science, reason, and progress. This gave the Ameri-can mind a weight and force of its own. The hostile Latin American image of the United States after 1890 was a false reflection of values, a distortion of North American culture, and an inverted *leyenda negra* of its own.

There was an even stronger opponent of cultural values as set up in this inter-American community. The chief weakness was an apathetic, ignorant people. In a hemisphere politically committed to republicanism and democracy, the voice of the people carried far. Schools and news-papers had the responsibility for spreading impressions and conveying "information." But cultural ideas of the sort described here take too long to percolate through to the popular mind. Moreover, by 1890, the entrance of United States government and early Pan-American or-ganization tended to dominate the picture, crowding the work of the societies to the background where they were lost from sight. Law, finance, commerce, diplomacy, tariff reciprocity, and foreign relations obscured the historic inter-American cultural tradition, putting out the light on a fine intellectual achievement, over a century old. Historians found in treaties, investments, newspaper headlines, inter-American conferences of states, corollaries of the Monroe Doctrine, and in the Latin American policy of the United States the apparent forces making for hemisphere history. The Muse of History must have looked very pained at this unhistorical division of the laurels. Man's shortness of memory is well known. How short is his memory of accomplished fact we can see from the failure of the historian to remember how old, how continuous, how precedented, and how inter-American is the North American cultural fondness for Latin America.

Not many nineteenth-century historians knew this either. Even in afteryears, from 1900 to the present, when Latin American history teaching and research in North American colleges and universities mastered an extraordinary subject-matter and gave it an important place in the course of study, it is noteworthy that the practice of cultural relations as organized by the societies did not carry over any influence upon North American academic teaching and research. It is almost as though higher education in the Latin American field rose up by its own bootstraps, without any derivation from individuals and institutions who had put in so much work for a hundred years past. There seem to be two intellectual processes at work here, quite unrelated and disconnected. Historic culture relations, even in the field of history, had not made a connection with the teaching of Latin American history, when it was begun after 1880. Latin Americanist professors of history in the universities and colleges owed and borrowed next to nothing from the antecedent North American historians and historical societies. History as taught was also fully individualist, and thus drew little from others in the same work.

Latin American history, when it entered the college lecture hall, was soon freed from the powerful influence of Spanish language and literature. In 1883 Columbia College in New York introduced the subject. Daniel de Leon was the lecturer. He made little or no mark as a Latin Americanist, but he did become, after separation from Columbia, one of the leading Marxists in North American radical and trade-union circles. De Leon was no scholar. He did little research and less writing in Latin American history than any of those greater names who came after him at Columbia, California, Texas, Chicago, Yale, and other universities. Still, de Leon's is the first name we come upon in college teaching of Latin American history.

Since de Leon's world as well as his views were influenced by current stress upon economics, international law, and diplomacy, his course was already intended to train Columbia students for careers in the State Department, business, or law.[22] As lecturer in international law and diplomacy de Leon preceded John Bassett Moore at Columbia, and as a specialist in Latin American history he paved the way for the course in the Department of History, given fifteen years later by William R. Shepherd. De Leon was not a historian nor did he have connection with the Department of History. Yet his course had much history, although he was a lecturer in international law. These are the instructional origins of the Latin American field at Columbia College, and for that matter, in the United States.

Daniel de Leon was West Indian by birth, a revolutionary by training, and certainly no student of the past. He had little connection with the historical societies, knew next to nothing of the efforts of Smith, or of the New-York Historical, Massachusetts Historical, and American Philosophical societies, which went to build up a cooperative basis for study of Latin American history. He was not so much concerned with history, ethnology, and other cognate subjects as he was with the contemporary materialist forces of a political and investment character. He was also a partisan of Latin American revolutionary tactic even before he came into contact with Marxism and his own version of Socialism. This viewpoint colored his teaching, and according to the notes taken in de Leon's class by William A. Dunning (Columbia's future professor of Political Science)[23] de Leon built into his lectures a republican enmity toward Brazil, whose Empire he compared with Tsarist Russia. Contrast with this the friendly cooperation which the learned societies sought with Brazil, the proposal with Brazil for an inter-American historical congress, and the fact of exchange of memberships. As Samuel Mitchill had room in his republican heart to praise the Kings of Spain so long as they favored science, so did the nineteenth-century societies ignore the form of government and the nature of politics, whether republican or monarchical. Pedro II, Emperor of Brazil, was a patron of the sciences.

De Leon was already fixed in his attitudes, and since the tendency all around him was to be the individual to an extreme and overlook the process at work, he went his own way. That is how he organized and taught his courses. It is interesting that Columbia's School of Political Science—soon to become the famous Faculty of the same name—was ready to get students into Latin American classes, although the First Conference of American States, better known later as the Pan American Union, was still some years off. Strictly speaking, de Leon's course was not Latin American or hemisphere history as we would now teach the subject, but rather a history of the legal and territorial problems of Spanish and Portuguese America. This turned out to be the equivalent of recent, that is, nineteenth-century, history, and he enjoyed a year's course in which to work out his approach and content. He may therefore be considered to be the first instructor of Latin American history in a North American college or university. He is also the first lecturer upon Latin American diplomatic history who taught that subject exclusively.[24]

As we reach the end of that century, the span from 1885 to 1895, cultural-mindedness lost ground to those forces with which the nineteenth century began: diplomatic, economic, strategic, territorial, and expansionist objectives. Government interest in cultural relations was still very small, especially since there were pressing problems which called for solutions along the lines of interest just cited. Nevertheless, far away in California, Bernard Moses began to teach Latin American history at the University of California. Moses, like de Leon, was unaware of the long history of inter-American cultural relations. Unlike de Leon, however, Moses was closer to the California-Spanish background. He also had the record of Bancroft's work and the asset of the Bancroft Library on which to draw. Moses knew very little about the inter-American connections which Middle Atlantic and Northeastern United States laid down with Latin America. He had been in Mexico and the Philippines, while de Leon was born in Venezuela or nearby. Both de Leon and Moses, like their contemporaries in that generation from 1880 to 1914, sensed the future role of the United States in Latin America. They worked in the present, toward the future. Neither of these two founders of historical instruction understood what had already gone into the inter-American record.

It is all the more remarkable, therefore, that Latin American history, as it finally matured in the colleges and universities of the United States, moved so rapidly to overtake and replace the leadership which was so painstakingly earned by learned societies and private institutions. It is just as unexpected to find that for all the cultivation of inter-Americanism in the older cities and societies of the Middle Atlantic and Northeastern seaboard the prestige of achievement fell to those in states of Spanish origin and history. Spanish influence in the American Southwest competed with the easterner's Anglo-American, hence artificial, attraction to Latin America and Spain. Both together should have combined into a strong North American basis for furthering inter-American studies. The appreciation of things Hispanic, however, was organized for teaching and research, wherever it arose. A young subject, growing and on the way to recognition in the curriculum before 1900, never really knew how old it was. Latin American history was being made in that generation of '98, as the subject and the age crossed into a twentieth century of expansion.

By 1900 the college professor of Latin American history had evolved, but his subjects of history, language, ethnology, and geology did not influence the tendency of knowledge to be of benefit to a few. University teaching had the same light weight upon the public mind that societies and individuals experienced from 1700 to 1900. The possibility was left open for extensive education, newspaper, radio, and magazine attention to Latin America, but that took another sixty years to develop. As for the public and popular mind, education and communications have brought new ways of reducing the *leyenda negra,* through their influence on opinion, but it is difficult to measure how much. By adopting its own methods, rules for research, and publications techniques instruction in Latin American history marked a higher stage of evolution, achieving a prominent academic place.[26] The Latin Americanist was heir to a rich legacy, the best in the North American culture, from which he might, much later, become an expert for government and an educator for the public mind. This was both his heritage and his challenge.

Notes

CHAPTER 1

1. For more material on this early period of contact see Harry Bernstein, *Origins of Inter-American Interest, 1700-1812,* Albert J. Beveridge Memorial Fund, American Historical Association (Philadelphia: University of Pennsylvania, 1945).

2. Cotton Mather, *The Diary of Cotton Mather, 1681-1708* (Massachusetts Historical Society Collections, Series VII, [2 vols.; Boston: by the Society, 1911-1912], VII, 284, 285.

3. Mather first called his book "La Religion Pura en Doze Palabras Fieles, dignas de ser recibidos de Todos." It was published in Boston as *La Fe del Christiano: En veynte quatro articulos de la Institucion de Christo. Embiada a los Españoles paraque abran sus ojos y paraque se conviertan de las Tinieblas a la Luz y de la potestad de Satanas a Dios. Paraque reciban por la Fe que es en Jesu Christo remis [ion] de peccados y suerte.* Por C. Mathero siervo del Señor Jesu Christo (Boston: B. Green & J. Allen, 1699). The original is in the library of the American Antiquarian Society; the New York Public Library has a film copy.

4. Samuel Sewall, *The Diary of Samuel Sewall, 1674-1729* (Massachusetts Historical Society Collections, Series V [3 vols.; Boston: by the Society, 1878-1882]), V, 485; VI, 53, 110.

5. Samuel Sewall, *Letter Book* (Massachusetts Historical Society Collections, Series VI, [2 vols.; Boston: by the Society, 1886]), I, 297.

6. Hawks Transcripts, I, New-York Historical Society. Francis L. Hawks copied the letters and minutes of the Society for the Propagation of the Gospel in 1836 but left the Sewall letter of 1704 uncopied. For the inter-American role of Hawks see *infra,* p. 117.

7. Sewall, *Letter Book,* I, 387, 405, 406; *Diary,* VI, 248. Also, Great Britain, Public Record Office, *Calendar of State Papers* (Colonial Series, America and West Indies, 1675-1733 [40 vols.; London: H. M. Stationery Office, 1860-1939], 1710-1711, 436; 1711-1712, 205.

8. Sewall, *Letter Book,* II, 156.

9. See the several contributions in A. P. Whitaker (ed.), *Latin America and the Enlightenment* (New York: D. Appleton-Century, 1942) or, second printing, Cornell University Press, 1961.

10. *Charter, Laws and Catalogue of Books of the Library Company of Philadelphia* (Philadelphia: B. Franklin & D. Hall, 1764).

11. *Catalogue of Books belonging to the Company of the Redwood Library in Newport on Rhode-Island* (Newport: S. Hall, 1764); *The Prince Library: Catalogue of the Collection of Books and Manuscripts now deposited in the Public Library of the City of Boston* (Boston: A. Mudge & Son, 1870); *Catalogus Librorum Bibliothecae Collegii Harvardensi quod est Cantabrigae in Nova Anglia* (Bostonii: Nov-anglorum, Typis B. Green, MDCCXXIII).

169

170 NOTES (PAGES 13-29)

12. Bernstein, *op. cit.*, pp. 52-65.

13. Charles Evans, *American Bibliography: A Chronological Dictionary of all Books, Pamphlets, and Periodical Publications printed in the United States of America* (12 vols.; Chicago: Blakely Press, 1903-1934), III, no. 6741.

14. *Ibid.*, III, no. 9333.

15. See *Catalogue of Books belonging to the Loganian Library* (Philadelphia: Zachariah Poulson, Jr., 1795).

16. Massachusetts Historical Society, *Proceedings*, I, appendix.

17. *Relación del Viaje hecho a los Reynos del Perú y Chile por los botánicos y dibuxantes enviados para aquella Expedición*, edited by A. J. Barreiro, S.J. (Madrid [first published edition], 1931); for the general situation in Spain, see Juan Sempere y Guarinos, *Ensayo de una Biblioteca Española de los Mejores Escritores del Reynado de Carlos III* (Madrid: Imprenta Real, 1785-1789).

18. American Philosophical Society, *Transactions* (Old Series) (6 vols., Philadelphia, 1786-1809), I, II, III, appendices.

19. Worthington C. Ford, *The United States and Spain in 1790* (Brooklyn: Historical Printing Club, 1890), p. 40.

20. American Philosophical Society, *Transactions*, III, appendix.

21. *Memorias de la Real Academia das Sciéncias de Lisboa, 1780-1788* (Lisboa: Oficina de la Real Academia, 1797), tomo I, appendix.

22. See José de Onís, *The United States as Seen by Spanish American Writers, 1776-1890* (New York: The Hispanic Institute in the United States, 1952).

23. American Philosophical Society, *Transactions* (New Series) vol. I (1818); *Catalogue of the Library of the American Philosophical Society* (1824).

24. *Memorias de la Real Academia de la Historia* (2 vols., Madrid: Imprenta de la Real Academia, 1796-1805), I, clviii. For the most recent study of this Hispanism, see Stanley T. Williams, *The Spanish Background of American Literature* (2 vols.; New Haven: Yale University Press, 1955). Before the Williams book appeared the best authority on Hispanism in the United States was M. Romera Navarro, *El Hispanismo en Norteamerica* (Madrid, 1917).

25. Manuel de Salas, one of the ablest thinkers of the era of Chilean Enlightenment and Independence, protested against the dogma of New World inferiority contained in such writers as de Pauw, Robertson, Buffon, and other Europeans. Salas pointed out that "we are vindicated by Peralta, Franklin, and Molina. Astronomy, electricity, and history have taken on a new aspect in the hands of these famous Americans." *Escritos de don Manuel de Salas y Documentos relativos á él y a su Familia* (3 vols., Santiago de Chile: Imprenta Cervantes, 1910-1914), I, 608.

26. *Early Proceedings of the American Philosophical Society, compiled from the "Manuscript Minutes of its Meetings from 1744 to 1835,"* see American Philosophical Society, *Proceedings*, XXII.

27. José Antonio Alzate (ed.), *Gazeta de Literatura de Mexico*, 1789-1794, I, 3 (1789), 22, 50; 15 (April, 1790); III, 32 (August, 1794), 250; 3 (October, 1794), 267. The Catalogue of the Library of the Philosophical Society showed in 1824 the possession of Alzate's *Nuevo Mapa geographico de la America Septentrional perteneciente al Virreynato de Mexico* (1768).

28. American Philosophical Society, *Proceedings*, I, 399.

29. Bernstein, *op. cit.*, chapters IV, VI.

30. American Antiquarian Society (Worcester, Mass.), *Proceedings*, I, 10, 55.

31. *Catalogue of the Books . . . Manuscripts in the Library of the New-York Historical Society* (New-York Historical Society *Collections*, 1st series, vol. II [New York: J. Seymour, 1813]).

32. Bernstein, *op. cit.*, pp. 61-62.

33. New-York Historical Society, *Collections,* II (1814), 206.

34. This activity of a political nature is well described in Arthur P. Whitaker, *The United States and the Independence of Latin America, 1800-1830* (Baltimore: Johns Hopkins University Press, 1941).

CHAPTER 2

1. Harriet Sylvester Tapley, *Salem Imprints, 1786-1825; a History of the First Fifty Years of Printing in Salem* (Salem: Essex Institute, 1927).

2. *Catalogue of All the Books printed in the United States with the Price and Places where Published.* Reprinted in Adolf Growell, *Book Trade Bibliography in the United States in the XIXth Century* (New York, 1898).

3. *Port Folio,* IV (January 7, 1804): "Mr. Thomas Dobson has in the press the Abbé Clavijero's History of Mexico. This useful, accurate and elegant work is derived from Mexican and Spanish documents, and from the ancient hieroglyphics of the Indians. It is illustrated by charts and ornamented with engravings and to the whole are appended critical dissertations on the land, the animals and the inhabitants of Mexico. . . . Mr. Dobson offers this work to subscribers at the moderate price of seven dollars and fifty cents for three large volumes in 8vo. It will speedily be published."

Sabin, *Dictionary of Books relating to America,* lists a printing of Clavijero at Richmond, Virginia, 1806, in three volumes, and one at Philadelphia: Thomas Dobson, 1806, 3 volumes. The former may be an error of date.

The Hawks MSS in the New-York Historical Society contain a Clavijero in the Cullen translation of 1787, printed at Philadelphia in 1804.

4. *Port Folio,* series III (July-December 1809), 282-283.

5. Harry Bernstein, "The Latin American Book Trade before 1900," *Publisher's Weekly,* CXLVIII, 22 (December 1, 1945), 2416-2419.

6. Compiled from book lists published in Sabin, *op. cit.;* Antonio Palau y Dulcet, *Manual de Librero Hispano-Americano* (7 vols. Barcelona: Librería Anticudria, 1923-1927); and from the Quarterly Book Lists of the *North American Review* since 1815.

7. James F. Shearer, "French and Spanish works printed in Charleston, South Carolina," *Bibliographical Society of America, Papers,* XXXIV, 1940; also Edith F. Helman "Early Interest in Spanish in New England (1815-1835)," *Hispania,* XXIX (1946).

8. *American Quarterly Review,* I (March-June, 1827), 358.

9. Comisión Nacional de Homenaje a Sarmiento (Argentine Republic), *Sarmiento: Cincuentenario de su Muerte* (5 vols. Buenos Aires: Imprenta Mercatali, 1939) IV, "Paginas Selectas de Sarmiento sobre Bibliotecas Populares," 64, 222.

10. For this, and other detail, see note 6, *supra.*

11. A copy is in the New-York Historical Society Library.

12. A few catalogues of the Lockwood firm still remain in the New York Public Library stacks, under the heading Lockwood Roe and Sons.

13. All the Lockwood material in Spanish was located in one bundle, somewhat disintegrated with age.

14. For Hallet's publications see note 6, *supra;* also a little work put out by the Instituto Cultural Argentino Norteamericano called *Amigos Inolvidables. Recopilacion de los folletos correspondientes a la primera serie de audiciones del programa 'Amigos Inolvidables'. Auspiciado por la Asociacion de Difusión Inter Americana. Transmitido por la LRI Radio El Mundo y la Red Azul y Blanca.* (Buenos Aires: n.d. [prob. 1944]). The brief account of Hallet is based upon

scattered material taken from Argentine histories, especially those of the local history of Buenos Aires, and of printing and the graphic arts in Argentina.

15. Zarzamendi became printer of *El Mundo Nuevo,* one of a large number of Spanish and Spanish American journals published in New York City during the past century. *Mundo Nuevo,* edited by Enrique Piñeyro, was, interestingly enough, published by Frank Leslie. Leslie acquired—either by way of Stephen Hallet, or by himself—favorable contacts and prestige in Latin America. This, at least, was the case in Mexico where in 1869 a reviewer, evaluating Leslie's *Ilustracion Americana* (Frank Leslie's Illustrated Weekly), printed the earnest hope that the journal would have the widest circulation in Mexico. See *Boletín de la Sociedad Mexicana de Geografía y Estadística,* epoca 2a, I (1869), 71. This was nearly one hundred years before the current era of Latin American issues of United States magazines!

16. James F. Shearer, "Pioneer Publishers of Textbooks for Hispanic America: The House of Appleton," *Hispania,* February, 1944, pp. 21-28.

17. Based upon careful reading of all the Appleton catalogues, 1848 to 1885, in the New York Public Library. Appleton's business, firm, and correspondence records were long ago burned by fire. A great many indirect references to the Latin American book sales of Appleton can be gleaned from Sarmiento's writings, some of which have been brought together, as in note 9, *supra.*

18. In César B. Pérez Colman, *Paraná: 1810-1860. Los primeros cincuenta años de la vida nacional* (Rosario [Argentina]: Emilio Fenner, 1946), pp. 353-355.

19. Note 9, *supra,* and p. 219 of the same work.

20. The first-mentioned periodical is the Spanish version of *Scientific Weekly.* Some individual books and journals may be selected from the *Catalogue of Title Entries of Books and other Articles entered in the Office of the Librarian of Congress under the Copyright Law* (Washington: Government Printing Office, 1891-1893), vols. I-IV.

CHAPTER 3

1. *American Journal of Science,* VIII (August, 1824), 382-384. For a glimpse of another proposal for intellectual cooperation as a model for the present, see the Philadelphia literary journal *Port Folio* and the project for cultural relations with German culture. *Port Folio,* series V, vol. XVIII (October, 1824), 340ff.

On Humboldt, see Helmut de Terra, *Humboldt: the Life and Times of Alexander von Humboldt, 1769-1859* (New York: Alfred A. Knopf, 1955); Arthur P. Whitaker, "Alexander von Humboldt and Spanish America," American Philosophical Society, *Proceedings,* CIV (June, 1960), 317-322.

2. There are several essays on Maclure, no complete biography.

3. *Catalogue of the Library of The Academy of Natural Sciences of Philadelphia* (Philadelphia: J. Dobson, 1837). Among the many scientific works in the Spanish language were those of Andrés del Río, Guillermo [William] Bowles, the botanist Larreateguí, and publications of the Spanish scientific societies.

4. Academy of Natural Sciences of Philadelphia, "List of Members and Correspondents of the Society," compared for 1841 and 1880.

5. Among the Samuel G. Morton Papers in the Library of the American Philosophical Society at Philadelphia are many letters from William Maclure.

6. Maclure to Dr. Morton, October 30, 1835.

7. Don José María Vargas to Dr. Morton, January 16, 1837.

8. See note 33, chapter I, *supra.*

9. *Charter, Constitution and By-Laws of the Lyceum of Natural History in the City of New York, incorporated April 20, 1818* (New York, 1826) ; *Annals of the Lyceum of Natural History of New York* (11 vols., New York, 1824-1876).

10. This letter is in the Archives of the American Philosophical Society.

11. Lyceum of Natural History, *Annals*, I (1823), IV (1836-1847), V (1848-1850).

12. *American Journal of Science*, XI (July, 1826), 304.

13. Instituto Historico e Geographico Brasileiro, *Revista Trimensal*, XII (1849), 284, and XIV (1851).

14. J. Fred Rippy, *Latin America and the Industrial Age* (New York: G. P. Putman's Sons, 1944) chap. IX, pp. 83-85, and chap. X, pp. 96-104. The Yale University Library has some interesting articles and papers written by Orville Derby. There are many articles on the United States Navy men who journeyed to Latin America and advanced the level of science there. See Wayne Rasmussen "The United States Astronomical Expedition to Chile, 1849-1852," *Hispanic American Historical Review*, XXXIV, (Feb. 1954), 102-113, which deals with Lieutenant Gillis, whose work in the promotion of exchanges with Chile was taken over by the Smithsonian Institution. See especially John P. Harrison, "Science and Politics: Origins and Objectives of Mid-Nineteenth Century Government Expeditions to Latin America," *Hispanic American Historical Review*, XXXV (1955), 175-202.

15. H. F. Peterson, "Edward A. Hopkins: A Pioneer Promoter in Paraguay," *Hispanic American Historical Review*, XXII (1942), 245-261.

16. American Geographical and Statistical Society, *Bulletin*, VII (1856), appendix D, 71-74.

17. Varas to Riley [Chilean Consul in New York], November 27, 1855; also American Geographical and Statistical Society, *Proceedings*, I (1862-1863), 19.

18. See Appendix.

19. American Geographical and Statistical Society, *Journal*, XVII (1855)— XXII (1890).

20. Republished in Brazil, in Portuguese translation, in the famous *Brasiliana* series.

21. This extremely interesting letter was found in the New York Public Library among the papers of Judge Charles Daly, president of the American Geographical Society, for whom the Daly Medal was struck. Hartt sought Daly's support for the position of "Geologist to the Empire," as he called it.

22. For a sketch of Hartt's life and work see Richard Rathbun, in the Royal Society of Canada, *Proceedings and Transactions*, V (1899).

23. See Appendix; also, Sociedad Mexicana de Geografía y Estadística, *Boletín*, II (July, 1849), 22.

24. Compiled from the Sociedad Mexicana de Geografía y Estadística, Boletín, for those years.

25. National Institution of Washington, *Proceedings*, February, 1842.

26. Sociedad Mexicana de Geografía y Estadística, *Boletín*, epoca 3a, I (1873), 592.

27. On Gould, see Academia Nacional de Ciencias Exactas existente en la Universidad de Cordoba, *Boletín*, I (1874). Argentines have always held him in the highest regard, not only for his work in astronomy but also for his pioneer role in meteorology, which still holds high importance in Argentine civil and military studies. Like Hartt, Gould left United States students behind him, to push ahead with his work and teach the next generation.

28. See the *List of Foreign Institutions in Correspondence with the Smithsonian Institution* (Washington: Smithsonian Institution, 1854, *et seq.*) ; George

H. Boehmer, *History of the Smithsonian Exchanges* (Washington: Smithsonian Institution, 1882); *List of Foreign Correspondents of the Smithsonian Institution*, corrected to 1882, January, Smithsonian Miscellaneous Collections (Washington, 1882).

29. [Cincuentenario de la Academia Nacional de Historia.] Ricardo Levene, *Mitre y los Estudios Históricos en la Argentina* (Buenos Aires, 1944). Article VI of the by-laws of the society (p. 274) made their relation with the North American societies quite clear: "El Instituto mantendrá relaciones con los sabios y las corporaciones literarias del exterior, abriéndola desde luego con el Instituto Histórico-Geográfico del Brasil, con la Universidad y la Sociedad de Agricultura de Chile, con la Sociedad de Medicina Montevideana, con el Instituto Smithsoniano de Washington y la Sociedad de Filadelfia [*sic*] . . . cultivando muy especialmente las relaciones americanas." These relations were achieved.

30. Boehmer, *op. cit.*, pp. 62, 63.

31. *Ibid.*, pp. 64, 65.

32. *Ibid.*, p. 94.

CHAPTER 4

1. This chapter is enlarged from my paper read before the New York Academy of Sciences and published as "Anthropology and Early Inter-American Relations," New York Academy of Sciences, *Transactions*, Ser. II, X, (Nov. 1947), 2-17.

2. Galvez to Peter Dupoinceau, letter in Archives of American Philosophical Society.

3. For more on Juan Galindo see Chapter V; a good sketch is in William J. Griffith, "Juan Galindo, Central American Chauvinist," *Hispanic American Historical Review*, XL (February, 1960), 25-52.

4. In John Russell Bartlett Papers, John Carter Brown Library, Providence, Rhode Island.

5. American Ethnological Society, *Transactions*, I (1845), 1-353.

6. Astor Library, *Annual Report, 1849* (1873), I, 16.

7. In Bartlett Papers. Morton held that even where one language was spoken or indicated, many races may have existed; that is, physical type was more revealing than language.

8. Victor W. von Hagen, *Maya Explorer: John Lloyd Stephens and the Lost Cities of Central America and Yucatan* (Norman: University of Oklahoma, 1947).

9. The Hawks Library in the New-York Historical Society is surprising in its wealth of Hispanic and Latin American items on a great variety of historical and literary topics. It is catalogued separately.

10. Hawks MSS., New York Historical Society.

11. See the sketch of Mayer in the *Dictionary of American Biography*. For more on Mayer see Chapter V.

12. The Squier Papers at the Library of Congress and the Bancroft Library at Berkeley, California, have not been used for this study. I have used the Squier MSS at the New-York Historical Society.

13. American Ethnological Society, *Transactions*, I.

14. *Revista Trimensal*, VIII (1846), 153.

15. *Revista Trimensal*, VIII (1846), 549-552.

16. Correspondence in Buckingham Smith MSS, New-York Historical Society.

17. Rathbun, *op. cit.*, p. 15.

18. Reports of the Peabody Museum of American Archaeology and Ethnology,

Vol. I, 1868-1875 (Cambridge, 1876): *Fifth Annual Report* (1872), and *Eighth Report* (1875).

19. In his "Ancient Indian Pottery of Marajó, Brazil," reprinted from the *American Naturalist,* IV (July, 1871), 270-271. *The Handbook of the South American Indian,* issued by the Smithsonian Institution (1948-1952), has gone definitively over the entire zone of Brazilian ethnology once surveyed by Hartt. Vol. III of the *Handbook,* "Tropical Forest Tribes," has articles by Alfred Metraux and Betty Meggers on *tupinamba* and Marajo, which are more complete than Hartt's work, but do not violate his conclusions.

20. From a paper of his in the *American Naturalist,* 1871.

21. Brinton's writings, articles, addresses, etc., are too numerous to cite here.

22. The Bandelier letter is among the MSS of the New-York Historical Society.

CHAPTER 5

1. For a more complete survey of this journalism see Whitaker, *The United States and Latin America, 1800-1830,* pp. 141-188.

2. Roger Wolcott (ed.), *The Correspondence of William Hickling Prescott* (Boston: Houghton, Mifflin, 1925); also, H. F. Cline, C. H. Gardiner, and C. Gibson (eds.), *William Hickling Prescott: A Memorial* (Durham: Duke University Press, 1959).

3. A volume of his essays is in the New York Public Library.

4. Poinsett has had several biographers; there is only one sketch of Brantz Mayer in the *Dictionary of American Bibliography.* His works on Mexico are being translated into Spanish in Mexico, it has been reported.

5. *Catalogue of a Choice Collection of Books . . . including the Entire Library belonging to Col. Brantz Mayer of Baltimore, Maryland* (New York, 1870).

6. There is an unsatisfactory sketch of Smith in the *Dictionary of American Biography;* he surely deserves a full-length biography.

7. American Antiquarian Society, *Proceedings,* no. 56, April 26, 1871, reported Smith's accidental death, and said that he was born on Cumberland Island, Georgia, spent his childhood at St. Augustine, Florida, and at the age of fourteen was with his father in Mexico City.

8. Josiah Smith, *Diary,* MS, in Buckingham Smith MSS, at the New York Historical Society.

9. Buckingham Smith, *Letter Book.*

10. B. Smith MSS.

11. Misc. MSS, B. Smith, Box III.

12. Misc. MSS, B. Smith, Box III.

13. Smith himself, in a letter to John Russell Bartlett, November 27, 1853, in which he sought Bartlett's recommendation for the appointment to Spain, explained his thought that "Bancroft, Prescott, and Sparks are beyond my reach." John Russell Bartlett MSS, John Carter Brown Library.

14. B. Smith, *Letters,* Box I. The printed New-York Historical Society *List of Foreign Members* is quite incomplete. For some reason the name of José Amador de los Ríos (as well as other Spaniards and Latin Americans) was left out. The unpublished Archives of that Society, however, very clearly prove that "José Amador de los Ríos was elected corresponding member on January 2, 1856. So that Buckingham Smith's recommendation from Madrid was acted upon quite promptly."

15. This invaluable letter, in the original Spanish, is preserved in the Buckingham Smith MSS.

16. The Latin American collections, holdings, and possessions in United States libraries were already outstanding at this time. There is no study of their contribution to inter-American culture.

17. A great many names were found outside the printed list of members.

18. *Revista Trimensal* II (1840), 368.

19. First mentioned in *Revista Trimensal,* III (1841-1842), the meeting of December 5, 1841. The acceptance by the Historical Society of Pennsylvania is noted in the supplement to III, 534.

20. The Instituto Historico e Geographico Brasileiro followed the existing pattern by nominating other Americans to membership, but this aspect of Brazil-United States cultural relations has not been undertaken here.

21. This letter is not in the records of the New York Literary and Philosophical Society. It was found in Volume V of the De Peyster Papers in the New-York Historical Society. The noted Peruvian Dr. Hipolito Unánue, already a member of several United States learned societies, was named corresponding member of this society in 1821.

22. The Columbia catalogues of these years give the information on the nature of the courses.

23. The notes taken by Professor Dunning, distinguished political scientist, could not have been complete notes of an entire course, or year's work, as it might be given today. A bound, typewritten copy was located in the Columbia Law School Library.

In preparing my forthcoming biography of Matías Romero, a correspondence between de Leon and Romero was discovered among the Matias Romero MSS, Mexico City. Romero gave de Leon much help on Latin American and Mexican historical sources, as well as some ideas about Mexican and Latin American independence.

24. For the rise of the college professor and the curriculum on Latin American subjects, see the excellent account by Jorge Basadre, in his Introduction to *Courses on Latin America in Institutions of Higher Education in the United States,* 1948-1949, compiled by Estellita Hart, Division of Education, Department of Cultural Affairs, Pan American Union (Washington, 1949), pp. ix-lxxiii.

Appendix

Latin American and Iberian Corresponding and Honorary Members of North American Learned Societies in the Nineteenth Century (A Selected List)

	American Philosophical Society *Philadelphia*	Lyceum of Natural History *New York*	New-York Historical Society *New York*	American Ethnological Society *New York*	Massachusetts Historical Society *Boston*	National Institute *Washington*	American Antiquarian Society *Worcester*	American Geographical Society *New York*	Academy of Natural Sciences *Philadelphia*
ARGENTINA									
Pedro de Angelis	1840				1845	184–			
Gregorio Funes					1825		1825		
Manuel Moreno					1825		1825		
Bartolomé Muñoz		1823							
Guillermo Rawson							1879	1879	
Julio La Croze									1852
H. W. Kennedy	1856								
German Burmeister							1910		
Juan E. Ambrosetti							1910		
S. A. Lafone Quevedo									
Wm. H. Hudson			1863						
H. D. Hoskold		1890							
Francisco P. Moreno								1909	
BOLIVIA									
Manuel Ballivián							1910		
Alcide d'Orbigny						184–			1834
Juan Ondarza		1859							
CUBA									
José de la Luz				1861					
Antonio de Gregorio		1883							
Wm. S. Jenckes							1819		
Andrés Poey			[?]	1861					
Felipe Poey		1851							
Alejandro Ramírez	1801								1867

Ramón de la Sagra		1835				184–			1829
Joaquín Velásquez		1851							1855
F. A. Sauvalle									1867
J. Gundlach									1818
Barón de Collins									
Antonio Bachiller y Morales			1847						1836
[Guillermo] Lobe									
José Silverio Joirin			1884			184–			
[Pedro] Auber									1835
Ignacio Carbonell						184–			
CENTRAL AMERICA									
José Barrundía			1850	1852					
Modesto Flores				1861					
Juan Galindo			[?]				1836		
Manuel Peralta	1836							1877	
Manuel Gálvez					1836				
Fernando Cruz	1889								
COLOMBIA									
Salvador Camacho Roldán	1828						1864		
A. P. Herrán				1845					
José D. Obaldía				1861					
Tomás C. Mosquera				1861	1825				
José M. Salazar			1828						
Ezequiel Uricoechea				1861					
Alfonso Pinart									
CHILE									
José S. Alduñate						1841			
G. A. Real Azúa						1841			
R. A. Philippi									1867
John N. Burr						1844			1829
Ignacio Domeyko						1841			
M. Carvallo									

Name	American Philosophical Society, Philadelphia	Lyceum of Natural History, New York	New-York Historical Society, New York	American Ethnological Society, New York	Massachusetts Historical Society, Boston	National Institute, Washington	American Antiquarian Society, Worcester	American Geographical Society, New York	Academy of Natural Sciences, Philadelphia
José T. Medina							1909		
Wm. Wheelwright						1842			
Manuel Bulnes						1844			
Joaquín Prieto						1844			
Manuel Montt						1844			
ECUADOR									
Wm. Jameson			1858					1870[?]	1836
Federico González Suárez							1910		
Vicente Pazos			1819						
Vicente Rocafuerte				1845		184–			
F. Villavicencio				1861					
BRAZIL									
Emperor Pedro II	1876		1856			184–	1858	1879	1876
Thomas Bedwell Jr.									1812
J. C. Rodriguez	1822						1910		
J. B. Andrade e Silva									
Viscount de Bom Retiro								1877	1877
J. M. da Silva Coutinho								1870	
João B. Calogeras									
Dr. Brunet		1867							
José Bento			1849						
Carvalho Borges								1877	
Dr. Ildefonso						1841			
J. C. Fernandes Pinheiro			1855						
Rev. James Fletcher			1855					1864	
F. I. Marcondes Homem de Mello									
Henry B. DeWey								1877	
Whitby E. Moore		1844							1850

Name				
Baptista de Oliveira			1864	1855
Joaquim Pimentel Oliveira			1872	
Viscount Porto Seguro			1879	
Viscount Sapucahy	1856		1879	1849
Manuel Ferreira Lagos	1825			
José de Silva Lisboa			1872	
D. S. Ferreira Penna				1876
José Saldanho da Gama				1855
C. A. Santos				1845
J. C. Reinhardt				
Marqués de Porto Alegre	1856			
Marqués d'Abrantes	1856			
Pedreiro de Couto Feraz	1856		1862	
I. Manuel de Macedo	1856			
Dr. Pacheco da Sylva	1856			
Chevalier de Lisboa	1856			
J. Nascentes de Azambuja	1856			
Viscount de Itaborahy	1856			
L. Antonio de Lacerda	1867			
José Silvestre Rebello	[?]	1842		
A. de Souza e Oliveira Coutinho		1842		
Barão de Boa Vista		1842		
Luiz Ferreira de Aguiar		184—		
B. F. Chaves		1844		
Marqués de Marica		184—		
Francisco Gonçalves Martius		184—		
Carlos F. Ribeiro		184—		
Bernardo Pereira de Vasconcellos		184—		
C. F. Hartt	1876			
Ladislau Netto	1890			
Orville Derby	1890			
Francisco G. Leão	1898			

	American Philosophical Society *Philadelphia*	Lyceum of Natural History *New York*	New-York Historical Society *New York*	American Ethnological Society *New York*	Massachusetts Historical Society *Boston*	National Institute *Washington*	American Antiquarian Society *Worcester*	American Geographical Society *New York*	Academy of Natural Sciences *Philadelphia*
Mexico									
[Baron von Humboldt]							1821		
F. de Arrangoiz			1850						
Lucas Alamán	1850				1850				
Mariano Roa Bárcena	1877								1874
Eligio Ancona							1880	1872	
Ignacio Altamirano									
Mariano Arista			1852						1874
José J. Arriaga								1872	
Joaquín Baranda								1870	
Juan José Baz									
José M. Bustamante	1828								1829
Walter Bayley			1848						
Mariano Caldas		1825							
Andrés Aznar Pérez							1879		
Tomás E. Carrillo		1833	1845	1845					
Francisco del Corroy								1872	
Manuel Cierol									
Crescencio Carrillo	1886								
Juan Ehlers		1835		1845					
Manuel Gómez Pedraza			1856						
Miguel Lerdo de Tejada								1872	
S. Lerdo de Tejada								1874	
Pedro de la Llave	1826								
Rodolfo Canton							1878		
José Pacheco			1863	1863					
Alonso Manuel Peon			1847						
Emilio Pardo									
Jesus Sanchez	1886								

Name								
Manuel Payno							1872	
Juan Pío Perez			1843	1845				
José F. Ramírez			1854	1861			1872	
Vicente Riva Palacio	1830	1817			1841		1872	1829
Andrés del Río							1872	
L. Rio de La Loza							1862	
Matías Romero								
Eugenio M. Aguirre			1863					
Francisco Pimentel			1863					
Lucius Woodbury		1824						
Antonio Peñafiel	1886							
Manuel Nájera	1836					1910		
Ignacio Mariscal							1872	
M. Velasquez de León					1841			1883
Alfredo Chavero						1881		1883[?]
Joaquín García Icazbalceta						1881		
Gumesindo Mendoza						1881		
Joaquín Hübbe						1881		
Justo Benítez						1884		
Nicolás León						1890		
David Casares						1904		
Genaro García						1907		
Juan Almonte					1841			
Isidro Gondra					184—			
José Manuel de Herrera		1890			184—			
Manuel Orozco y Berra		1891		1864				
Antonio del Castillo		1892						
José G. Aguilera								
J. de Mendizábal								

PERU

Name								
Pedro Abadía		1820						1821
Mariano Rivero				1845				1821

	American Philosophical Society	Lyceum of Natural History	New-York Historical Society	American Ethnological Society	Massachusetts Historical Society	National Institute	American Antiquarian Society	American Geographical Society	Academy of Natural Sciences
	Philadelphia	*New York*	*New York*	*New York*	*Boston*	*Washington*	*Worcester*	*New York*	*Philadelphia*
Manuel Vidaurre		[?]			1829		1829		1821
José H. Unánue									1867
Antonio Raimundi								1879	1855
José del Solar									1866
J. M. S. Thackara									1855
José M. Garcia y Garcia			1866						
Puerto Rico									
C. Carbonell									1859
Venezuela									
José Páez			1850			184–			
Manuel Carreño			1855						
José de la Cruz Carreño			1855						
José María Vargas			1855						1835
E. Chadwick			1890						
Vicente Coronado			1890						
Jacinto Pactiano									
Isidro Barriga				185–		184–			
Coronel Codazzi		1878				184–			
Adolfo Ernst						184–			
Juan José Flores									
Fernando de la Cuesta									1844
Portugal									
Cipriano Ribeira Freire	1796								
F. J. Borja Garcia Stockler	1806								
Joseph Correa da Serra	1812		1813						
J. P. Cassado de Güiraldes	1827								
José N. Dantes Pereira	1828								

Name					
Viscount Santarem	1833				
J. S. da Costa Macedo	1836				
Laurenço Malheiro					
Bernardino Machado				1906	
Alexandre Herculano		1872			
Antonio José d'Avila		1872			
José Maria de Casal Ribeiro		1872			
Antonio da Cunha Pereira		1876			1876

SPAIN

Name					
Manuel de la García	1802				1817
J. González Hidalgo	1801				1867
Valentín Foronda	1796				
José Joaquín de Ferrer	1796				
José de Jaúdenes	1789				
J. B. Cuñat	1789				
Luis de Urbina	1789				
Diego de Gardoquí	1784				
José M. de Flores	1801				
Francisco de Gardoquí	1802				
Conde de Campomanes	1804				
Francisco Peyrolón	1804				
Carlos de Yrujo	1804				
Manuel Godoy	1829				
Pedro Cevallos	1831				
Antonio de Cavanilles	1832				
Francisco de Paulo Quadrado	1831				
M. Fernández Navarrete	1861	1844			
Juan Martínez					
Francisco González					
Pascual de Gayangos		1844	1845		
Jayme Salvá		1844			
J. Amador de los Rios		1856			

	American Philosophical Society *Philadelphia*	Lyceum of Natural History *New York*	New-York Historical Society *New York*	American Ethnological Society *New York*	Massachusetts Historical Society *Boston*	National Institute *Washington*	American Antiquarian Society *Worcester*	American Geographical Society *New York*	Academy of Natural Sciences *Philadelphia*
G. Fernández Duro			1884						
Conde de Tureno			1878						
J. Martínez de la Rosa	1840								
Alvaro de Gandara									1876
Juan J. Marin									1876
Justo Zaragoza							1882		
M. Jiménez de la Espada							1882		
José R. de Olañeta								1880	
Angel Ortiz								1877	

Index

ACADEMY of Natural Sciences, Philadelphia, 15, 71, 72, 73, 113

Alzate, José Antonio, Mexican scientist, 23

Amazon Valley expeditions, 80, 86, 122, 133

America, Conquest of, 1, 139, 145

American Academy of Arts and Sciences, Spanish correspondents, 24

American Antiquarian Society, and Latin America, 25, 111

American Ethnological Society, 107-109, 111, 120, 121, 122

American Geographical Society, 80-85

American Journal of Science, 69, 70, 71, 77-78

American Philosophical Society: and Latin America, 13, 15, 18, 20, 78, 88, 92, 106, 128, 161; elects Spanish Americans, 18, 23-24, 37; relations with Spain, 19-20, 22-23; with Cuba, 22-23

American Quarterly Review: attacks Mexican culture, 43

Appleton, D. & Co., publishers, 47, 52; books for Latin America, 59-63, 64, 95

Arango y Parreño, Francisco, Cuban: contact with American Philosophical Society, 22

BANCROFT, Hubert H., historian of Spanish West, 16, 19, 66, 147, 152, 153, 154

Bandelier, Adolphe, anthropologist, 137

Barba, Álvaro Alonso: Spanish book on mining, translated, 14-15, 33

Bartlett, John Russell, secretary, New-York Historical Society and American Ethnological Society, 109-110, 120, 122, 124, 127, 160

Barton, Dr. Benjamin Smith, scientist: in Latin America, 13; his writings in Latin America, 28-29, 68, 104

Behrendt, Carl, Maya specialist, 109, 129, 134

Book trade: in books on Latin America, 14, 16, 32, 33-67; with Latin America, 42, 51, 68, 69; children's books on Latin America, 49-50, 53-54

Boston: interest in Latin America, 6-7, 8, 11, 24, 25, 37, 44

Brazil: cultural relations, 20, 69, 70, 77, 79, 83-84, 85-86, 87, 120, 122-126, 127, 160-161

Brinton, Daniel G., University of Pennsylvania, 28, 136-137

Burlington, New Jersey, Library Company, 13

CALAVAR: fictional Brazilian figure, 41

Caldas, Francisco de, New Granadan scientist, 21, 92

Campomanes, Count Pedro Rodríguez de, 19, 20, 21

Carey & Lea: Philadelphia publishing house, 37-38, 42, 43, 58, 70

College of Philadelphia, 13

Cultural relations: inter-American, 4-5, 10, 13, 19-21, 22, 23, 24, 29, 31, 32, 67, 122, 163. *See also* Inter-American cultural relations

DE LEON, Daniel: at Columbia College, 165-166

187